The Heart of Success

The Heart of Success

Conversations with Notable Achievers

By

Dan G. Tripps, Ph.D.

Foreword by

Walter Cronkite

Afterword by

John Wooden

BAINBRIDGEBOOKS
Philadelphia

Published January 2001
By
BainBridgeBooks
an imprint of
Trans-Atlantic Publications Inc.
Philadelphia PA

Website: www.transatlanticpub.com

PRINTED IN CANADA

ISBN: 1-891696-12-2

Library of Congress Cataloging-in-Publication Data

Tripps, Dan G.
     The heart of success : conversations with notable achievers / by Dan G. Tripps ; fore-
word by Walter Cronkite ; postscript by John Wooden.
        p. cm.
     ISBN 1-891696-12-2 (paper original)
Success. I. Title

BJ1611.2 T75 2000
158.1—dc21

                                                                00-044475

Dedication

To all of you who have recognized your responsibilities and fulfilled them, discovered your dreams and pursued them, and through it all made a contribution to just one life. You have left the world a better place, and you have found the heart of success.

Acknowledgements

Always fascinated by those who excel, I had for a long time wanted to talk face-to-face with exceptional people in a variety of occupations to find out what made them rise above the rest. If I could find some common elements among them, I would be able to provide a marvelous personal and professional resource for my students. But who should I meet? My first task was to formulate a list of individuals. With the help of my long-time friend **Ev Dennis**, Distinguished Professor of Business at Fordham University, I developed a fascinating list of extraordinary people across an array of representative achievement areas. Perhaps, more importantly, through his good name and reputation, I had access to many of them. Thank you, Ev, for opening my mind and opening the doors.

Throughout the first year of the project, I phoned, faxed, and sent email messages to set up the interviews. The idea that I could actively meet with the people on my list was not a prospect many took seriously. I owe to my sweet friend **Ann Marie Hanel**, Executive Director for School Administration in the Bellingham Public Schools, more gratitude than these lines can express for believing in me, my idea, and my plan. Without her encouragement and logistical support, the endeavor would still be only an idea with an unworkable plan. Thank you, Ann Marie, for nourishing my soul and enabling my dream.

During the three years of interviews, I traveled around the U.S. on planes and trains and in my car, meeting with those on my list and taping our conversations. I returned to Seattle each time with a satchel full of tapes. Every interview was transcribed, word for word, through the labor and supervision of my two wonderful secretaries **Cori Miller** and **Karyn Kiemele**. Thank you so much for building the bricks of the edifice and for enduring throughout with a smile.

As the 2,000 pages of conversations began to fill a row of binders on my worktable, I wondered if I might have something that could talk to readers beyond the halls of my university. It was clear I needed help to create a public concept and to find a trade publisher. By chance, I met one of America's truly notable international literary agents **Roslyn Targ** who helped me shape the concept and in the process became one of my dearest friends. No less serendipitously, I developed a wonderful friendship with a gifted Kean University professor **Ruth Piatnochka,** who meticulously edited my work and in the process guided my path through the publishing process. Thank you, both, for transforming my odyssey into a publication. Roslyn, if it were not for you, I would never have thought myself to be a writer. Ruth, if it were not for you, no one would have ever read what I wrote.

Of course, that brings me to the publisher. Thank you **Ron Smolin** for seeing potential in my work and providing the vehicle for its public debut. Thank you, too, **Lane Startin** for honing it into a comfortable format.

There are many people who helped make this endeavor possible because they performed those tasks without which nothing ever happens. While it may seem unfair to single out any among them, I hope the others left unnamed will see their place in this paragraph. To all the members of the administrative corps, such as **Marlene Adler** and **Cori Martin** and the hundreds like the two of you who facilitated my various requests and enabled me to meet with this extraordinary group of achievers, thank you. And to all my students and colleagues, in particular my department head, **Grant Hill**, and my comrade-in-ideas, **Bob Grams**, who gave me the freedom to pursue my dream and kept my classes humming, thank you.

Finally, without question, I have an enormous amount of gratitude for all the interviewees, for it is their lives and their stories and their wisdom that form the substance of the book. To all of you, thank you. To **Walter Cronkite** and **John Wooden**, two men whom I have admired all my life, who were gracious enough to be interviewed and kind enough to create the bookends to my work, a special thank you for your contribution to my research and to my life.

CONTENTS

The Heart of Success:
Conversations with Notable Achievers

Foreword

By Walter Cronkite

In the last half of the 20th Century, Americans became somewhat confused about achievement. Among other things, they were increasingly unable to separate success from notoriety. I've always perceived success to be the result of an accomplishment that is worthy of admiration, perhaps even noteworthy in our history. Today, it is not that at all; it is the number of times one gets into the gossip columns. Notoriety has become success. That is hardly the proper definition.

When I look back at the first half of the 20th Century, our national heroes tended to come out of science, the military, and politics. Beginning with the 1950s, particularly since the development of television, athletes and entertainers have dominated the public's attention. Few of these individuals will achieve lasting fame. Their notoriety is a reflection of the culture of the last half of the 20th Century, a manifestation of the Andy Warhol notion that everyone is famous for 15 minutes.

The media obviously is the guilty party in the creation of such notoriety, but it also remains the basic recorder of those who can lay legitimate claim to historical fame. By and large, the media does as good a job as we should expect of it. It identifies the Nobel Prize winners, and presents individuals in politics and world affairs, so the record is there for future generations to appreciate and understand.

Money, too, is now very definitely a part of notoriety. But even in sports, where money is so dominant a criterion for notoriety, it is the person's accomplishments that go into the record books, not the amount of money that was made.

While I am not optimistic that this malaise of notoriety is going to change, neither am I terribly disturbed by it. There is no inherent harm in this exaltation of personalities for less than substantial reasons. Where it does make a difference is when these personalities and the events in which they are involved edge out in the media those matters that the public ought to be interested in. There are so many major issues that we should be concerned with today that aren't getting a proper exposition because notoriety is taking up the pages of our newspapers and the time on the airwaves.

Thus, it is well and good that *The Heart of Success* calls our attention to the difference between achievement and notoriety. It is important to reinforce the notion that truly successful individuals make a contribution in their field that has an impact beyond their own lifetime, regardless of the recognition they receive. Now, for historical greatness, that achievement requires public recognition.

It is also important to reinforce the notion that making a major contribution of impact does not require that the individual necessarily meet public approval in every other way. With the White House scandals that plagued the Clinton administration, we were nudged to look at former leaders and their peccadilloes, and there are few whose private lives would meet all the public's expectations.

In addition to presenting some well known people, this book calls our attention to the many people out on the streets of our cities who are doing great things without wide public recognition. A person can achieve something notable without bringing notice to themselves. For many, achievement comes within their own profession or through service to the community.

As Dr. Tripps points out here, the real significant component of success is devotion to the principles of the achiever's craft, a devotion to the goal. At the core, there's an impassioned, almost spiritual quality to their quest. And the heart of success is a legacy that goes down in history even if it goes unrecognized by the public.

One of the most respected names in journalism, Walter Cronkite was anchor of "The CBS Evening News" from 1962 to 1981. During his tenure at CBS, he was considered one of the most recognized and trusted individuals in America. His trademark broadcast signoff, "And that's the way it is," was known universally throughout the country. Since retiring from network news, Cronkite has been active producing and hosting documentaries on science and space exploration.

Chapter 1

The Lure of Success

The Lure of Success

In 1953, my father took me to my first college football game, and I marveled at the grace and speed of USC running back Aramis Dandoy, and something began to bubble inside my soul. In 1954, I was glued to our tiny television as New York Giant center fielder Willie Mays made "the catch" in the Polo Grounds. A year later, I saw Hall of Fame quarterback Norm Van Brocklin. I still have the trading card he signed that day. The following spring, I sat spellbound as Charlie Dumas eliminated the 7-foot barrier in the high jump. In the fall, I attended my first opera and felt my body quiver to the sounds of Beverly Sills. There was a stream of remarkable people that flowed through my childhood. Adali Stevenson and Dwight David Eisenhower. Mickey Mantle and Stan Musial. During my college years it became a river. John Kennedy and The Beatles. Pablo Picasso at the Getty Museum and Aba Eban at the United Nations. Alan Shepard on the moon and Allen Ginsberg on life. The names and achievements were, and still are, amazing.

I was not alone in the fascination. Whether in first grade or graduate school, in my office or at a pub, it was clear to me that chanting the litany of achievers or trying to become one of them is part of an American ritual. Like so many others, I joined the choir. I pursued the dream of achievement as a performer, as an athlete in high school and college. I shaped the dream of achievement as a mentor, as a coach for dozens of All-American, professional and Olympic competitors. At every step of the journey, I was surrounded by people devoted to reaching their dreams. I was also engulfed by three nagging questions: Why did some make it while others did not? Was it worth it when they got there? What was success after all? Now, as a professor teaching about achievement, it seemed like the right time to go looking for answers.

I did just that. For three years, I crisscrossed America to talk with those who had made it. In hotel lobbies and penthouse apartments, on back porches and pool decks, following their recitals and in between their meetings, at their labs and their vacation retreats, I had the privilege of spending time with some of the most notable people in the land. They have won the World Series and the Nobel Prize, conquered Mt. Everest and Wall Street, held stage at Wimbleton and La Scala, gathered Olympic and Emmy gold, changed history and themselves.

In the pages that follow, you will find profiles of 40 of the 160 I met. They share personal reflections of their careers and their lives. Their remarks are often inspirational and reveal the people behind the accomplishments. In the first eight chapters, they discuss critical factors common to their achievements: focused will, self-discipline, intuition, hard work, overcoming obstacles, going the distance, taking risks, and working with others. In the closing chapters they offer two powerful perspectives on the real merits of achievement: understanding self and making a difference for others. All together, the ten chapters serve to define the heart of success.

Many of those you will read about are famous, due of course to the media attention extended to their careers or intruded into their lives. Many are not, because of the anonymity of their medium or the privacy of their lives. But all of them offer comments and perspectives about achievement, its relationship to success, and the impact of the journey that I hope will remind you of similar points along your path.

A book about extraordinary achievement built on interviews could be challenged with regard to the individuals or the accomplishments selected. While extraordinary achievers and extraordinary achievements have been the consummate symbols of success in America, our nation is a complex and diverse society, and what Americans deem to be extraordinary has taken many different forms. But I truly believe the individuals interviewed constitute a representative sample of achievement. Let me explain my thinking and introduce the individuals.

Adventurers have always been viewed as extraordinary achievers. In the early years of the nation, it was frontiersmen like Davy Crockett, pioneers like Calamity Jane, and explorers like Robert Peary. At the dawning of the 20th Century, extraordinary achievement for the adventurer was conquest of the sky. The Wright Brothers soared in flight. Chuck Yeager broke the sound barrier. John Glenn ventured into outer space. Today, with few places to explore, all that is left of the adventurer are the daredevils who claim attention through courageous feats reported by the media; sailor **Karen Thorndike**, land-speed fanatic **Craig Breedlove**, and mountaineer **Tom Hornbein**, all profiled in this book, are among them.

Capitalists have often been among those deemed successful. In the late 19th and early 20th centuries a host of industrialists succeeded in ways so extraordinary that, measured in dollars, their achievements remain hard to comprehend. Nearly all began poor. Few were formally educated. They earned the admiration of the nation for rising up and making it on their own as did J. P. Morgan, Andrew Carnegie, and John D. Rockefeller among many. Although most American CEO's today are among the most wealthy people on the planet, they are not given the esteem of their predecessors. While America is a country where the love of money is epidemic, it is the manner in which it is obtained that matters. Success is characterized by entrepreneurs who have amazing instinct, like IMG President **Mark McCormack**; who are courageous enough to take risks akin to desktop publishing inventor, **Paul Brainerd**; or who lead a small band of comrades from vision to victory, similar to public relations founder, **Daniel Edelman.**

Politics was an achievement area that regularly produced icons of success across the years from George Washington to Abraham Lincoln to Franklin Roosevelt to John Kennedy. But the advent of television and the quasi-tabloid approach to investigative journalism have made politics a quagmire, muddying the waters by creating a skeptical, if not cynical, public. The result is that image has become the single most important criterion for political success. Just listen to former presidential candidate **Bob Dole**, who talks about it in the pages ahead. Ironically, the Justices of the Supreme Court have no regard for image and shun personal publicity and media coverage. Of course, that may explain why so few can name all nine and why law today is short on John Marshalls or notable figures at all, except **Sandra Day O'Connor**, as the profile clearly suggests.

Arguably, the military has produced more esteemed Americans than any other institution. Army Generals George Patton and Douglas MacArthur, Navy Admiral William Hasley, Air Force General William Mitchell, and Marine Colonel Gregory Boyington earned their honors as America fought the Mexican War, two World Wars, and Korea. But the attack on the morality and efficacy of the U.S. military that began during Vietnam altered our traditional high regard for the military. Subsequent incidents such as the Iran hostage rescue, Lebanon peacekeeping force, and complicated operations in Panama, Iraq, Somalia, Haiti, Bosnia, and Kosovo explain why few military heroes have emerged since and why the nation views POWs as the real heroes of the war. It also explains why the nation looks to officers of principle and dignity, like **General Harry Brooks**, as the real leaders of the armed forces.

Scientists have occasionally been included in the pantheon of success. Thomas Edison, Albert Einstein, and Jonas Salk are as familiar as Erector sets. But like the toy, they are from another time. Today, despite having unlocked the secrets of DNA, James Watson and Francis Crick are practically anonymous. So are those who give life to the dying, like heart transplant surgeon **Margaret Allen,** and **Belding Scribner**, whose work paved the way for kidney dialysis. While the Nobel Prize represents the pinnacle of achievement for scientists, it is more famous than its recipients as the research that won the crown, like that of physicist **Leon Lederman**, is usually beyond understanding. Biologist **Paul Ehrlich,** who made his work understandable in a simple book, had the fame, appearing on the Johnny Carson show more than two dozen times, but never won the Nobel Prize. Complicating the matter, scientific breakthroughs such as in-vitro babies and cloned sheep have given rise to public questions about the limits and morality of science altogether.

Ironically, moralists — philosophers, clergy, educators — have seldom been seen as models of success. Thomas Jefferson and Martin Luther King were deemed men of noble thought. And in survey after survey, Americans report that teachers are the most influential people in their lives. But rarely, however, do teachers mount the podium, as in the case of **Jaime Escalante**, whose riveting story portrayed in the movie *Stand and Deliver* reminded us of their value. We have always admired people of faith and virtue but we also seem to enjoy seeing them fall from grace. And there have been a lot of tumbles. Jimmy Swaggart was involved with prostitutes and Jim Bakker bilked his congregation. More dramatically, morality has changed as strong opinions about homosexuality and abortion have led to divergent moral views. As made obvious in his profile, reinforcing morality in order to renew relationships and leadership is what Promise Keeper founder **Bill McCartney** seeks to achieve. President Emeritus of Notre Dame and recipient of the Medal of Freedom, **Theodore Hesburgh**, seeks even more. He wants all humanity to be part of our relationships and leadership to become a synonym for service that makes a difference in others' lives.

Historically, success was characterized by individual achievement that resulted in a better America. But during the 20th Century, with the rise of mass communications, the traditional meaning of success faded into history and Americans redefined success in terms of notoriety. The media helped make Joe Lewis, George Gershwin, Mary Pickford, and Babe Ruth larger than life in an earlier era and it is the media that have enshrined sport and entertainment stars as the global models of success today. Largely the result of film and television, actors who portray notable moments in history have become more celebrated than those who originally created them, and hitting a home run or a high C offers a whole new meaning to notable. From Madonna to Michael Jordan, success has come to be defined by momentary triumph in an illusionary world. As with our notions about appropriate behavior, our notions about noteworthy achievement are gradually adapting to the mass consensus coaxed out by media and marketing. The result is that extraordinary achievement and success are now most frequently defined by the accomplishments of those in sports and entertainment.

The passion for sports is extremely complicated. It is part spectacle and part religion. But many argue that sport is one of the rare places where success and failure are measured against objective standards and excellence is the filter for achievement. These are the virtues that Hall of Fame baseball manager **Sparky Anderson** and Hall of Fame football coach **Bill Walsh** advocate for their teams and use to live their lives. And we appreciate that because we live in a world where there is little objectivity. In other occupations, success can be the result of circumstance: the achievers knew the right people or they were born into it. In sport, there is no other way but to combine talent with the passion of Olympic ice hockey hero **Mike Eruzione**, the commitment of swimmer **John Naber**, the work ethic of two-time American League Batting Champion **Edgar Martinez**, the determination of Olympic gymnast **Kathy Johnson Clarke**, and the tenacity of six-time Ironman Champion **Mark Allen**.

Since most people do not have great talent, watching sports lets them at least identify with success vicariously. From the grandstands, fans are often more captivated by the athlete's intense and often entertaining personality than by the performance. Along with talent, today's athletes possess a charisma that few others can match. America's Cup captain **Dawn Riley** and retired Boston Celtics basketball coach **Red Auerbach** have it in spades, while ultra distance athlete and TV commentator **Diana Nyad** and the best doubles player in tennis history **Pam Shriver** have it in hearts, literally and figuratively.

But in contemporary American society, the epitome of success is not the All-Star but the entertainment star. Movies have enormous power over people. They enable people to escape safely from their reality. In the 1920s, an industry arose to bring good stories and intriguing people to the silver screen. Award-winning cinematographer **Ken Burns** talks about the rigor it takes to become one of the best at the craft. In the late 1940s, another industry arose to bring those stories home and make their stars a part of every household. Television became the nation's electronic campfire. In movies, the audience could live out the dreams of what and where they would like to be. In television, viewers found a mirror to their own worlds and found themselves as heroes. Real world television star **Judge Mills Lane** minces few words in telling you how to reach for your dreams in real life. Former fantasy world television star and model **Rebekka Armstrong** does likewise, telling you what can happen when they are not the right dreams.

In part because of television, all the arts are alive and well in America. Novelist **Chaim Potok**, choreographer **Mark Morris,** and saxophonist **Don Lanphere** explain their path to the top of those careers. Classical music, the performance medium with a list of achievers that spans more centuries and more continents than any other medium, is also flourishing, enabling Oregon Symphony maestro **James DePreist** and former St. Paul Chamber Orchestra music director **Hugh Wolff** to stand on the podium of success while working in two of America's smaller towns. Despite the fact that only five percent of the public has any encounter with classical music, television has helped violinist **Hilary Hahn**, pianist **Vladimir Feltsman**, and cellist **Lynn Harrell** to acquire stardom from a public that often knows little about the music they play. Even opera has seen a renaissance in America substantially due to the global broadcast of the Three Tenors concerts that catapulted Pavarotti, Carreras, and Domingo from extraordinary voices appreciated by an elite niche to superstars. Despite its highbrow reputation, opera does not require an intellectual appreciation. It has visuals, energy, words, and music that are now packaged and sold as mass entertainment instead of high culture, making it an occasion for everyone. Singer **Frederica Von Stade** talks about the magical moments of opera and its relationship to her life.

If the magic is in the visuals, energy, text and music, then there are no greater magicians than rock musicians. It is they who are America's elite. No athlete, actor, or artist enjoys the adoration of so many people. Their celebrity is worldwide. Their achievement is built on passion. For some it is intellectual, like the lyrics of Bob Dylan. For others it is emotional, like a Janis Joplin wail. They are also the voices of freedom. Some of it is sexual but some of it is political. When the Berlin Wall was falling down and Eastern Europe was changing, teens there were inspired by rock messages of hope. The essence of the message, the genre, and success within it are the subjects of the **Roger**

McGwinn profile, founder and lead singer for what may arguably be America's first supergroup, The Byrds.

While on first glance sport and entertainment may appear to be strange bedfellows, they are far more compatible than you think. Both suspend time. Both involve the unexpected. Both are powerful emotional and social experiences where you are surrounded by people sharing the same hopes, dreams, and champions. Through sport and entertainment, individuals can get beyond their daily humdrum existences and escape into another world. When everything works, it really is magic, and they talk about the performance for the rest of their lives.

These are exceptionally good times for sport and entertainment. In a world bolstered by a vibrant global economy, television and the Internet deliver, for the first time in history, sports and entertainment twenty-four hours a day, seven days a week, every day of the year, making us constant and intimate spectators to the rich and famous. It really is no wonder Americans believe that recognition is essential for success. And the data support the concept. Among the leading uses of discretionary income, Americans take lessons, attend seminars, and hire personal trainers to be like those they deem successful. Fascinated by those who have it, they purchase tickets to events and seek autographs, take photos, and line highways to wave and to touch and compensate for their perceived ordinariness. As a result, Americans cannot separate success from notoriety, extraordinary accomplishment from extraordinary people, and achieving great things from living great lives.

That brings us back to the three questions. Why do some people make it while others do not? I think you will find in the profiles that a single answer to achievement is a myth. Yet, I think you will also find that certain personality traits and personal needs characterize achieving individuals and influence their ways of pursuing their goals and responding to the opportunities and challenges en route. Is it worth it when you get there? I think the profiles will suggest that there are some heavy costs as well as some surprising benefits to a life devoted to achieving. What is success after all? That is a tough one. I hope through the profiles you will come to understand the energizing, if often troubled, closing decades of the 20th Century and at least differentiate success from stardom. In doing so, you will have learned something about the heart of success.

But more of that a bit later. Let's take a look at success through the eyes of those who seem to have it.

Chapter 2

It Takes Absolute Will

Mike Eruzione

Captain and Hero of the 1980 U.S.
Olympic Hockey Team's Miracle on Ice

In February 1980, Americans were hard pressed to find something positive about life. US hostages were still being held in Iran, the doomsday diplomacy of the Cold War was in full swing, and the economy was colder than the weather. The mood in the country was dour. But with one swing of a stick, it all changed as a rag-tag collection of hockey players lifted the spirit of the nation by winning the gold medal at the Winter Olympic Games in Lake Placid, New York. That stick belonged to team captain Mike Eruzione, who remains today a symbol of hope and the hero of the team that will be forever remembered for the "Miracle on Ice."

"At the time, we didn't know how big the event was," Eruzione says, still stunned by its significance today. "I had scored game-winning goals before and they were big goals. But because it was the Olympics and against the Soviets, and because of all the atmosphere the goal generated, it was certainly my biggest goal."

The Soviet Union national team was one of the best ice hockey clubs ever assembled, amateur or professional. Incredibly disciplined, superbly coached and with years of experience playing with each other, they were virtually invincible. Going into Lake Placid, the Soviets had won four straight gold medals and were heavy favorites again. They hadn't lost a single game in Olympic competition since 1968. In 1979, they shut out a team of NHL all-stars 6-0 in Madison Square Garden while playing their backup goaltender. Shortly before the Olympic Games, they crushed the United States 10-3 in an exhibition.

The American team by contrast was a collection of college players and minor leaguers groomed for international competition on a 60-game exhibition tour. Seeded seventh in a field of 12, they were not expected to contend. But led by Eruzione, coach Herb Brooks, forward Mark Johnson, goaltender Jim Craig and future NHL all-star Neal Broten, the Americans hung tough throughout the tournament, skating to a tie with Sweden in the opening game and winning three straight — including a contest against the formidable Czechs — to set up their match with the U.S.S.R in the medal round.

With exactly 10 minutes left in regulation, Eruzione's 30-foot shot went past Soviet goaltender Vladimir Myshkin to give the United States a 4-3 lead. Despite intense Soviet offensive pressure in the closing minutes, the scrappy Americans hung on to win, assuring the United States of its first Olympic medal in hockey in 20 years. The game-winning goal not only stunned the world, it revitalized the spirits of the American people as the win came against a nation that inspired political fear and athletic awe across the country.

Twenty years later, US media converged to celebrate the anniversary of the win. "With all the media attention it has received and all the people calling, I now realize just how big it was," Eruzione says happily.

The celebration on the ice after the Soviet victory was electrifying, as might be expected, but the celebration on the medal stand following a come-from-behind 4-2 win over Finland two days later to clinch the gold was nothing less than an emotional mirror of the American psyche. During the awards ceremony, the gold medal was presented to Eruzione as the team captain. Then, in a moment that will go down in Olympic folklore, Eruzione called his teammates up to the podium to share the moment with him. Even some of the Soviets, who were on the stand wearing their silver medals, were seen applauding the team.

"The 1980 US Olympic team wasn't just Mike Eruzione. It was a team. It wasn't right for just me to be up there," he says. "We have become much more than buddies. There is a bond that will never die. And that bond would exist even if we had lost. The friendship and respect we developed for one another during that six-month period would have overshadowed any defeat." Eruzione stays in contact with his teammates to this day.

Eruzione, who played for minor league teams in Toledo, Ohio, and Philadelphia before the Olympics and was considered a marginal prospect by NHL scouts, reflected on his options following the triumph. He chose not to further pursue a professional hockey career, effectively retiring after Lake Placid. "Success is when one achieves the goal that they set out to achieve in any environment: athletics, music, business. It doesn't matter," he proposes. "Failure is when a person does not do everything they could have done to achieve their goals. After the Olympics, I looked at my life as an athlete and realized I had done all that I could and I had accomplished what I wanted. It was time to move on and do something else. What greater way to move on than having won the gold medal?"

Today, Eruzione serves as the director of development for athletics at his alma mater, Boston University, where he is primarily responsible for raising money for the athletic program. But he also helps out with the university hockey team and scrimmages with his sons, staying fully connected to the game he loves.

You don't have to be an ardent hockey fan to recognize success in the sport demands a very competitive — even aggressive — personality. But tenacity might just be Eruzione's middle name. "I am very goal-oriented. I have a great work ethic, an enormous desire to be successful, to achieve the goals that I intend to achieve. I am fiercely competitive, maybe driven. But those are all things you have to have to be the best," Eruzione exhorts. He also extols the virtues of environment, temporarily the winner in his own analysis of the battle of nurture versus nature. "I grew up in a three-family house with cousins, and we were competing all the time. So it was instilled in me at a young age that in order to achieve your goals, you've got to work hard and you've got to fight for everything you want. We grew up in a working class environment and there wasn't a lot of money, so whatever you wanted to get you had to be very competitive, very aggressive, and never give up."

Eruzione does not see the same characteristics in many young players today, as the blue collar world is quickly being replaced by shirts and ties. "Kids today are a lot more comfortable than we were," Eruzione suggests. "Look at the time they spend in front of the television or on the computer. We didn't have a TV when I was a kid, so we were out playing. You are really a product of your environment." And the comment hits home. Eruzione acknowledges his sons have a completely different approach to hockey and to life than he, and he finds the differences perplexing. "They don't seem to be as competitive as me. They want to win, they want to do well. But when I watch them play hockey, I think, 'Why doesn't he go after that person?' I don't mean in the physical sense, just to work him."

> "We didn't have a TV when I was a kid, so we were out playing. You are really a product of your environment."

If you want to be a hockey player you had better be competitive and aggressive. If you are not, you are going to get hurt or you are not going to play. So like a gold miner digging into rock beds, Eruzione tries to extract those nuggets from his children. "I tell them, 'When the guy has the puck, you got to play with a passion. You've got to go after people. You can't just stand back and wait for things to come to you.' But I don't think they're convinced."

In his classic jovial Italian manner, Eruzione switches from nurture to nature to explain the dilemma. "They are very quiet, go about their business, like my wife's side of the family. I have a nephew like them. I told my wife and my sister one day, 'He's the nicest kid. I would want him to marry my daughter, but I wouldn't want him to stand in my first line.' There's nothing wrong with him. He's still young so that drive could kick in at some point."

In his playing days, the drive propelled Eruzione beyond the opposition. "You have to have a dislike for your opponents because they're trying to take something away from you. You set a goal and they've set that same goal themselves. You have to say inside of you, 'I'm not going to let them take something that I want to achieve.' Hate is not the word, but dislike is a good one."

In the highly competitive and aggressive world of ice hockey it is only the respect each player has for the opponent that keeps the game from becoming violent. "You have to want to hit that guy, but you must respect him as a person, follow the rules of the game and hit him a certain way."

That drive in Eruzione is still evident today and it oozes out in his speech and in his actions. "You have to love what you're doing," Eruzione advises, nearly shouting to make his point. "I have a passion for hockey. I've always had it. If you don't have it, then you're not going to work and strive for your goal as hard as you should. Improvement stipulates that you are getting better. But improvement is not the end where you want to be. It is nice to get better, but how much better are you if you still don't reach your goal?"

> "You have to have a dislike for your opponents because they're trying to take something away from you. ... You have to say inside of you, 'I'm not going to let them take something that I want to achieve.'"

Whether you are Wayne Gretzky or Mike Eruzione, at some point in your life, the career must come to a stop. But that doesn't mean you stop setting goals. "Life goes on," Eruzione submits. "At some point in your life, things start to change. You just set goals for yourself in other endeavors. So you prepare your life, and you take the same competitiveness, the same energy, and find something else to apply it to."

We all know sport is not the end. It is a vehicle. It is a part of one's life.

The road ends for players at every level, and then the next part of life begins ... but not for everyone. "You get those guys that remain frustrated athletes all their lives," Eruzione chuckles. "I play against them in hockey games. There is this guy who is 45 years old and he still thinks he's going to play in the NHL. Those people have to get a grip on things a little and realize that it is over and enjoy the game. They need to go back to the reason they played it in the beginning, because they liked to do it." More importantly, they need to be happy with who they are now, not with who they were then and measure success on what they are doing now, not what they have done.

"The most important thing you can always have in your life is peace of mind. I am very happy with who I am, and I am no different personally than I was 20 years ago. Things around me have changed. I have a house; I have an opportunity to make good money. When you are given an opportunity in life, it's what you do with your opportunity that's important. But I'm the same person. I firmly believe that as long as I am doing what I want to be doing, whatever that is, I would be just as happy as I am today."

Not everyone, even those who bring such intensity to the stadium, is going to reach the pinnacle of an Olympic dream. Aware of the potential for defeat, Eruzione nevertheless always counsels his listeners to proceed full steam ahead. "Not everyone is going to succeed," Eruzione concedes. "You have to accept the results because someone is going to win, someone is going to lose. I arrive every day, prepare every day, to win. And when I don't win, that's OK, because I worked damn hard trying to do it. Things just didn't fall into place for me. So I get up the next day and work harder, and try to win again. Neither then or now is there any intention of turning back! I am determined to make it."

In one of the most inspirational movies ever made, *Rudy*, a determined 24-year old Daniel "Rudy" Ruettiger sits with his father on the bus stop bench. Against the counsel of his family, teachers, and coaches, the poorly-skilled Rudy is resolved to leave his job at the mill and go to Notre Dame to play football. In his impassioned response to his father's gloomy predictions, Rudy boldly tells his father he is tired of everyone telling him he cannot make his dream come true. Eruzione, animated and equally impassioned, stands in for Rudy's dad and replays the scene. "You've got to live your own life and go for your dreams. You have to go out and do what you think you have to do," Eruzione pleads. "I would have told that to Rudy. I tell that to kids today. If you want to go to school or do something, go do it. If it doesn't work, at least it's your decision. You have to make your own decisions on your life and what you want to do with it. And don't let anyone tell you otherwise. The Miracle on Ice was not a miracle. It was a matter of will."

The winter of 1980 is long gone. The Cold War has thawed. The Russians are no longer the evil empire. The hostages are home. The Berlin Wall has crumbled. There is no enemy out there any more. The only one left may be the one inside of us that dares us not to dare at all. If that one appears, remember Mike Eruzione and the Miracle on Ice.

Chaim Potok

Author of the Award-Winning
1967 Novel, The Chosen

His father, Benjamin Max Potok, emigrated from Poland to the United States in 1921 and sold stationery before the Depression and jewelry thereafter. Benjamin and Mollie Friedman Potok, he once told the *New York Times*, raised him in a Hasidic world "without the beard and the earlocks."

Rabbi Chaim Potok is the quintessential Jew. His educational résumé includes preparatory work at the Talmudic Academy of Yeshiva College (University), a BA in English literature at Yeshiva University, and a master's in Hebrew literature and rabbinical ordination from the Jewish Theological Seminary of America, all in New York City. He met his wife, Adena, at a Jewish camp in the Poconos in 1952 and married her six years later. His brother became a rabbi and his two sisters married rabbis. He wears a wonderfully full beard but no earlocks. He is 70 years old, now living in Philadelphia. At last count, Potok is the author of eight novels, four non-fiction books, four plays, four short stories and three children's books.

Potok started writing fiction at the age of 16. His first submission was to *Atlantic Monthly* a year later. The piece was not published but Potok received a complimentary note from an editor asking if he was writing a novel. Potok's journey into writing was not an accident. "There are no choices involved," Potok asserts softly but sharply. "Nobody who is going to be serious about his life sits down and says, 'Well, I could be a doctor, I could be a lawyer, I could be a salesman. I think I'll try and be a lawyer.' It doesn't work that way. Something reaches out and grabs you."

Several things have grabbed Potok. Among other things, he defines himself as a novelist, playwright, historian, theologian, and philosopher, the latter the result of his Ph.D. in philosophy from the University of Pennsylvania. Clearly, he is qualified to talk about complicated principles of life. As for being grabbed from somewhere, Potok is quite sure it is not what some might describe as a calling. "That's a theological word," Potok retorts politely but decisively. He is clearly qualified to talk about that subject too, having served as chaplain in Korea, an instructor at the University of Judaism in Los

Angeles, a scholar-in-residence at Har Zion Temple in Philadelphia, managing editor for *Conservative Judaism*, and editor-in-chief for the Jewish Publication Society of America. "All disciplines have a term for this experience," Potok expounds. "For me, it occurred as a teenager. I read novels one after the other and I knew when I finished the second novel, I was going to learn this craft and spend the rest of my life writing stories and I was going to shape my world and life through them."

Now it helps if you have some talent and, as simple as this may sound, you learn very quickly whether you've got the talent or not because the hints are all over the place. "If you've been grabbed this way and you don't have talent, the world really stomps you down," Potok notes with amusement. "But, if you've got talent, you will come to know it and then begin the apprenticeship." Musicians, for example, are often discovered as children and then begin years of study under a mentor to learn their instruments. And in pedagogically sound elementary classrooms, teachers are telling students they have talent and they begin to learn.

That's what happened to Potok at 16. "This grab from somewhere reaches out and pulls you in. I don't know what it is. I don't think anyone knows what that is," says the theologian-philosopher. "I don't think Freud knew what it was. I don't think we've come to a point in our understanding of ourselves that we can, with any measure of certainty, describe that dynamic. But there is a shift that occurs inside the individual as a result of an experience or series of experiences, and the individual is forever changed. That's a prerequisite for extraordinary accomplishment."

The world has a very ruthless way of telling you whether you've been grabbed or not. If no one has discovered your talent or you're getting C's in a particular discipline, Potok says, "the world is telling you to cool it, back off, try something else." That is hard to accept for anyone. But if you listen and make the change and you are finally grabbed in a particular domain, Potok says, "give it 10 or 15 years of your life. It's not going to happen in one or two years. BUT, there had better be hints along the way because it's foolish to do it if there aren't hints that there's real quality there."

The transformation of talent into accomplishment is a struggle of enormous proportions. It does not come easily or quickly. Ego and ambition are prerequisites and more than that, the two must be merged into what Potok calls focused will. "You have to be absolutely convinced that what you're

> " ... there is a shift that occurs inside the individual as a result of an experience or series of experiences, and the individual is forever changed. That's a prerequisite for extraordinary accomplishment."

doing nobody else can do… In other words, you have to be convinced you're bringing something radically new to the scene and nobody else can bring that radically new thing to the scene. That's what I mean by a focused will. And that means that you will drive yourself and everybody around you crazy."

The wall between focused will and obsession is permeable. In fact, Potok's philosophy and his life suggest focused will is merely another word for obsession with the difference being the support system around you. "If you're lucky, you marry someone who understands what you want to do and supports you," Potok concedes pointing to his wife of more than forty years, "but who tells you when you're going overboard, and you learn to listen."

Harvard Psychologist Howard Gardner has suggested that one of the most extraordinary forms of accomplishment that we've lost sight of today is that of nurturing other people and that such was a significant gift of women that has been lost in their effort for equality. "Absolutely," Potok nearly shouts. "I consider myself such a fortunate man to have met and married this woman and to have her as the mother of the children we've brought into this world, because she's not only smart, Phi Beta Kappa, OK, that's terrific, but she is a nurturer par excellence. And I'm grateful for it."

> "You have to be absolutely convinced that what you're doing nobody else can do."

Like his wife, Potok's children also became part of the support system for his literary pursuits. "The children learned very early on," Potok reports, "that when I was staring off into space it's not that I didn't love them, it's that I was somewhere else. I was sitting at the table and they were talking to me, and I was there and not there at the same time because I was in the middle of something I was working on." That can be confusing, even frustrating to children who may not identify with their father's focus as they seek his time and attention. "They learn to live with it," Potok maintains, "and you compensate for it in other ways. You try to make it a normal way of living."

More often, it is not. Data suggest that marriages among highly accomplished people break up at a far higher rate than marriages in the average population, which break up about one out of every two. So focused will can leave you deficient in some other places of life. "It certainly does," Potok accepts. "It leaves you deficient in your relationship with your family. It leaves you deficient in the number of friends you have, because there are times when you can't fully participate in the life of a community." But ever the philosopher, Potok is quick to point out that "you find out fairly easily who your real friends are, because the ones who aren't your real friends take umbrage and disappear. And you don't need more than a handful of friends anyway. At least I don't because the friends that I have are really deep friends. But, there is a price to pay. And it's a high price."

Across four decades, from his award-winning novels, including *The Chosen* (1967) and *My Name is Asher Lev* (1972), to his latest children's book, *Zebra and Other Stories* (1998), Potok has shaped his world and his life through stories. He looks back and agrees the price has been worth the cost. "The changes are simply awesome," Potok announces. "I construct the world in a way that is altogether different today from the way I constructed it 40 years ago. I have a new sense of human nature, of the cosmos. I have an awareness of the interaction of human beings and the world around us, that we're all creatures in contexts and the contexts are given. To that extent we're creatures of accident, depending upon where we're born. I did not think that way before."

You can see the evolution in Potok's thinking through his novels that become more and more complex throughout the years. His 1992 novel, *I Am the Clay*, was about the removal of a woman's grave from one site to another. Potok saw that happen when he was stationed in Korea as a young man. "I couldn't have written that 45 years ago," Potok concedes. "I could never have gotten into those people and I was in Korea for 16 months. I had that experience in me, but I carried it with me all these decades because I had to be at a certain level in my thinking and feeling and growing before I could get into the hearts and the minds of those Korean farmers."

There is a path or trajectory of change in the ways we think, the ways we see the world, as we strive to achieve. One could argue that people who don't go through that process are only repeating rather than growing; they are merely spinning their wheels, dead in the water. One could argue that such personal transformation, in and of itself, without any public recognition, is an extraordinary accomplishment. After all, discovering self and bringing it out to the open, being comfortable with one's self, is a difficult journey. "That's the great adventure of life," Potok exclaims. "To be open to that kind of trajectory. And the person who isn't open to that kind of trajectory has tossed the anchor overboard and just circles around where the anchor has stuck in the mud on the ocean bottom and is just circling around instead of navigating or sailing dangerously where real meaning and real accomplishment occur."

But even adventurous journeys require some guidance. Potok is sure he has discovered a map, what he calls the construct. It came to him when he was done with *The Chosen,* and he has been exploring it in all of his work ever since. And the construct is this: we face an ascending order of confrontations, each more difficult than the previous one to resolve, each requiring us to give up something in order to resolve the confrontation and move on. "What I'm doing now in my work is writing about individuals who are trying to reconstruct the pasts they abandoned," Potok explains. "They're reconstructing them late in life when they're close to being old and wondering whether the abandonment was worth it or not. That's the trajectory. Because there's going to be abandonment on the part of many individuals, and the questions will follow: What did they abandon? What did they get for the abandonment? Was it worth it? Where are they now? That's the agenda."

Heavy-duty stuff. It has been the focus of Potok's will for nearly half of his life and he still has many more stories to write to get it all explained. Does he worry about the limited number of years ahead? "It's my agenda to write it. Whether I can finish it or not, that's Someone else's agenda with a capital S."

Focused will, after all, only takes you so far.

Karen Thorndike

First American Woman to Sail
Around the World Via the Great Capes

Karen Thorndike completed her 33,000-mile sail around the world on August 18, 1998, when she returned to San Diego two years and 14 days after she began on August 4, 1996. When Thorndike docked, she became the first American woman to circumnavigate the world alone in open ocean around the five Great Capes: Cape Horn (South America), Cape of Good Hope (South Africa), Cape Leeuwin (Australia), South East Cape (Tasmania), and Southwest Cape (New Zealand). While there have been six other women to sail around the world, at age 56, Thorndike was the oldest ever to accomplish the feat. "What I did would not be considered great by everyone," Thorndike says without a hint of defensiveness, "but it was for me because it required reaching beyond my limits. It was the hardest thing I've ever done. I had to put every bit of my financial and emotional resources, and all of my energy, toward it to accomplish it. It proved to me that you can do anything you want to do if you just set your mind to it."

Storm damage to her 36-foot yacht *Amelia*, unseasonably bad weather, medical problems, and moments of despair threatened to scuttle her 10-year dream. During the most difficult part of her odyssey, Thorndike did not see land for more than three months while sailing from Mar del Plata, Argentina, to Hobart, Tasmania. "There were some really low times in the Indian Ocean," she admits, pausing briefly to reflect and then adding tongue-in-cheek, "but I wasn't close enough to land to give up."

Isolated from everything, Thorndike endured relentless gales day after day after day. Ironically, off the Cape of Good Hope, she was hit with near hurricane-force winds and had to fight at the helm for 12 exhausting hours. The worst weather was yet to come. As Thorndike approached New Zealand's Southwest Cape, the last of the five, the wind howled through the rigging at well over 65 knots producing seas with 40-50 foot swells. In retrospect, Thorndike got what she had asked for. "I wanted to do one enormous, huge, very difficult adventure in my life. I wanted to test everything: emotionally, physically, spiritually, mentally. I wanted to see just how far I could go."

Most people do not sit in their living room and fabricate a way to push the edge of their psychic envelope. Most people sit in their living room because it is comfortable. Thorndike was in that space. With commercial real estate holdings that were returning well on her investment, she was setup to be financially comfortable for life. In one gigantic moment, she spent all of it. "I could always come back and go to work, find a little comfortable niche somehow," Thorndike offers in retrospect. "Maybe I wouldn't have a new BMW or the most beautiful clothes, but I could always come back and make something happen again. I couldn't always do this trip. The physical and emotional aspects, the energy it required would not always be there." Thorndike sold her holdings and when the transaction collapsed two months before she was to depart and it appeared she would not be able to attempt the voyage, she panicked. "Not being able to try was worse than trying and failing because you cannot fail if you try to do something. That is not the failure. The only failure is in not trying."

In the United States, sailing is not a sport that wins much public acclaim. There are ostensibly no sailors benefiting from product endorsements and televised ads. However, in Great Britain, New Zealand, Australia and France, homes of the other women who have circumnavigated the globe, more money is available, and sailors even enjoy some fame. Thorndike did not launch her boat for notoriety. "I love sailing. That was the big factor," Thorndike explains. "I really, truly feel at peace when I'm out in the ocean. And it's a complicated activity, to handle the boat, navigate, take care of the problems that arise. I had sailed for a long time before I even thought about doing this and it was ten years more before I tried. It took that long to feel that I had the skills to do all the right things."

It truly did take Thorndike a long time to learn how to sail. She did not grow up with a tiller in her hand. Her family didn't sail. She had never been on a boat until her 30s, but she fell in love with it all the same. "Anything I learned, I learned the hard way. It doesn't take talent to sail around the world. It takes absolute will. So, I hoped that I might be respected for having done it."

Thorndike's naiveté caused many to doubt the sensibility of her dream. Shortly after she conceived the plan, she shared her goal with a male friend who frequently sailed with her during a grooming period when she worked as a delivery skipper sailing between Seattle and Hawaii. Even though she had demonstrated her competence, he told her the idea was ridiculous. "He was a good friend who respected me as a sailor and yet he said it was impossible. I decided I would not share it with anyone else until I had everything in place," Thorndike reports, still slightly miffed. "I didn't want to risk getting negative at that point. I was still a little too fragile. I knew what I wanted to do and I didn't want to deal with negative reactions."

Thorndike picked up her boat and sold her property and then announced her plans to her friends. "Most of them talked around me to others. 'This is crazy. What does she think she's doing?' They even took a negative viewpoint about the name of the boat saying it was named after a woman who never returned. I thought then, and still do, it was good luck." Even after Thorndike rounded Cape Horn, the first in her five landmarks, there were people those who said she would never make it to Australia. "I simply didn't listen to negative folks at all. I chose not too."

Thorndike sustained the attitude nearly flawlessly throughout the voyage. She never looked at the problems. She always looked at the goal. When the electrical system experienced trouble, Thorndike did not focus on her limited electrical proficiency but turned her attention to the horizon. "I would never say, 'Oh my gosh, I don't know how to solve that.' For every problem that came up, I had a way to solve it in my head. I had all the contingencies on the boat for repairing almost everything. To achieve anything, you cannot depend on anybody else. You can't say, 'I'm going to sail around the world, and I want you to help with the boat.' You have to be totally in control and in charge or you can't solve problems when they arise."

Thorndike did have e-mail. And as circumstances demanded, Thorndike would contact friend and master sailor John Oman who would enlighten her on possible solutions. But ultimately it was her responsibility. "Besides, when you come against rather formidable odds, you have to reduce them down to the real problem: am I still sailing? Yes? Then I am fine. When you get down to that level, everything becomes simple." Thorndike had only one fear: the ultimate disaster, of course, was losing the boat. This was possible. But she did not try to solve that one. "If I'd lost it close to land I would have a chance of survival," Thorndike points out astonishingly clinically, "but if I didn't, well... I just didn't think about it." If she didn't, Thorndike had made out a will.

"The most important thing for me was not whether I accomplished it, or how the story ended ... Going out there and trying was the most important thing."

But the unthinkable was all too thinkable. The seas and the winds and the noise pounded on Thorndike and the *Amelia* repeatedly. Prior to the journey, several boat enthusiasts had tried to reassure Thorndike by telling her the boat was unsinkable. But then again, that's what the White Star Line said about one of their ships in 1912. "I did cry after moments here and there," Thorndike divulges. "But that helped me leave those incidents behind and look at the ocean and not be afraid of it. I was able to put those fears in proper corners where they belong and not feel paralyzed by them."

That is not to say that Thorndike was not scared to death at times. She was, but she put her fear into perspective and from that vantage point she now looks at her voyage as a metaphor for living. "I can apply it to my own personal life in almost every aspect. In dangerous moments, all you can do is make yourself very responsible and hang on for the ride and hope for the best. There is no true security in life. The stock market can crash. Your health can go. Once you realize the couch isn't any more secure than the boat, you take a little different perspective on risks. The freeway is clearly more dangerous than crossing the ocean."

Among her great discoveries on the high seas, Thorndike found out more about herself than about sailing. What started as a dream ended as an awakening. She expected the big payoff to be the sailing but things happened that she did not expect. "Stopping in the different places and meeting the people was the ultimate reward. I've made wonderful friends in my odyssey around the world that I will keep in touch with for the rest of my life." In addition to those whom she met in port, there were thousands of school children following her journey on the web and sending her messages of encouragement. "Thanks to technology, I knew they were there. OK, 15,000 miles away, but they were there emotionally for me. And that was very important."

During her two years alone, Thorndike discovered the power of introspection, the significance of friends, and the meaning of life. Despite occasional bouts of loneliness and the deep sadness of spending two Christmas mornings alone at sea, Thorndike views the isolation as the key to her new understanding about living.

"When you are alone for a long time, you tend to focus on the things that are really important, like family, friends, and lifestyle." Good thing, because since she has come home to her quiet Northwest town, she has been confronted with dozens of proposals and agents outlining how she can get rich from her triumph. "If I wanted to be rich, selling everything I had certainly is not the way to do it. That was not my goal," Thorndike responds. "It's nearly impossible to return to the American tunnel vision we display by how we drive on the freeway. We don't take time to enjoy the little things in life because we're way too financially oriented. I'm not going to do that anymore."

Having fulfilled her 10-year dream, Thorndike recognizes that everything has changed, that nothing can be the same again. No longer under the unrelenting pressure of the boat, the sea, and the journey, Thorndike combats the emotional let-down by working on the boat. "It's like a crutch. It prevents depression," Thorndike diagnoses. "But I need to put it out on the water soon because I am really getting excited about going somewhere again. Had I known how difficult it would be, I probably would not have done this. Now that I'm back I can say hands down, I'd do it again. It is interesting how once it's over the pain becomes less uncomfortable, less difficult. You can't forget. But it's different."

It's different for a lot of people. Traditionally women have not been accepted in the sport of sailing because it has always been a gentleman's domain, although many have not acted very gentlemanly. A lot of men feel that women cannot sail and they do not care to be with women on the same boat. Thorndike is not flying the flag of emancipation, but she does acknowledge, "My voyage was important for women that sail, but who think that they can't or shouldn't or never will be able to do so without a man, to know that it is possible. I have some friends that sent me messages while the journey was in progress telling me about things they were changing in their life as a result of me doing what I was doing and that they were a lot happier for it. So it has made a difference."

Thorndike is the first to admit that before she left she did not have any idea how the story was going to end. As the world has come to know, it ended well. She did not lose the boat. She did exactly what she said she wanted to do. And it was the doing of it, the story, not the end of it that mattered. "The most important thing for me was not whether I accomplished it, or how the story ended," Thorndike muses. "That didn't matter. Going out there and trying was the most important thing. The thought of finding myself in a rocking chair at some point wishing I had tried it was frightening. And at my age, I don't have very far in the future to look. I will be there pretty soon and I just couldn't allow that to happen."

Thorndike takes a sip from her cup of coffee and a healthy bite from her muffin and jam. With no prompting whatsoever, she gives her ideas full sail and sets the course for those who would listen. "I feel very passionate about life and what's out there. It's an incredible world. More and more people are losing their passion. They get on the freeway, lock themselves in and time punch the clock of life. I want them to tear up their punch cards and go do something."

When Thorndike tied up in San Diego at the end of her journey, she indeed had done something. In doing so, she also found something. "When I stepped onto the dock, immediately I felt at peace. I had really accomplished my goal on a very personal level. I always felt like I had to prove myself. Now I don't have to prove anything to anybody. I'm done. Whether they like it, appreciate it, think it's crazy, or think it's weird. It doesn't matter. I accomplished something."

We should all have such peace about our lives.

Bill Walsh

Former Coach of Three-Time
Super Bowl Champion San Francisco 49ers

Few coaches in American professional sports history have had the quick and longstanding success of William Ernest Walsh. In 1979, Walsh took over a poorly performing San Francisco 49ers football team that had won only two of its 16 games the previous season. Just three years later, Walsh's 49ers were Super Bowl champions. The Niners would claim two more world championships in the 1980s under Walsh, in addition to seven postseason appearances and six NFC West titles. Twice, Walsh was named NFL Coach of the Year and ultimately named NFL Coach of the Decade for the 1980s. In 1993, he became only the 14th coach to be elected to the Pro Football Hall of Fame in Canton, Ohio. His .617 winning percentage built from a 102-63-1 career record includes a formidable 10-4 postseason mark. But the man who is one of the most extraordinary coaches in NFL history struggled to get there and has struggled even more since he left.

Walsh's first significant head coaching job came at Stanford University in 1977, 22 years after he had graduated from nearby San Jose State University. "My ultimate goal in coaching was to be a head coach at a major university," Walsh says in a tense voice. "It took a number of years to make it and when I became head coach at Stanford I was satisfied that I had reached my goal. Everything after that was a surprise in a sense."

A wonderful surprise. Walsh guided the Cardinals to a 17-7 record during his two years there and captured wins in the Bluebonnet and Sun Bowls to crown both seasons. The faltering 49ers turned to Walsh to work similar magic in the National Football League. "Having been in the NFL for 10 years as an assistant (with the Cincinnati Bengals), I had an excellent grasp of the game as it was played there, but I didn't anticipate going back. I had reached the pinnacle of my expectations."

The journey to the mountaintop of his coaching dream was arduous at best and downright harsh at worst. Like many young graduates, Walsh started out quickly as a high school head coach right out of graduate school. "I was very young and certainly not prepared for the job," Walsh says in a somewhat self-defacing tone. "I was just plain fortunate to move into the college level very quickly as an assistant to Marv Levy at the University of California and I was fortunate again to move on to Stanford with John Ralston who was a good friend." At 33 years old, Walsh was riveted on finding the next step up, but it did not happen. "There were several head jobs that I was passed over for, like Fresno State or Cal Poly. So I felt fortunate to go with Paul Brown into the NFL as an assistant with the Cincinnati Bengals, although at the time it sure didn't seem like it because we were moving 2,500 miles away."

Walsh did well as Cincinnati's offensive coordinator. Several NFL teams expressed interest in him as a head coach. Again, nothing came of it. "Either Paul Brown wouldn't recommend me because he wanted me to stay there or I was one of two final candidates. In every case, it never worked out." Walsh turned his attention back to the college ranks and when the job came open at his alma mater, San Jose State, Walsh felt he finally would get the call. "My own school passed me over," Walsh says still stinging from the rejection, "even though I was with the Bengals and had developed quite a reputation as an offensive coordinator."

The string of eliminations kept unraveling, and Walsh became depressed. Disconsolate and frustrated, he turned to one of his college friends who had an advertising agency in New York City. "I was making $18,000 a year and I told him I'd come to New York, learn the business, if he'd pay me $20,000. I was so naive I didn't even realize I couldn't have lived in New York on that salary," Walsh recalls, shaking his head at the foolishness of the idea. His friend was enthused and promised to get right back but he never did.

Walsh won a few more games in Cincinnati. The urgency passed but not the sadness. "I didn't think I was going to make it at all. I felt I would always be an assistant football coach, a respected one and a good one, but that was going to be my destiny. After my own school passed me over for the job, what could you expect?" Of course, they also passed on Dick Vermeil, who came out of retirement to coach the long-hapless St. Louis Rams to an improbable 13-3 record in 1999 and a Super Bowl XXXIV win over the Tennessee Titans.

Walsh, disheartened and depressed, stayed with the Bengals. As his reputation for offense grew, so did his salary and, as time passed, many thought he would become the head coach when Paul Brown resigned or retired. When Brown did leave the field for the front office after the 1975 season, he did not give Walsh the post, "probably because I was just different enough from him that he might have felt I was someone he couldn't control like he would hope or expect to," Walsh theorizes with a hint of bitterness in his voice. "He hired someone he thought was a safer candidate, assuming that I would remain as an assistant coach. But, it was very, very evident I couldn't stay in Cincinnati if I ever wanted to be a head coach because I had been passed over. I had to leave." Walsh resigned, and then Brown "proceeded to make it tough for me to get a head coaching job anywhere."

Coaching professional football can be a cruel, divisive and tough business. At the same time the brutality on the spirit coexists with the very positive aspects of molding a team, strategizing a game plan, the excitement of the contest, and the camaraderie of players and coaches. "Working with the people is what obviously draws coaches to it," Walsh suggests. But being fired, and the rejection that goes with it, is devastating on coaches. They seldom realize how impersonal it can be, how quickly they can be discarded — because they love their work and they thrive on it. "Coaching football is just like guys standing on these girders on tall buildings. There's always a chance they could fall, but it's what they do. You exist in an environment where you know people are thrown out, fired, rejected, embarrassed, and you assume it won't be you because you're so intense on what you're doing, and you're doing a good job, and you'll handle anything. You don't realize the perils of it until you're a little bit older, and you say, 'My God, how did I ever get through that?'"

But Walsh was still young and would not be dissuaded. "The key to finally making it is to find your passion," Walsh proposes. "Passion starts and demonstrates itself fairly early in your life. You have to thrive on its very existence, develop an inventory of knowledge, an expertise that is so solid you are valuable to other people and you feel valuable yourself."

During the years of rejection and disappointment, Walsh became a pure student of the game. He read any books on football and coaching he could get his hands on. He studied. He drew diagrams. He had a passion for the artistic or technical side of football and a competency for using it that was as good as or better than anyone. "I knew the game. I was a student of football. Call it creative or inquisitive. I was impetuous and adventurous about new concepts. I had that as part of my very existence, so I knew I was of value. I knew that couldn't be taken away. I knew, if ever given an opportunity, I would succeed. I just had that much confidence in myself. That's what carries you through."

Not a bad lesson for a young coach to learn. If you do not ground yourself in the fundamentals and the nuances of your work, you have nothing to fall back on when disappointment occurs. Learning the buzzwords, the minimum, only gets you so far, logistically and emotionally.

Walsh pursued a series of jobs after being passed over by Cincinnati and landed a short-term assignment as an assistant with the San Diego Chargers when, once again, opportunity appeared on the horizon. Stanford University needed a head coach. Walsh, having been an assistant there, had excellent rapport with key people and they had a lot of respect for him. Finally, at age 45, Walsh reached his goal. "There must be an energy that drives you, that can take on your competition," Walsh says as he looks back on the odyssey. One has to develop the mental or emotional toughness to absorb disappointment, to accept it and carry on. That comes in part from confidence, but more from "a swelling of energy that overcomes disappointment," Walsh exclaims. "I can recall thinking after all those years that I was never going to be a head coach. I became melancholy facing up to my lot in life, that I would never have an opportunity. And, by certain strokes, it worked out, but it very well may not have. I have many dear friends and associates who didn't have the opportunity to be as successful as I was for one reason or another."

Two successful seasons later he was back in the pros as the head coach of the San Francisco 49ers. "I was very fortunate to be at Stanford, right in northern California where I'd started. When the 49ers job was offered, I thought I was the most fortunate guy in the world."

Success didn't come immediately. The 49ers under Walsh finished 2-14 in 1979. In 1980, thanks in part to the play of a new starting quarterback named Joe Montana, the team improved to 6-10. Better, but not good enough. "The team did very poorly and we weren't coming close to being as competitive as we had to be," Walsh recalls. "Then all I would say was, 'Why did I leave Stanford? What am I doing here?'"

The next season, at first San Francisco looked to be mediocre again, losing two of its first three games. But then it all came together. With Montana leading the offense and rookie Ronnie Lott making a huge impact defensively, the 49ers won 12 of their last 13 regular season games to lead the league in wins, won their division for the first time in nine years, sent six players to the Pro Bowl and — best of all — won their first Super Bowl 26-21 against none other than Walsh's old team, the Cincinnati Bengals. Including the playoffs, San Francisco's 1981 record of 16-3 was at the time the fourth best in league history.

"Coaching football is just like guys standing on these girders on tall buildings. There's always a chance they could fall, but it's what they do."

Over the next seven years, Walsh led the 49ers to football success never reached prior to his arrival and never matched since, the zenith coming in 1984, when the Niners lost only once all season, pounded the Miami Dolphins 38-16 in Super Bowl XIX and fielded an incredible 10 players in the Pro Bowl — including the entire defensive secondary. In addition to serving as head coach and field commander, Walsh was appointed the team's general manager in 1982 and ascended to the role of president in 1985. During his coaching tenure, Walsh laid the foundation for the success the 49ers have achieved over the last 20 years, including the beginning in 1983 of an unprecedented streak of 16 consecutive 10-win seasons.

Walsh's impact on the coaching industry is still apparent by the plethora of former assistants and players who succeeded under his influence. In 2000, Montana and Lott joined Walsh in the Pro Football Hall of Fame. No less than three current NFL head coaches, Mike Shanahan of the Denver Broncos, Mike Holmgren of the Seattle Seahawks and George Seifert of the Carolina Panthers, first worked on Walsh's staff. Since Walsh left coaching, the three have combined for five Super Bowl victories and are considered at the top of their profession.

After the 1988 season, Walsh retired and the next year joined NBC Sports to team up with award-winning announcer Dick Enberg for three seasons as the network's top analyst on NFL and Notre Dame telecasts. But Walsh returned to Stanford in 1992, desperately missing the magic and mayhem of the game. He promptly led the Cardinals to a 10-3 record that concluded with a New Year's Day win over Penn State in the Blockbuster Bowl. It was the school's first New Year's Day bowl game victory in 21 years. Walsh remained at Stanford through the 1994 season and retired again. "I realized I had already taken myself beyond that kind of work. I was no longer interested in the recruiting aspect of college football," Walsh reports sadly about what was once the pinnacle of his expectations.

> "The drive I've had to succeed, the drive I've had to excel often has taken me beyond an appropriate limit. It's gotten me there, but it's often taken me beyond."

In 1994, Walsh was instrumental in the establishment and management of the World League of American Football, now known as NFL Europe and continued to serve the league as a consultant and representative in various NFL ventures. He is author of two books, *Building a Champion* (1995) and *Finding the Winning Edge* (1997) and he is a frequent speaker to corporate clientele.

But despite his extraordinary achievements on the field and significant contributions off the field, Walsh is plagued with disappointment. "When people call me a great coach, there is a hollow ring to it for me. I have a hard time with it," Walsh agonizes. "I didn't run out the string of a coaching career. I left it early. I did not fulfill the tenants of greatness. It's that simple. Was I creative? Yes. Was I dynamic? Sure. There are some areas where I was as competent as anybody in sports. But great, I don't believe."

Walsh struggles in his chair, uncomfortable with the topic and sadly uncomfortable with himself. Eyes gazing out the window into the Portola Valley sunlight, Walsh continues as though he were talking to himself. "I should have continued on. Greatness is being able to take it all the way to the finish. And it has to be a logical finish. It can't be, 'Here he is again trying to get another coaching job' or, 'He is staying too long.' In my case, I was at the peak of my career. I had the best team in football, and the youngest team, and there was every reason to think that I could go for two, three, four more years. Then I could have conceivably been considered a great coach because we would have won two or three more Super Bowls. But I left early and that is a haunting feeling for me."

Walsh is fixated on the topic. His commentary expands and he begins to probe the dark force that haunts him. "The drive I've had to succeed, the drive I've had to excel often has taken me beyond an appropriate limit. It's gotten me there, but it's often taken me beyond," Walsh concludes. When Walsh left the 49ers, Seifert succeeded him as head coach and Holmgren took over as offensive coordinator (Walsh had held both positions simultaneously). But each play or drill was designed by Walsh. Holmgren played more conservatively than Walsh and, by Walsh's own admission, "The team functioned much better offensively after I left it because the crazy professor left also. Holmgren stayed with what had worked but, with me, that wouldn't have been enough."

As he had done throughout his career, Walsh would have tried something new, expanding the envelope of his legendary West Coast offense. Walsh was never satisfied with the status quo, and his compulsion to take it all one step more carried him right out of coaching. "I had my foot to the floor so hard. I was the president, general manager, head coach and offensive coordinator all in one person for 10 years and I just had emotional, mental, and physical exhaustion. I wore myself right out. Had I been more conventional and more conservative I would have lasted longer and probably done better. Whatever traits I have that are most positive, they're excessive."

Perhaps in a career where the need to win is excessive, where anything short of maximum success results in rejection, the only way to survive is to be excessive. Perhaps the career is that way because the men and women who participate in it are that way. In any case, Walsh says, "I never took my eye off the road when I was successful. I didn't stop and look around and say, 'I've made it.' It was always a continuous drive to succeed. The fear of failure is a major part of the makeup of a very, very intense and aggressive person and has been a major part of whatever success I've had."

Failure is devastating whether it is failing to be selected for a job or failing to score the necessary touchdown. But successful people always bounce back from failure. "I did not want to fail and I wasn't going to let that happen. It was a matter of keeping my head above water all the time and thinking failure was just around the corner. And I would measure failure a lot differently than others. Often, only I would feel I failed, and I would be somewhat chagrinned or embarrassed about it when other people didn't even note it. That was just always there."

It is a vile business, winning and assessing yourself on how much winning you do. But there are some parameters to it. If you cheat, if you don't win fairly and honestly, then it's awfully hard to measure that as victory. So there are some ethical parameters in which you must operate. "But, that doesn't mean that you don't take everything to the limit of your ethics," Walsh admits. "Within the parameters of moral and ethical competition, winning is the bottom line."

Within those parameters to get to that bottom line, every week Walsh found a reason or concocted one so his players would dislike the other team. The opposition insulted them. They didn't have respect for them. "I would bring to the team the theme that they had contempt for us and I would bring it in all kinds of ways," Walsh admits. "Some of it would be rather theatrical and dramatic. It worked very well except when we were facing a good opponent and the other coach was doing the same thing. So, you just held your own."

There is an intense rivalry among coaches. They all know they are standing on those girders and the guy across the field could cause them to fall. "I felt a major rivalry with (former Washington Redskins coach) Joe Gibbs. I felt one with (former New York Giants, New England Patriots and New York Jets coach) Bill Parcells, (former Chicago Bears and New Orleans Saints coach) Mike Ditka." But the rivalry doesn't mean you didn't respect them. "It didn't mean that Joe Gibbs and I weren't very friendly. We just weren't friends. He would say the same thing. When it came to competing, our two organizations were very serious." Within such an environment, it hardly seems possible that a coach could be as successful as Walsh and be a contented or satisfied individual. "By and large, unless they have incredible good fortune, happy, competent people are still assistant coaches somewhere or looking for an assistant coaching job."

The intensity in the room is electric. Walsh has exorcized the demon and sits calmly in his chair silhouetted against the sun-filled window. Calm and articulate and philosophical, he puts then and now into perspective. "I would hope people would say that I had sensitivity and feeling for others, that I aggressively demonstrated that by my acts I was a thoughtful, socially conscious, and compassionate person. And I would hope they would say that I was as good a technician, or artist, in my field, as there ever was. But, I don't know what they'll say."

Walsh pauses. "You have to go on with your life. You have to come to the realities of the life cycle," Walsh adds. "You have to take satisfaction in where you've been and what you've done and your personal relationships with people. And then as you reach a certain stage of life, you can serve as an alter ego or a conscience for the game because you're removed, you're not directly connected, and you can observe and remark like an elder statesman. Gee, I hate to say elder. God, that's tough to say. But that is just part of the life cycle. And, if you struggle with this part of it, this stage of life, you really can make a fool out of yourself."

In January 1999, the San Francisco 49ers announced Walsh's return to professional football, naming him vice president and general manager and predicting he would guide the team to success in the new millennium. As it was 20 years before, the assignment gives Walsh daily management of the organization and football operations, including personnel decisions, the college draft and training camp. With most of the great players of Walsh's coaching era now retired, the 49ers have fallen on hard times, finishing 4-12 in

1999. It is once again Walsh's objective to bring the team back to the top of the NFL.

Walsh is equally exceptional in being a mentor as he is at being a coach. In addition to the crop of coaches he has directly tutored, Walsh created the Minority Coaching Fellowship Program in 1987 that has produced, among others, Tyrone Willingham, Stanford's current head coach. Walsh is also committed to changing the current ethos of player arrogance and ego. "You almost embarrass people out of demonstrating too much ego," Walsh explains. You might say, 'Fortunately here we don't have those kinds of men who do these things,' or something like that. You do it in every venue you can. You plan it. You just keep hammering at it, and it makes it tougher and tougher for someone to split off. And when they do the other guys will pull them back."

For many years, the 49ers had great team personality, with few individuals trying to attract attention to themselves. That is getting now difficult to control because television media have glorified some of the most aberrant behaviors. "Bringing together, collectively, a group of people to accomplishing something, then organizing it, mobilizing it, and moving forward to do it is an art form. One of my strengths has always been my ability to communicate with anybody and everybody. And when I say communicate, that can be anything from body posture to harsh, severe language to caring language. Interacting with others is absolutely critical. I have a sensitivity, a feel for where they are, what they're thinking. Only in a few cases have I failed in that."

In football and — if you ask Bill Walsh — in life, success is most often measured by whether you win or lose. Perhaps we ought to rethink that definition.

"The fear of failure is a major part of the makeup of a very, very intense and aggressive person and has been a major part of whatever success I've had."

Chapter 3

It Starts With Discipline

Hilary Hahn

Grammy-Nominated Violinist
and Sony Recording Artist

Born in 1979, Hilary Hahn has already established herself as one of the most accomplished and compelling artists on the international concert circuit. Admitted to the Curtis Institute of Music in Philadelphia at the age of 10, Hahn made her major orchestra debut a year and a half later with the Baltimore Symphony. At 13, Hahn played with the Philadelphia and Cleveland orchestras, the New York Philharmonic and the Pittsburgh Symphony.

Photo credit: Janusz Kawa

She characterizes the beginning of her career as "sort of a fluke." Hahn and her father were taking a walk through the neighborhood when they saw a sign that they had never noticed before. The sign offered music lessons for four-year-olds. "I was almost four," Hahn notes. "We rang a bell and walked in. I watched a lesson with a little boy playing 'Twinkle-Twinkle' on a tiny violin and I wanted to try it. So I started the next week." That is typical of how Hahn does most things. She sees something she likes and tries it.

Following a year in the Suzuki program, she began five years of study at Baltimore's Peabody Conservatory with Klara Berkovich, a native of Odessa, Ukraine, who taught for 25 years in the Leningrad School for the Musically Gifted. "It was never like anything was pushed on me," Hahn explains. "I always decided to do whatever I did." Consciously or unconsciously, achieving with her violin has been at the forefront of her imagination.

When she was seven, Hahn and her family had just come back from a vacation at the shore and she drew a picture of the beach replete with umbrellas and people lounging in the sun next to the water. Then, for no reason she can explain, she drew "a plane flying overhead with a banner streaming from the back that said, 'Come hear Hilary Hahn play in Carnegie Hall tonight.' At that point, being onstage at Carnegie Hall was just a figment of my imagination. I never really expected it to happen." At ten, Hahn gave her first full recital. The experience was an eye opener for Hahn and for her family. "Of my friends, I didn't know anyone giving a recital, so I thought maybe there was something here."

There was also the time when Berkovich informed Hahn she had taken her through the repertoire she usually taught in Russia, and offered to help Hahn find her next teacher. A professor at the Peabody told them that the only person she would trust Hilary to was 83-year-old Jascha Brodsky at the all-scholarship Curtis Institute of Music in Philadelphia. That would require an audition and Hahn was skeptical, since she had college age friends who had auditioned there and were denied. "I didn't think I could get in," Hahn admits. "But I decided to do the audition because I needed a trial performance of a particular piece and didn't have any other place to play it." When the institute's director, Gary Graffman, called to say she had been admitted and told her that the faculty decided she should study with Brodsky, Hahn "began jumping up and down and running all around the house. I was just going nuts because I was so happy. I had fallen in love with Curtis when I went to audition and had heard so many wonderful things about Mr. Brodsky, even though I hadn't officially met him yet. I couldn't imagine going anywhere else."

For two years, Hahn's father drove her the 100 miles from Baltimore to Philadelphia and back twice a week for lessons. Then, at 12, she and her father took an apartment in Philadelphia so she could study her music and attend classes full-time. Hahn's mother retained her full time job in Baltimore. On weekends they went back to Baltimore to visit her. "I took my bachelor degree classes during the week for four years," Hahn explains. "When I finished the requirements I stayed on at Curtis, taking elective classes in writing literature and languages." Hahn started German at Curtis when she was 12 and later participated in a seven-week intensive program. "I didn't get much practicing done, but I learned a lot of German. Since my first trip to Germany at 15, I'd been doing my interviews in German, but that program brought my fluency to the next level." She is currently studying French.

She also gave more and more concerts each year. At 15, Hahn made her German debut playing with Lorin Maazel and the Bavarian Radio Symphony Orchestra in a concert that was broadcast throughout Europe on radio and television. At 16, Hahn finished her bachelor's degree requirements, obtained professional management with IMG Artists, signed a recording contract with Sony Classical, and made her Carnegie Hall debut. She has since played there again and will undoubtedly be playing there often.

"Curtis was an extraordinary place to be and I got very attached to it," Hahn reflects, now five years into her professional career. "I had a teacher in Mr. Brodsky whom I respected and adored, and the school had a wonderful familial, nurturing atmosphere. I virtually grew up there and I was very happy. My first orchestral arrangements came in my first year at Curtis, and my teachers — both academic and musical — encouraged me to pace the beginnings of my career with caution, so it wouldn't disrupt either my education or my life. Following their advice, I came to everything gradually and in a well-paced way, adding a few more concerts and media events each year, so by the time I began performing more or less full time, I was ready."

Like all performers, Hahn has her moments of frustration and uncertainty, but "I don't have stage fright," she asserts. "I love to perform. I love being onstage and interacting with the audience and with the musicians around me." Knowing she must discipline herself in order to perform well, Hahn devotes hours every day to practice, dividing the music up into bits and pieces, polishing details and analyzing her interpretations as she works in the practice room. On stage, if something goes wrong, Hahn maintains, "there's nothing I can do about it at that point. So before the concert I prepare as carefully as I can, and then once I get out on stage, I just enjoy myself and play. Performances are one of the few times I get to play pieces straight through. Besides, you're up on stage, you're not performing for yourself; you're playing for the audience."

Hahn views her performance as her chance to give the audience a piece of music the way she hears it. "Mrs. Berkovich said 'It's like you invite them to a party and you give them a gift. You prepare your gift well, you wrap it nicely and you present it. Then they thank you with their applause.' So, there's really nothing to be scared of there."

> "I've gotten a lot of really good advice from people. But in the end, I'm the one who has to live with the results of my decisions."

Throughout the process, Hahn's father has been at her side. "My mom has always been the breadwinner, the one with the career, and my dad's the house parent," Hahn explains. Like most involved dads, he tries to help everything progress as smoothly as possible for his daughter's endeavors. "He answers the phone, sends faxes, does the laundry, and goes shopping for groceries." He also accompanies her when she travels, wheeling the duo's luggage through airports and sometimes carrying his daughter's violin. While Hahn's parents have always been supportive, Hahn is the first to admit, "I've always made my own decisions." But Hahn has been lucky because she has always had very good people standing in the wings.

When Hahn started at Curtis, many of her classmates were college age. "It was great because it was like I had a whole lot of older siblings without the arguments. I had a lot of support from everyone around me; no one really cut me down or did anything mean to me, or pushed me in any way." Hahn has also been blessed with remarkable mentors. In the business of child prodigies, some mentors do not allow their students enough room to be themselves. "I have a life that's my own," Hahn notes.

When she played with her hometown orchestra, the Baltimore Symphony, conductor David Zinman counseled her not to do too much too soon.

"He told me to take it slowly, not to do lots of concerts at a young age, not to record before I was ready, not to get management too soon, and, above all, to stay in school." The message was clear. Don't change your life for the career, for the music. Hahn has heard the same advice from her teachers, her managers, and nearly all the musicians and conductors she has met over the years. "I've gotten a lot of really good advice from people. But in the end, I'm the one who has to live with the results of my decisions. So I've always listened to the best advice I could get; then I've done what seemed right to me. That way, if there are mistakes, they are mine, and I'll know better next time. In my case, that's proven to be the best way to do things."

But the imprint of her greatest mentor is unmistakable. Hahn cannot say enough about her teacher Jascha Brodsky, with whom she studied for seven years until he died in 1997 at the age of 89. Brodsky was 83 when he began working with Hahn. As a young man he studied with the legendary Belgian violinist Eugène Ysaÿe, who was born in 1858. Brodsky was first violinist for the Curtis String Quartet for 50 years. "There is one generation between me and the middle of the 19th Century. It makes my link to the playing of that time very direct, and that's rare in the early 21st Century. It's an honor to be part of that legacy. There are recordings of Mr. Brodsky playing. I just love his playing, his sense of style and takes in music, the spirit and sophistication of his interpretations. I truly admired him as a teacher and he was a wonderful person."

Hahn marvels at Brodsky's contemporaries: Nathan Milstein, Jascha Heifetz, Mischa Elman, and Fritz Kreisler. "Mr. Brodsky was friends with these people and he had the most interesting stories. Once he beat Heifetz at Ping-Pong at a party. Heifetz was not one who liked to be beaten at anything. So Heifitz put the paddle and ball down on the table, picked up his coat and hat, and walked out the door without saying a word. He was competitive, no doubt about it!" Hahn is not quite as competitive. While critics draw comparisons between Hahn and her contemporaries, Hahn views it matter-of-factly. "Everyone goes in their own direction. I have my path and they have theirs. It's not like we're really colliding or conflicting with one another."

Hahn views her contemporaries as different artists playing what they want to be playing the way they want to play it. And being "you" is all that matters for Hahn so she doesn't compare her own performances to those of others. "Every listener perceives music differently. I interpret it in my particular way. People can take it as they like it. There are some people who like my playing, some people who don't. It's all a matter of perception, like art. So it's hard for me to describe what I am, because there's no solid measure of what I do, no statistics like there are in sports. Even the instrument doesn't make much difference. Mr. Brodsky liked to use the expression, 'It's 95 percent player and five percent instrument.' So it's mainly personality that defines your style and interpretations, and comes through in your playing." The personality that comes through her music and her conversation is that of a young woman very comfortable with her gift and herself.

But Hahn's life is anything but typical of a young woman. Her travel schedule whisks her from Jerusalem to Lithuania to Australia and across Europe and the US. But she has a lot of friends, several in most every place she goes. "The way the music world works, with regular re-engagements and people moving from orchestra to orchestra, I know that whenever I make friends, I'll see them somewhere in a couple years, though I don't know precisely where or when," Hahn says. And whether it is in Warsaw or Seattle, she makes time for people. "I like to go to movies or go to lunch or shopping, just hang out with my friends. I do normal things. I take ballet, read, write poetry, or go to the gym."

Hahn makes a lot more money than most people her age. But like everything else that could separate her from normality, she has placed that in personal perspective too. "It's not like I've gone out and bought a six-bedroom house or a Ferrari or anything like that," Hahn chides. "I'm able to support myself, but like every touring musician I also have to cover hotels, airfares and food on the road, plus concert attire, commissions for agents, maintenance and insurance on the violin and bow, international phone bills, taxes, health insurance, replacement luggage, rent for my apartment, and the usual day-to-day expenses that everyone has."

Hahn puts her earnings in three accounts. Besides a savings account she maintains a sabbatical account, in case she ever decides to take a year off from performing. And there is the instrument account. Violins can be very expensive. Although she now plays a 135-year-old J.B. Vuillaume violin, "I'll never have a Stradivarius or Guarnarius," Hahn allows. "It's impossible for a violinist to own one of those unless they have money from some other source. I have friends who play on Strads worth $4.5 million, but I'm uncomfortable borrowing instruments. I bought my violin — not a rare one — six years ago for a small fraction of the cost of a Strad or Guarnarius. Now, I save to buy strings, pay for bow repairs and to be able to buy a new or second violin if I find one that works well for me."

There's a bit of risk in accomplishing as much as Hahn has because at some point she will have been nearly everywhere and done nearly everything. Despite her accomplishments and her acclaim, she is not ambitious to

> "Every year I do something interesting and eye-opening that takes me another step forward. I'm working with artists I have a lot to learn from, and there are plenty of people I still hope to work with."

rush ahead. She continues to do only those things that interest her and that she enjoys, and she has been very careful not to do them all at once. "That's one reason why I keep enjoying it," Hahn speculates. "Every year I do something interesting and eye-opening that takes me another step forward. I'm working with artists I have a lot to learn from, and there are plenty of people I still hope to work with. I'm learning new pieces and there are many, many more ahead of me that I want to learn, that I need to learn. Sometimes it surprises me to think about all those I've worked with and where I've played, because it's all still relatively new for me."

A lot of aspiring musical artists who have yet to stand on the stage of Carnegie Hall must wonder how it has all come to pass so magically for Hahn. Perhaps it was her talent or that she has worked so hard, "And that's true to a great extent. But for me," Hahn explains, "it also felt like a lot of circumstances did fall right into place."

She was at the right place at the right time during her childhood stroll with her father. She did have exceptional mentors, extraordinary teachers, and supportive parents. "You can have talent and not have any of the right situations, and nothing may happen. Yes, in my case maybe part of it was talent. But the way everything fell together probably also involved the fact that I've always liked what I do, and I especially enjoy performing. People seem to pick up on that."

As she stands acknowledging the enthusiastic applause of the audience who has clearly picked up on that, you can't help but wonder where her gift and her spirit and her pleasure and her decisions will take her next. "Oh, it's hard to say. So many things are possible in a musical lifetime. I expect I'll continue to work hard and go with whatever comes. I just hope to keep enjoying whatever I'm doing. Because if I don't enjoy it, I won't do it. I like the way my life is going and I hope that it continues to be as nice as it is now."

Let's hope the years don't change Hilary Hahn either.

Mills Lane

Legendary Boxing Referee and
Star of the Judge Mills Lane Television Show

On June 28, 1997, boxing referee Mills B. Lane disqualified Mike Tyson for biting Evander Holyfield's ear during their now-infamous title fight in Las Vegas. Later that week, the Nevada Athletic Commission fined Tyson $3 million of his $30 million purse and revoked his license for at least a year, the most severe penalty in boxing history.

Lane, the best-known and most respected referee in professional boxing, who among other things has been immortalized in clay in the raucous MTV animated series "Celebrity Death Match," had worked over 100 title fights and over 20 heavyweight championships. In a voice astonishingly similar to Ross Perot's, an angry Lane emerged from the hearing and assailed Tyson's behavior. "(His) action was such a violation of protocol ...I mean ... Judas, that someone would ... damn! ... It's just outside of good order."

Order and discipline are virtues to which Lane has devoted his life whether in the ring, or in Washoe County District Court in Reno, Nevada, where he served as a judge for eight years, or on his nationally syndicated daytime television show, *Judge Mills Lane*. Lane is at his desk early every business day surrounded by photographs of his championship fights and dozens of honorary public service awards.

His credo is clear. If you're skilled and you're disciplined, you have a chance at real achievement. His manner of expressing it is characteristically direct. "If you're a fighter and you tend to business," Lane advises, "you can be great." Lane takes an oblique path to explain his point. "The best pure fighter I've ever been in the ring with is Roberto Duran. But Duran can never be to me a complete professional. Duran would go from 135 pounds to 190 pounds between fights and he was good enough to get away with it. But by doing that he abused his tools.

"Now a good workman, a good carpenter, wouldn't leave his hammers and saws outside in the rain," Lane continues. "They're his tools. A fighter's tools are his body. A great fighter never gets overweight after a fight. He's always within striking distance of his best weight. But Duran? No way."

Lane never pulls his punches when it comes to advice. Duran felt the full brunt of that many times. "I'd say 'What the hell is wrong with you, man? You've got an office. Your office is the road and the gym and you got to go to your office every day. You take one day a week off, maybe. You take one vacation a year, maybe. You got to go to the office. A good businessman or a good businesswoman goes to his or her office every day. You don't do that and you cheat yourself. You're not great, you can't be great because you won't pay the price.'"

"Nothing will take the place of persistence. Talent will not. Genius will not. The world is full of educated derelicts. Determination alone is omnipotent."

For Mills Lane, life and achievement are simple. The person that lives without discipline dies without dignity. Everything is discipline. As Lane bluntly puts it, "It's about getting your ears back and getting after it."

Lane's path to the bench exemplifies his faith in discipline. Growing up in South Carolina, he was an average student in high school, but he avoided juvenile problems because of his passion for sports. Enlisting in the Marine Corps in 1956, Lane quickly became a force on the armed forces boxing circuit. A modest success as a business administration major at the University of Nevada-Reno, a school he chose because of its boxing reputation, he maintained a B average despite a heavy amateur fight schedule. He obtained his law degree in 1970 from the University of Utah through sheer willpower.

"You have to put a check on doing some things you want to do," Lane exclaims. He learned the philosophy from a high school football coach who doled out the advice in a chalk talk after practice one day. "Coach said, 'You know, this Saturday you all are going to go down to town and probably going to go to the drugstore. Now if you have a chocolate milkshake it won't make you any less of a football player but you're conceding something to the other guys.'" Lane took this to heart and became a starting linebacker despite being the smallest member of the team.

Lane believes you have to get your mind set not to concede what you don't have to concede, same kind of thing he did to become a lawyer. "If I took an IQ test with a group of folks I'd be right average," Lane admits. "My LSAT scores for law school were low. I got in and through it because I worked hard. That's the name of the game. To me greatness is in discipline, in being able to do what you have to do. I call it tending to business."

Lane certainly tended to business in the ring, winning 60 out of 64 amateur bouts and the NCAA welterweight championship with the Nevada-Reno Wolf Pack. He also came within a whisper of making the 1960 US Olympic team. As a professional, he put up an 11-1 record. But ever the pragmatist, Lane realized he was not going to be a great fighter himself and hung up his gloves in favor of his referee shirt after a rather brief career.

To be a great fighter one has to be blessed with physical skills and combine them with discipline. Lane had only half of the equation. "I always say when the good Lord passed out the credentials, he gave some folks great discipline and no talent and he gave other folks great talent, no discipline. Every now and again he gave somebody both. Ray Leonard or Ray Robinson — they got it all. Without great tools if you have the discipline, if you work hard, you can succeed but you're never going to be great without some gifts. I got hit a lot."

Lane believes part of discipline is introspection about what you're doing. Doubt may arise from self-examination. Doubt is real but you have the discipline to press forward. "Doubt is those butterflies in the stomach," Lane attests. "The butterflies are your friends. The day you lose them, pack it in and get out." Trying to accomplish big things, you can easily get nervous. You have to be concerned, to ask yourself if you can do it, if you're doing it right. Are you doing the best you can? You must have that conversation. You must have that kind of doubt but despite that doubt you move

Lane as referee for the "Bite Fight" — Tyson vs. Holyfield

forward and, as Lane advises, "You conquer that doubt, conquer that fear and triumph. When I was fighting I lived in fear of two things and two things only. One was walking up to that ring and saying I'm not going in there tonight and walking back to the locker room. I was always scared to death every time I got in there but you just overcome it. The other thing I was always scared of was taking off my robe and I didn't have any trunks on."

There is no doubt about one thing: ego and pride are critical, maybe even a little vanity. Discipline grows out of a strong sense of self, from wanting, choosing to be a success. Without it, Lane believes you are beaten. "Rule out metabolism, rule out thyroid, and show me someone who's fat and I'll show you someone who's probably lazy. Now, someone who is fat may not necessarily be lazy in the sense that they direct their energy and interests in some other way, but no one has to be fat if they are willing to pay the price not to be.

"I travel a lot and the only things that go inside the airplane with me are my sweats." Lane continues. "You can run in San Francisco. You can run in

Central Park. It's just a question of if you want to do it." Easy thing for a man to say who has maintained his fight weight into his 60s.

But virtually every day Lane finds this same malaise standing before him in his courtroom. "I'll have somebody say, 'Well judge, you know I've got this bad drug problem.' Well, I say, 'Sonny, it's not drugs, it's not because you weren't breast-fed. It's not because your mama didn't change your diapers. It's not because your daddy yelled at you; it's you.'"

Discipline implies responsibility. When we can look at ourselves and recognize that we are the ones at fault and take responsibility for our actions, then we are well on our way to living disciplined and ordered lives. But as long as we are willing to pass the buck, we can rationalize anything if we work at it hard enough.

For Lane, part of the price we are paying today in our society was "hacked out by social workers and mental health people that blamed everything on something else." Lane riles up and goes on. "Defendants tell me, 'Don't blame me, it was my mama. Don't blame me, it was my daddy. I was abused.' Don't give me that. People are using that as a parachute and people that do that can never be great, never, because they shirk their responsibility."

Lane speaks enthusiastically about his life in the Marine Corps where he learned the notion that even if you don't like something, you do the best you can at what you are doing because it is there to be done. The result is that many people discover potential they never knew they had. "Nothing will take the place of persistence," Lane stresses. "Talent will not. Genius will not. The world is full of educated derelicts. Determination alone is omnipotent. The slogan 'press on' has solved all of our problems in the past and will always solve them. You've got to police yourself and be prepared to do what has to be done."

For Lane, that's one of the good things about boxing because a fighter has to police himself. It's about waking up at five a.m., getting out of bed and starting your training. As a judge, Lane could just sit there with his feet up on the desk, not read the legal briefs, pretend to know what is going on, call a recess, come back and have the law clerk draft an order. He could do that, but he won't. Lane knows "you can get away with that. That's not tending to business. You need to tend to business to be great."

Lack of order and discipline and the determination that arises with them can destroy talented people. Even if they have all the tools, it is easy to quit. Every year in his adopted home state of Nevada, Lane gives a talk at Boys State, a conference of high school student leaders held each summer in 49 states by the American Legion. "Things have been easy for most of them. They are at the top of their class. They skim the book one time and get an A on the test." Lane admonishes his audience about complacency and the danger of quitting that follow close behind. "One of these days as you go on in life you're going to meet people that maybe didn't have the same tools you got but who'll outwork you. And they're the ones you've got to start worrying about because they're going to kick your butt because they know what it is to work hard. They've had to do it all their lives and they're used to it. You're not. You must work long and hard and you can't give up."

Lane admonishes adults too, telling young prosecutors it won't hurt them to keep their nails clean or keep their shoes shined or get their hair cut, and if they wear facial hair, to keep it neat. Those things don't cost much, but such discipline will give them the edge because they are not conceding anything to their adversaries. "In order to be great," Lane advises, "however we define that word, you have to be willing to give up something. You have to be a Spartan." Lane is quick to acknowledge that tending to business is learned. "No matter who you are or wherever you get, if you don't remember the folks that helped to get you there, you're nothing but a damned ingrate," he says in his quintessential no-nonsense rhetoric. "Best thank that teacher that put his or her arm on your shoulder and said 'You can get it done,' or that coach that kicked you in the ass when you were laying down and not giving enough."

Order, discipline and determination. His famous pre-fight invocation, "Let's get it on," says it all.

John Naber
Winner of Four Swimming Gold Medals
in the 1976 Olympic Games

At the 1976 Olympic Games in Montreal, American swimmer John Naber won four gold medals, one silver medal and broke world records five times — including one on two consecutive nights. His standards in the 100- and 200-meter backstroke lasted an amazing seven years after he retired. During his career, Naber won 25 national titles and a record 10 NCAA individual titles while leading his USC team to four undefeated seasons. In 1977, he was presented the James E. Sullivan Award as the nation's Outstanding Amateur Athlete.

Today Naber is a motivational speaker. He preaches the importance of expecting a positive outcome. There is a psychological question that poses whether an eight-ounce glass with four ounces of water is half full or half empty. Says Naber, "It's full of water, there's no half involved and that's the attitude I carried with me to every workout, every pool, every meet." Naber views every experience as something that will help him get to where he wants to be. "My goal never was to win a race," Naber reports. "My goal was to be the best I could be that day so I brought to the pool the notion that this day's going to be great — something good's going to happen."

Naber follows an eight-step process for achievement that serves as the bedrock of his optimism. The first step is to seek a positive emotional response to something you do. It is not something you attain or acquire. It is a feeling that arises from the results of what you do. The second step is to have a realistic appraisal of the attainability of that feeling. "I would love to fly by flapping my arms," Naber illustrates whimsically. "I'd love to feel the freedom of flying without an airplane but it will never happen. It's a good feeling to want but it fails step two."

Step three is to translate the feeling and the appraisal into a concrete goal. Naber did this by setting his standard against one of his sport's all-time greats: seven-time Olympic medalist Roland Matthes of East Germany. In 1968, Matthes became the first Olympian to break the one-minute mark in the 100-meter backstroke. He won gold in the event again four years later, clocking in at 56.58 seconds. "I figured he would swim the distance in 55.5

seconds in 1976, so that became my goal," Naber said. "It wasn't beating Matthes, but beating the time that I calculated would likely beat Matthes. That way the target wasn't going to move."

Step four is to have a strategy. Now that you know where you're going, how do you get there? Step five is identifying bite-size stepping stones. "To be the best in the world in 1976," Naber recalls, "I wanted to be one of the top three in the world by 1975, one of the top three Americans by 1974, and one of the top 10 Americans by 1973." The last three steps are timeless attributes of achievement: work, will, and performance, or paying the price for the dream, overcoming the obstacles in your path, and delivering the goods when it actually matters.

While the first five steps are analysis, the final three are action. According to Naber, these are bound together by discipline. "Commitment is the act of making a promise," Naber explains. "Responsibility is the ability to keep the promises you make to other people. Discipline is the ability to keep the promises you make to yourself." When Naber's parents allowed him to join his first swim team, they didn't know it would lead to Olympic medals. They did know it would require teaching their son how to make and keep promises. "When my dad said, 'Last night you said you were going to morning workout, are you still going to keep that promise?' he was challenging my discipline. And if you want to become a champion, it starts with discipline."

Discipline by nature demands sacrifices but Naber did not and still does not mind making them because he considers a sacrifice "a wise exchange of alternatives." When you are on a diet, you sacrifice the hot fudge sundae to look better in your clothes, which is the wise exchange. A sacrifice as so defined isn't a bad thing; it's a good thing. Naber gave up weekend parties, didn't have girlfriends, and his grade point average could have been better, but if he had it to do over he'd do it the same way.

A few months before Naber's multi-gold medal performance, at the 1976 Winter Olympics in Innsbruck, Austria, American Sheila Young won the 500-meter speed skate. She would go on to win two more medals that year. At her awards ceremony, on television, when the silver medalist was receiving her award, viewers saw Shelia's lips move as though she were talking to herself. Naber met Young later and asked what she was saying. "She said, 'I was thanking God that I was willing to work hard enough five years ago so that I wouldn't have to stand on the silver platform today.' At the time it's a sacri-

> "I would like to be considered great not because I swam fast but because I was able to take my experience and help other people to do what they want to do."

fice, but later on it's a wise exchange of alternatives. I don't regret a single price I paid."

Naber is clearly a confident individual. Confident people believe they are capable, that they have the ability to do what they set out to do. If you don't believe you have the ability, you cannot win. Confident people possess an ego that says it is possible. In contrast, egotists cannot believe it might not be possible. Naber remembers one moment when his confidence got out of control. "I said to a competitor, 'Hey, we've got the 200 back coming up and I don't see anyone who can touch us; let's go one-two.' He and I both knew I was saying, 'You go two and I go one.' That was an egotistical remark and I'm embarrassed to admit that's what I was thinking and I was playing that game."

But the ego to win is primordial and essential. In the most pull-it-out-of-your-gut race of his life, Naber was trailing Peter Rocca at the NCAA finals in 1975. He had never been behind an American in college at the 75-yard mark and "something inside said I can't let him win and I pulled ahead and won by 1/100th of a second."

In the mid-70s, Naber was nearly invincible as a swimmer. But even nearly invincible individuals have doubts. They just don't last very long. During his sophomore year, USC swam against the Canadian national team. Naber lost the 100-meter backstroke to Steve Pickell, the Canadian record holder. He agonized over the upset. "I thought, 'I am no longer the best. Maybe I'll never be the best again.' Then I realized that he was just best on that day. I call it temporary negative evidence." Just because you can't play a Beethoven concerto after a few lessons doesn't mean you will never play it. We tend to think what is current is permanent and that's not true. "Champions are able to disregard temporary negative evidence or at least acknowledge that it's only temporary," Naber adds. He never lost in the event again.

In fact, Naber never lost a race in any stroke that he thought he was going to win. He remembers losing only when he thought he might lose and that included his silver medal in 1976. The 200-meter freestyle was the very next men's race after the 100-meter backstroke. Naber was the first and only athlete to try that double. "I was swimming for the silver," Naber admits, "so I took a silver as a victory." But had he been surprised in any of the other four races where he felt confident of victory, Naber believes, "My parents' training would have taught me to congratulate (the winner), let him feel his moment, give him his time. Then, I would have probably gone home and cried. If the victory is guaranteed, there's no feeling of accomplishment."

Naber does understand disappointments. In March 1972, 16 weeks before the Olympic Trials, Naber dove off a diving board and broke his collarbone. It was June before he got back in the water but he still qualified for the trials. He finished fifth, falling two spots short of the three spots allowed on the team. "It was a great lesson," says Naber. The fact that I didn't make the '72 team made me that much hungrier for '76, which perhaps gave me the ability to do better than I otherwise would have done. But I never once contemplated abandoning that goal."

In the final analysis, in order to achieve you must risk failing.

Achievement requires that you challenge your preparation with the unknown results of your effort. It is like sitting in a ski lift while it crosses a deep ravine. Achievers don't think they are going to fall, but the fact that they could fall is always on their minds. So it was in that long-awaited moment when Naber met Matthes for the 1976 Olympic gold in the 100-meter backstroke. In the preliminaries the night before, Naber had broken Matthes' world record. For the finals, Matthes was in Lane 3, Naber in Lane 4. The starter said, "Take your marks" when Naber's dream began to unravel. "I'm pulling up to get ready to start and I see him go, then the gun fires. I was certain the officials saw it too so I didn't move." After everyone else had hit the water, the starter fired a recall gun. "It dawned on me that the starter is calling them back because he noted I hadn't left, not because he saw the false start. The bottom line was I could have screwed up. He could have not called them back and I would have been sitting here on the blocks and they would have been 10 meters down the pool."

Photo credit: ABC Photo

In 1976, the first false start that occurred was charged to the field. As Naber remembers, the mounting anxiety led to a growing awareness of the possibility of failure and with it a greater meaning of success. "My heart was racing as they came back for a second try. I looked at Matthes and saw a smile on his face. He'd done it on purpose. He'd tried to catch me on my heels and he tried to catch the starter."

Again, the starter said, "Take your marks" and, again, Matthes went early but this time Naber did too. The recall gun brought the field back for a third start. Now there were two false starts on the field. A third false start would disqualify the swimmer who committed it. "I realized I could easily slip or something on the third try and never swim the race. But it's the possibility of failure that makes the eventual success so much sweeter."

He won the gold in that race while Matthes had to settle for bronze. And remember that 55.5-second mark Naber set for himself? Well, he crossed the finish line at 55.49 seconds, nearly a full second ahead of the silver medalist,

Naber's old NCAA nemesis and countryman Peter Rocca. The time would stand as an Olympic record until 1988, when it was finally eclipsed by a group of medalists led by Japan's Daichi Suzuki.

The sweet successes in Naber's career also included beating Matthes and his formidable teammates at a USA-East Germany dual meet in 1974. The outcome of the dual meet rested on the backstrokes. If Naber won, the USA won. If he lost, East Germany won. They also included leading the USC Trojans over the Indiana Hoosiers in the 1974 NCAA Championships. The final score: USC–339, Indiana–338.

But success does not buy contentment. In November 1977, after the Olympics and the talk shows, Naber finished studying at the library and went back to his apartment to sit in his beanbag chair with the lights out, alone. There, he faced his biggest challenge; he faced himself. "The rain was coming down and there was a spotlight illuminating the parking lot that was lighting the drops and it was quiet, and it was the first time since the Olympics that the treadmill stopped and there was a real emotional letdown because I realized I did not have a feeling to chase anymore." An individual without a goal or without a dream is a bit like a water-skier that lets go of the rope and gradually starts sinking. It took from July to November for Naber to slip down. "That was a real scare for me, a lonely period. I felt purposeless for a while."

> "Winning a gold medal doesn't make you great. If all you've done is do things for yourself, you are selfish and very good at it."

Naber used his highly introspective mind to devise his eight-step plan that enabled him to succeed in his date with destiny and Roland Matthes. He used the same philosophical perspective to resolve his emptiness and recognize that the dream and the dual were part fiction.

"Being a millionaire is only one dollar more than being a nine hundred ninety-nine thousandaire. It's just a title," asserts Naber. "Being a world record holder is a title and they can't ever take that away from you. But there is no inherent value in swimming quickly while on your back. Unless you're pulling somebody to safety it's no big shakes. Titles are merely public declarations that in a skill where you competed against others who wanted the same reward, you were a bit better."

Despite his incredible athletic performance, Naber didn't get lost in the glitter of his gold. "Winning a gold medal doesn't make you great. If all you've done is do things for yourself, you are selfish and very good at it." When he thought it over in the quiet of his room and as he continues to do in the still of his life, Naber realized that greatness is about doing something that is good for others as opposed to doing something that is good for you. "I would like to be considered great not because I swam fast but because I was able to take my experience and help other people to do what they want to do. You try to have life as it occurs because of your input to be better than life as it might occur without your input."

The reason most educators encourage young people to get into sports is not to win something, but rather to learn something; to learn goal setting, discipline, and sacrifice. Sports should be a character builder. Naber says, "the pot of gold is what's inside of you after you're done with sport, not what you wear around your neck."

When Naber began the rigor of training, as he confronted the obstacles along his path, as he prepared for the swim of his dreams, he always went back to step one of his process and lived out the feeling and anticipated the reward. Like a narrator in his own video, Naber relives it one more time. "I'd close my eyes and I'd imagine the rumbling sound of 12,000 spectators. I'd imagine Roland Matthes pulling himself up to the blocks in the lane next to me. I'd imagine the echo of the sound of the gun. I'd imagine the slap of the water hitting me in my back after the start. I'd imagine the tension in my shoulders and my shallowness of breath as I got to the 75-meter mark. I'd imagine the ache and the burn in my thighs. In the privacy of my bedroom I always won. That I was willing to try to make my dreams come true, that is the real gold medal."

That is also why John Naber is considered one of America's true champions.

Sandra Day O'Connor
*First Female Justice of the
United States Supreme Court*

Former Supreme Court Justice Lewis Powell once said, "Being asked to serve on the US Supreme Court is a little like being struck by lightning in both the suddenness and improbability of it." It is not a position to which people can reasonably aspire. It occurs as the result of unique circumstances that create a vacancy at the exact moment when a would-be Justice is qualified, available, and politically aligned with the incumbent president. "It is very unlikely for anyone and certainly it was for me, a cowgirl from Arizona," says Sandra Day O'Connor, who in 1981 became the first woman appointed to the Supreme Court in the nation's history.

O'Connor's family had a small, remote cattle ranch in Arizona that was reached by a road in New Mexico. Her grandfather started the ranch in 1880 when Arizona was only a territory and it was where her father, Harry A. Day, was born in 1898. The nearest town was more than 35 miles away and the roads were poor. The ranch was so remote that when it came time for her mother, Ada Mae Day, to give birth, she went to a hospital near her parents in El Paso, Texas. O'Connor was the couple's first-born child on March 26, 1930.

As a young girl, O'Connor lived in an old adobe house surrounded by a screen porch where the ranch hands slept. There was no running water, indoor plumbing or electricity. "We didn't have those things for many years," O'Connor recalls. "Eventually my father installed an electric generator which he could crank up at night so we'd have lights for awhile. When I was in high school, he put up more than 10 miles of telephone poles so we could have a party line phone."

At first, Mrs. Day tried teaching her daughter at home but she quickly decided it would be better for her to attend school. But that meant making a very difficult decision: whether to leave her husband and move to a larger town so her daughter could go to school there or stay with her husband and send her daughter away. Because her grandparents were still in El Paso, O'Connor left home to attend the Radford School for Girls. Obviously a very astute teenager, after attending Radford for several years, O'Connor thought, "It would be nice to be in closer proximity to boys so I moved over to Austin High School."

If ranch life wasn't enough to make improbable her rise to the highest court in the land, her small town schooling came close to making it impossible. "The only place I wanted to go to college was Stanford," O'Connor recalls. There were not many students in Austin High School that planned to leave the state to go to college so the principal informed the few who were that he would let them know when the college entrance exams were given, which Stanford required. He forgot. "I missed the exams," O'Connor exclaims. "I was just stricken because I intended to apply to no other school. He was stricken, too." The principal contacted the admissions office and begged that they allow O'Connor to take the exams when she arrived on campus and they agreed. It is highly unlikely they would do that today.

At Stanford, O'Connor made the dean's list her first semester. She majored in economics as a last resort. "I liked many things," O'Connor says with a smile. "I loved geology and languages, and there were all kinds of options. I just didn't know what to do." O'Connor finished her degree program in three years and spent a fourth taking elective courses, one of which was an undergraduate law class. "It was simply marvelous and the professor was an inspiration. He held seminars at night at his home. It was a quasi-religious approach. He believed very strongly in the ability of the individual to make a difference. And he was sure that each of us would go out and do some good and he tried to persuade us that that was how we should spend our lives. I was very impressed with him and because of that class and the experience of knowing him, I decided to apply to law school."

In those days, women seeking admission to the law school were interviewed. Following hers, O'Connor was granted early admission. Her academic performance was distinguished and she was invited to join the *Law Review*. "It opened entirely new ways of looking at the world. It was a way of analyzing problems, pulling the pieces apart and putting them together in a way that makes sense. It turned on major floodlights to the world's affairs, how the world worked, and what some of the rules were that made it work. It was a great experience."

In 1952, Sandra Day graduated from Stanford University Law School and married John Jay O'Connor III. Following commencement, she served as a deputy county attorney in California and as a civilian lawyer for the Quartermaster Corps while her husband was on military duty in Germany. When the couple returned to Arizona, O'Connor was unable to find work with any law firm because of her gender. Rather than retreat, she established her own successful law practice and, in 1965, was named Assistant Attorney General for the state. From there, O'Connor was appointed and subsequently reelected to the Arizona State Senate, serving a total of six years. Following four years as Superior Court judge in Phoenix and two years on the Arizona Court of Appeals, she entered history.

When President Reagan put a woman on the Court, the first in 191 years, it opened other doors for women all across the world. Nearly 20 years later, O'Connor continues to receive letters from female students who want to write a report about her and from young career women who want to do what she did. "The letters have been wonderful," O'Connor admits. While it is clear that she is a role model for women, O'Connor is not one who views role models as essential for achievement. "I hear the notion you have to have role models," O'Connor adds. "I didn't have any role models, for heaven sakes! And as to the notion that you have to have female role models for women, the hope is that people see through the gender and see to the dream."

The Supreme Court has come a long way since its first days. There were only five members originally. Then, the justices still had responsibilities as circuit judges and met only as needed, living together in a boarding house near Washington where they would work morning, noon, and night to accomplish their tasks. But the charter remains the same, not to make law, but interpret it. "When you review a case," O'Connor explains, "you look at the statute Congress has written and try to interpret it as it was written. You may think it's a lousy idea personally but you're not writing it, you're trying to interpret what Congress thought was a good idea. I may think it's good policy to mean this or that but I have to look at those words and figure what was intended."

A noble ideal, but O'Connor views everything she does in noble terms. While her gender-breaking appointment has given her extraordinary notoriety, O'Connor responds quickly that the "decisions rather than the members of the Court are what's important." In fact, O'Connor has no illusions of grandeur about being a Supreme Court Justice nor does she extend privilege to any member of government. "We have acknowledged leaders in a democratic society," O'Connor lectures. "We elect them. We've gone to great pains to make sure they're not royalty. They're subject to laws like anyone or, in the common vernacular, even the president puts his pants on one leg at a time, just like everybody else."

O'Connor attributes her sense of responsibility to her rural roots. In the flatlands of Arizona, everyone had a role to play. Everyone had to learn how to solve problems, do things for themselves. "If the truck broke down there was no mechanic to call; you fixed it," O'Connor reports. "If a person got sick there was no doctor for hundreds of miles. You solved the problems yourself. My father set bones in animals and people and when a cow's uterus would come out, we cleaned it off, put it back in, and sewed her up."

O'Connor's circumstances are much different today. Her chambers are elegant and meticulous. A Court receptionist and a personal secretary guard entry to her office. The entourage and Renaissance paintings and enormous oak doors and accouterments of power and royal blue tailored suit all belie her humble roots. "I had to take lunch to the round-up crew in a remote place," O'Connor describes, "make a fire, make the coffee, have the food hot and ready when they came in. I was supposed to be there before 10 o'clock in the morning. I was driving the truck and I got a flat. I was young and the lug bolts were frozen on but I changed the tire and got the truck on the road again but I was late. I got lunch ready but it meant my father started branding first instead of letting the men eat first. He was very irritated and he said, 'You're late.' I said, 'I had a flat tire.' He said, 'You should have started earlier.' He was right. You have a job to do and you're responsible for doing it. Don't expect sympathy. Get the job done. Now that's a good lesson for a kid to learn."

It was an idea good enough, in fact, to become part of her own parenting strategy. When O'Connor was raising children, she was a working attorney and wasn't always available. She kept her children busy with chores so they'd stay out of trouble and learn a sense of self-reliance. Her plan proved successful when one afternoon their dog was hit by a car and needed medical attention. Her boys didn't drive, but they remained undeterred. "They figured out where there was a veterinarian, got a door off the hinges, put the dog on the door, and carried him there. Now, that was very responsible," O'Connor boasts. "I was very impressed that they were willing to figure out what to do and did it. And that's what everyone has to do. It really helps if people learn that."

> "I didn't have any role models, for heaven sakes! And as to the notion that you have to have female role models for women, the hope is that people see through the gender and see to the dream."

O'Connor loves to talk about her father's ranch. The values she learned there are central to her world view of and for American society. She also loves to talk about American society because she is terribly worried that children today no longer have the opportunity to learn those values. "Why do we have all of these urban problems, incapacity, unemployment, and boredom? It's because we have this mass of young people who aren't required to be doing chores every minute to help the family survive. We lose something in an urban society, and it's the kind of substitutes we're going to find that will make the difference in whether we succeed as a nation."

As an emerging judicial leader, O'Connor learned that while there are only a limited number of leaders, they're not genetically limited to men. As a Stanford student, O'Connor learned that while this is a huge world, the individual can make a difference. From her family, she learned there is a role for everyone in life that they must find and embrace. "Everybody can have an impact by participating in a public sense," O'Connor argues. "Whether it's on a school board or a city council or a community commission or a voluntary organization or in your job, you can make a difference. Those who dedicate themselves to trying to provide a solution can meaningfully affect the solution that is selected."

O'Connor is a pragmatist. She does not believe you can legislate solutions to America's social problems. Some laws are needed, but that is not the solution. Instead, O'Connor believes solutions require thoughtful collaborative approaches. "We need to develop a culture of respect for other people, what we used to call civility. That is diminishing today. I care about my country and I want the world to survive peacefully. We all ought to want that, so we all ought to care; we all ought to be thinking. Care is something else that's missing. There seems to be indifference to community, but there can't be. You have to be a caring, civil, thoughtful person."

During her confirmation hearing for her appointment to the Supreme Court in front of the Senate Judiciary Committee, one senator asked O'Connor what she would want her tombstone to say about her life. O'Connor replied, "Here lies a good judge."

A good judge indeed.

Chapter 4

It's Intuitive, Intuitive, Intuitive

Leon Lederman
High Energy Physicist and
Winner of the 1988 Nobel Prize

When we take a walk in a park, we are bombarded every second with nearly 400 trillion neutrinos from the sun, another 50 billion neutrinos from the natural radioactivity of the earth, and up to 100 billion neutrinos from the plants all over the world. Fortunately for us, neutrinos don't collide much with the body and so we can still appreciate a good picnic on the grass.

Photo credit: Fermylab Visual Media

Fortunately for us too, physicist Leon M. Lederman opened the door a little wider to understanding these particles through his discovery of the muon, or "two neutrino," for which he was awarded the Nobel Prize for physics in 1988 with his associates Melvin Schwartz and Jack Steinberger. If you've never heard of a neutrino don't worry, you're not alone. "Remember the Periodic Table in high school chemistry with hydrogen and the other stuff? Well, that was the best organization one could make then. But it was made by chemists," Lederman exclaims with a hint of disapproval. "Those elements were believed to be the basic properties of matter. The designers of the table thought these were uncuttable objects. But it turns out we can cut them, and it turns out we have an array of basic particles that are the core of those elements."

Neutrinos are almost nothing, one of the smallest quantities of reality discovered by science. Despite that or perhaps because of that, they raised a lot of questions for physicists and headaches for those who tried to detect them. "Three types of neutrinos are known and there is strong evidence that no additional neutrinos exist," Lederman explains emphatically. He places no emphasis at all on his place in history as the father of a new table that physicists were able to create only after the discovery of the two neutrino. "Well, the second neutrino certainly helped people to say it has to be this way," he acknowledges.

The new table greatly reduced the number of elementary particles of matter from the old Periodic Table. According to the Standard Model, 12 particles form the basis for all matter: six types of quarks (a name taken from a James Joyce novel) and six types of leptons (derived from the Greek word for tiny, *leptos*). Among the six leptons, three are electrically charged and three are uncharged or neutral. These uncharged leptons are the neutrinos.

Lederman graduated from City College of New York in 1943 with a chemistry degree. Eight years later, he received a Ph.D. in physics from Columbia after conducting research at the Nevis cyclotron, the university's atomic accelerator. He spent the next 28 years at Columbia, directing the Nevis Lab from 1961 to 1978, before becoming director of the Fermi National Accelerator Laboratory, or Fermilab, in suburban Chicago where he completed his neutrino research. Now director emeritus of Fermilab, Lederman has published more than 200 papers, sponsored research of 52 graduate students, and won a Nobel Prize during his nearly 50 years in physics. The 78-year-old Lederman is still looking for answers to mysteries of the universe. "Our world is dominated by quarks; 99.99 percent are just two of them." Then the question that dominates his life: "Why?" he asks.

"The answer is we are living in a very cold universe," Lederman explains, answering his own question. "The average temperature is three degrees above absolute zero. I live in Chicago where it's warmer fortunately. But once upon a time the average temperature was billions of degrees. In the early universe all quarks coexisted and smashed into each other and had a wonderful time. When the universe cooled, the heavier ones went into limbo and so we're left with mostly lighter ones in our current world. If we want to understand the world, we have to understand what's there."

Does it really make a difference whether there are six quarks or two quarks or no quarks at all? "A big difference if we want to understand the world," Lederman answers. "It enables me to know that Halley's Comet will appear in 2061. I know that because somebody was curious about the motions of comets and planets and now we can make a prediction and, no question about it, in 2061 Halley's Comet will appear. That's an achievement of curiosity-driven science. And if there weren't this many quarks, it wouldn't take place, nor would natural selection and evolution."

And what about those neutrinos? "They are the first serious candidates known to exist that may explain dark matter or black holes. They may have even played a role in the creation of galaxies. Isn't it amazing?" Lederman asks amazed that anyone would not find it so.

If you find it hard to understand, Lederman has an answer for you. "Everything's hard," Lederman says. "If you ask, 'Why are clouds white?' you get, 'Because they reflect all colors equally.' Why do they reflect colors or anything for that matter? Because clouds have droplets of water. Well, then, why does a droplet of water reflect light? And so on until, pretty soon, you get down to the atomic structure of water and when you get to atomic structure, it comes down to quarks. That's what we're trying to find out about. It's not frivolous."

Such a line of questioning invariably gets us down to the fundamental properties of matter. Understanding the fundamentals has been Lederman's life work and he has mastered it. In 1990, he was elected president of the American Association for the Advancement of Science, the largest scientific organization in the United States. His list of awards includes the National Medal of Science in 1965 and the Enrico Fermi Award given by President Clinton in 1993.

"The deepest impulse of man is to understand," Lederman says slowly and intentionally. "The first attempts were to build a wonderful, mythological, literary picture. 'The earth is shaking because Zeus is mad at us. We did something wrong.' Kind of clumsy, but at least it was an attempt to understand, a pre-scientific attempt to explain the common terms of a frightening world. Why is it dark at night and light in the daytime? Now we have a system of rationality and, maybe by accident, invented a way we can get an objective understanding of the world. So it's not frivolous. It's why we're here, to understand the world into which mankind is imbedded."

Lederman possesses a curiosity to understand without being passionate. If he believes there are dangers facing humanity, he does not put his conclusions before his research. That, he claims, is the domain of social science. "You may have biases," Lederman admits, "but you're not supposed to tilt the machine. The skill of the scientist is to make sure your experiment is correct." Science, with a capital S, is value-free. It is about how the world works. It is about knowledge. It gets into values through decisions made by citizens and their representatives on how to put science to use. Lederman does not suggest uses for his conclusions; however, as a scientist-citizen, he works tirelessly for science as essential to human welfare.

Photo credit: Fermylab Visual Media

"When you've satisfied your curiosity, you go on to the next problem," Lederman states. He leaves the social applications of science to technology, which is "thousands of years older than science. The first technology was the club. You beat somebody with it, then it evolved into a sharp horn on a stick and so on. Science is relatively new. It started in 650 BC on a Thursday afternoon at 4:15 in Greece," Lederman quips, irritated in having to make the distinction. "Fire was a technological instrument and the technologist never asked, 'What is fire? How does it work?' That's science."

In 1831, Michael Faraday discovered electromagnetic induction and invented the generator by tinkering with batteries and wires. Fifty years later London was electrified. But the difference between tinkerer and scientist has never changed. "When Faraday was working on electricity, Prime Minister

William Gladstone came to visit him and said, 'What good is all this stuff?' Faraday's famous answer was, 'I don't know, but someday you'll probably tax it.' He was not interested in its usefulness."

In fact, Faraday never patented the motor or generator. He was interested in electrical and magnetic phenomena. In the course of exploring those came the motor and generator and changes in the way we live. "The tinkerer and the scientist are both driven by curiosity. Technologists are driven by science," Lederman asserts, "and with the basic understanding of how atoms work, they are now developing useful things like gene therapy."

Science is also different from philosophy, too, because it uses objective criteria that require experiments. Philosophy does not get involved with experiments, with posing questions that are answered by doing them. "There's a famous story of philosophers who were discussing how many teeth a horse has," Lederman begins. "A bitter argument ensued and a kid who was just admitted to the group, maybe it was Plato's club, suggested there's a horse outside and they could go out and count the teeth. Well, he was beaten up by the other guys and thrown out."

While Lederman finds the subatomic world of quarks and leptons beautiful, he sees the big outside world as a contentious mess.

"There's a gap. The public isn't educated," Lederman declares. "If I spent all night in the lab and made this incredible discovery and got a call saying, 'On your way home pick up a dozen rolls,' well, I'd want to talk to somebody. If I go to the grocer and tell him what I found, all I'd get is a blank stare. That's a gap and a failure of our educational system which is widening the gap instead of closing it. I spoke at a high school and during the question period a kid said, 'What do you remember from high school?' I said, 'Josephine.' It was the right answer; everybody applauded."

Lederman speaks candidly about education. He is founder of the Teachers Academy for Mathematics and Science, founder of a public high school for the gifted, and active in the training of primary school teachers. "Society is changing rapidly. I just downloaded CD-ROM data off a Yahoo! web site. Five years ago that would have been gibberish. Our language and behavior are changing because of technology. We are a society driven by technology yet ignorant of the science that produces it. There are those who hate science. They adjust their pacemaker, roll their lumbar chair up to their word processor, and denounce it."

The ignorance, the gap, and the disdain for science are mind-boggling for Lederman who believes that without understanding our world we will never resolve its problems. "The only way we can escape the problems of 10 billion people on the planet or global warming or the enormous gap between

"The deepest
impulse
of man
is to
understand."

rich and poor is with science," Lederman urges. "Science ultimately empowers humanity to rise to incredible heights and fix these problems." But science immediately leads to technology and it is technology that exacerbates the gap between the rich and the poor because people who are comfortable with technology get richer and those who are uncomfortable get poorer. "The key word is ultimately. We have to change the Bill of Rights to life, liberty, the pursuit of happiness, AND access to knowledge," Lederman, now animated, fervently pleads.

That, of course, requires a change in ethics. And for the first time, Lederman is stumped. "I don't know how to teach morality and ethics. It would be wonderful to figure out how but you have to go on because it's too late to turn back. You can't go back to an agrarian society where everybody grows their own food. We're on the back of a tiger called technology. Technology creates wealth. The question is how to distribute it, use it more wisely. Technology gave us the drab cities that take over landscape and technology can get us out of it if we make the right choices."

The relationship between science and social science is fragile. At the base of the pyramid of knowledge is mathematics. Physics sits on mathematics because it is a convenient language. You can write an explanation in English, but it would take 30 pages to say what one line of mathematics says. Chemistry sits on physics, biology on chemistry. From there, you stand at the door of social science with psychology on biology. After that, the picture gets blurry. "A lot of us believe artificial intelligence and neural physiology, what might be called cognition science, are starting to form a bridge between science and social science. Do the properties of quarks determine something as exotic as love? We're beginning to dare to understand those things."

When one thinks about scientists who dared to understand, one thinks about Albert Einstein. Einstein opened up a whole new world. He transformed our notions of space and time. The theory of relativity is extremely profound. It enabled us to glimpse the origin of the universe. Without it, we would not have nuclear power or nuclear weapons or their consequences. But technologies were not what drove him; Einstein didn't invent nuclear power and was strongly opposed to nuclear weapons. It was, as Lederman has repeated, to understand the world.

The only other figure in science that approaches Einstein's stature is Sir Isaac Newton. There have been other scientists who did very profound work but not at the level of those two, Lederman among them. "My achievement was not at all like his," Lederman states without any hesitation. Despite the fact that his restructured model has impacts on the thoughts of scientists everywhere as they explore our universe, fame is not what drives Lederman. "It means nothing to very little. It's useful to be anonymous. I'd hate to be Michael Jordan, always drawing a crowd. On the other hand, it would be nice if, when you're introduced, they say, 'Oh yes, I've heard of you.'"

Some people act as if they seek prizes. Prize winners don't. They don't even think about it until long after the work they did is in the history books. The great quest for real achievers is to get through each day. "The chance of a major discovery is small. You have to learn to enjoy someone else's discovery, take pleasure in it, appreciate it. That's a hard thing for humans to learn. And you must have fun in the day-to-day operations, the little triumphs and discoveries."

There is another great discovery like Einstein's to be had. It will take us very deep. Since Einstein, we have relativity, a tremendous theory about the cosmos. We have quantum mechanics, a tremendous theory about atoms. But the two theories are independent, side-by-side and non-communicative. "If we truly ever want to understand how it began in the big bang, those two theories will need to be joined because they both don't apply to this beginning. They're inadequate. Somewhere, a kid being turned off by an insensitive third-grade teacher, has in him the seeds to combine those two theories in some way. And that will be something totally new. That's big stakes, that's really big stakes."

"The only way we can escape the problems of 10 billion people on the planet or global warming or the enormous gap between rich and poor is with science."

Scientists everywhere are competing for that prize. They compete against colleagues across the hall and against scientists in other countries. Yet while they are competing they are also collaborating. "There's a lot of post-modernist, multi-cultural BS that says there are many different ways of looking at the world. It's all baloney. There's only one science and if there's a Maori doing science, he will do the same science as an Argentinean or a Greek or the Chinese. There's one science and it happened to have started in Western Europe and it was a gift to civilization."

Sometimes it gets a little unpleasant. Not all scientists are sweet, loveable people; some can be obsessive and secretive. Remember, Leonardo DaVinci coded his notes so no one would steal his ideas. And it is not that much different today. "The opposite number of this lab is in Switzerland. There are two big labs in the world and we collaborate," Lederman acknowledges, while quickly adding, "But we want to beat the hell out of them."

Lederman puts in long hours day after day to do just that, following a regimen that is so rigorous "you don't know it's Monday because you've worked all weekend anyway." It is an obsession, but one Lederman thoroughly enjoys. "The whole point is to get up in the morning and say, 'Oh no, I overslept. I've got to get to my job.' That's a wonderful life. If you never achieve anything, you could become very frustrated and not have any fun at all, and then not even want to get out of bed. Achievement tends to add to the fun."

If Lederman ever decides to close the door and not walk back to the lab, science will lose one of its great achievers. Will it notice? "What do I care?" Lederman retorts crisply. "I don't have the ego to think I am that important except to family." Somebody thought he was. There is a center on the Fermilab campus that bears his name. "I didn't do that. Had to get special permission. You can't name a government building after someone who's alive, so I had to play dead. They got a dispensation."

Probably from Albert and Isaac.

Mark McCormack
Founder and Chairman of
Sports Marketing Giant IMG, Inc.

Photo credit: Berliner

Over 40 years ago, Cleveland attorney Mark McCormack shook hands with golfer Arnold Palmer and started his business. Today, the undisputed leader in global sports management and marketing, McCormack functions as agent and impresario for hundreds of the world's biggest names and biggest events. With nearly 3,000 employees and more than 70 offices in 29 countries, International Management Group is a billion dollar empire with a client list that includes tennis champion Pete Sampras, violinist Itzhak Perlman, broadcaster John Madden, fashion model Lauren Hutton, the Nobel Foundation, and the All England Lawn Tennis and Croquet Club at Wimbledon. American sports media have called McCormack the most powerful man in golf, tennis, and sports. The *London Times* named him one of the "Makers of the Twentieth Century."

As a young man, McCormack did not have grandiose visions of being President of the United States or Nobel Prize winner or sports marketing magnate for that matter of fact. He just loved sports and loved to play them. "Like everyone, I imagined hitting home runs that won the World Series," McCormack reminisces. "But I didn't really know what I was going to do, even when I went to college." While attending the College of William and Mary in Williamsburg, Virginia, McCormack majored in French primarily because his mother and father convinced him that he should get a good liberal arts education and then concentrate on something at the graduate level. Even when McCormack went on to law school he didn't want to be a lawyer. "But I knew it would show me how to write and think better and that a legal degree would help me in whatever I did."

While he had no idea of his future career, he did play sports. Golf was McCormack's game and he played exceptionally, competing four times each in the US Amateur and British Amateur championships and once in the US Open. "I played pretty well," McCormack recalls, "but I knew I wasn't good enough to be a professional so I tried to figure out something I could do with my golf and legal training. In those days nobody represented athletes, so I started doing that."

From a single client, McCormack has developed and diversified his business to become an enormously successful multi-national corporation. Today, IMG is the world's largest athlete representation firm; the world's biggest independent source of televised sports; an agency representing world class musicians; a literary agency and lecture bureau; three international modeling agencies; a licensing agency; and a financial planning firm that serves hundreds of business executives and sports celebrities.

McCormack speaks candidly about the ingredients of his success, which he claims are simple and obvious. He has published his thoughts in two Bantam Books, *What They Don't Teach You at Harvard Business School: Notes from a Street-Smart Executive* (1986), and the sequel, *What They Still Don't Teach You at Harvard Business School: Selling More, Managing Better, and Getting the Job Done in the '90s* (1990). "People will tell you that luck is important and, to a degree, that's true," McCormack agrees.

One could argue McCormack was lucky. His first three clients were golfing legends Arnold Palmer, Gary Player and Jack Nicklaus, all of whom signed before they became famous. At the time Player, a native of South Africa, had only played once in America, Nicklaus was still an amateur and Palmer had won only one major championship. Perhaps he was lucky, too, that the three of them started winning everything just as sport television coverage expanded and golf was suddenly getting more exposure and their names were getting bigger. But McCormack clearly believes it was not purely luck. "I am always reminded of what Gary Player always says: 'The harder I practice, the luckier I get.' There's real truth to that," McCormack emphasizes.

McCormack had an intuitive sense about the men that he selected and he was creative with their good fortune. "I went to businesses and told them to use golf to promote their products and to use my golfers. If I didn't have the right golfers, the idea could have failed. Instead it was brilliant. I did something about my circumstances."

McCormack believes that anyone could achieve his level of success in any business if they set aside money as motive and, as Nike might say, just do it. McCormack argues that "the big problem with MBAs today, in fact maybe everyone, is that they expect $70,000 a year right out of school." He counsels would-be achievers to volunteer in the business of their dreams instead and demonstrate their talents. "You diffuse all those people who say they haven't got any budget to hire anybody else. Everybody thinks they're overworked and that their departments are understaffed. If you can supply help without forcing increases in their budgets, you'll get the job. And, if you get the job and you're really good, you'll start getting paid to do what you enjoy." That was pretty much what McCormack himself did with IMG.

Whether it was judging the potential of his golfing trio or picking the right executives for his clients, McCormack maintains the most important attribute to success is people sense, building relationships and building them with the right people. "Relationships are critical to the whole thing," says

McCormack. "You've got to have relationships with the people that can make something happen." And the CEO is not necessarily that person. CEOs are always good relationships to have, but CEOs often do not stay on top of details because most of them do not have the time to do that. "I can go to the CEO of a company and win his approval and he can tell his marketing guy to sponsor my event. Fine, but if he isn't on top of how that works and the marketing guy doesn't want it to work, it won't work. So finding the right person to get the action you want is the key and that can be very complicated."

McCormack simplifies it, as he is prone to do, with one word, dependability. "On a scale of 10, most people range from six down to one. I'm a 10," McCormack notes with absolute certainty.

In McCormack's first meeting with one of the most powerful businessmen in America, he learned that the executive's daughter was attending Tulane University in New Orleans. McCormack knew that Bjorn Borg was going to play a tennis exhibition nearby. Since Borg was one of McCormack's clients he told the executive he would give his daughter tickets. Weeks later, McCormack wrote and sent the tickets. Years later, and by then one of McCormack's sponsors, the executive told McCormack he started doing business with him because anyone that would have that degree of follow up on such a small matter would be equally as professional with his business. "The single most important thing for developing relationships is dependability," McCormack declares, "and that means keeping your word even if the keeping of your word costs you a lot of money."

McCormack has kept his word and he has made a lot of money. After Palmer, Player and Nicklaus, his agency continued to attract top-shelf athletes, including Australian tennis star Rod Laver, French skier and Olympic gold medalist Jean-Claude Killy, Scottish auto racer Jackie Stewart, John Havlicek of the Boston Celtics, and so on. Like Bill Gates and Microsoft or Babe Ruth and the Yankees, McCormack and IMG are so successful they are often the man and the company people love to hate. Competitors castigate IMG as impersonal and McCormack as arrogant. They mistrust his personal style and motives. The media are similarly antagonistic and vilify IMG for a ubiquitous industry presence that includes annual marketing solicitation to more than 1,200 companies, tour promotion for Pope John Paul II, and clients as diverse as the Mayo Clinic and the Ringling Brothers Circus.

Despite the success and the criticisms, McCormack continues to build. He could easily retire with no financial worries but one of the powerful nuances of achievement, ego, drives him onward. "Ego drives a lot of people," McCormack admits. "But to me ego means 'self' and it means getting gratification from achievement. If you're developing a cancer cure, you're developing it for the world, to be sure, but the ego element is certainly there. You are happy and comfortable saying, 'I developed the cure for cancer.'"

McCormack deals with egos every day from the corporate executives he solicits for sponsorship to the celebrities and athletes he represents. There is no question that Jack Nicklaus plays golf today partly to give gratification to his fans. But McCormack notes he is also playing to "receive the ego gratification that he gets when he plays and he is applauded. He knows he's still competitive and he knows he can't win on the regular PGA tour but he still does it because his ego drives him to do that. Ego is always there in varying degrees and drives people to make more money or be recognized as the best."

It clearly drives McCormack and is rooted in three aspects of his job. One is mastery. McCormack has attained a level of competence in what he does and he still has the ability to do it as well as ever before. "It's different than Arnold Palmer," McCormack explains, "who attained a certain level a proficiency but no longer has the ability to do so." McCormack wants to stay at the top of his game for as long as he can and is comfortable in proclaiming that. "I want to keep being someone who is driving the most successful sports marketing, sports management, sports television company in the world, rather than someone who built it, created it, and is no longer driving it."

The second aspect is the milieu. McCormack exudes enthusiasm for his work and enormous satisfaction with working in the industry. "I love playing sports and going to sports events," McCormack exclaims. "Most people retire to do what I do every day which is play tennis and golf." And McCormack plays with some heavy hitters. He's returned volleys with Monica Seles and teed off with Tiger Woods. As the king of sports marketing, McCormack can be with nearly anyone in the sports world he wants and is treated like royalty at sporting events.

The third is medium. Sport and society are different today in large measure because of McCormack and IMG. There is little debate that McCormack has been the primary factor in the globalization of sport. He views that as socially valuable. "I can look back and see that the world of sports is better for my existence and that is a very gratifying thing," McCormack acknowledges. "Sports is, by and large, a good way for societies to interact and sports, by and large, has set up good role models for the youth of the world, and so I feel very good that I've been a part of that."

While a good number of sociologists might disagree with his noble analysis of the industry, McCormack is clearly pleased with who he is and what he has done and the pleasure drives him on. "It isn't the money," McCormack states unequivocally. "I have enough. It's personal satisfaction. That's a big part of success."

> "The single most important thing for developing relationships is dependability, and that means keeping your word even if the keeping of your word costs you a lot of money."

Mark Morris
Award-Winning Choreographer
Acclaimed as the "Mozart of Modern Dance"

Photo credit: Marc Royce

From film to television to Broadway, Mark Morris has given new meaning and new life to dance. Morris has literally danced around the globe with performances in communities as different as Kansas City and Istanbul. He has danced on "Sesame Street" and his Mark Morris Dance Group has performed with the Boston Pops. He so loves the arts, he has commissioned a backdrop from painter Howard Hodgkin, collaborated with Isaac Mizrahi to design costumes for the Royal Opera, and shared the stage with Yo-Yo Ma. The *Washington Post* has called Morris the "Mozart of modern dance."

Whistling all the way from the coffee bar to his room, Morris is always in motion, physically or mentally. After rearranging the clutter in his room, he finally sits and is ready to speak. Dressed in a sarong, tank top and sandals, Morris is always vintage Morris as he sips on his Starbucks and pours out unabashed, unedited, and unending commentary on the things which are most important to him: music and dance.

"Rhythm, the pulse of music, moves everybody," Morris exclaims. "We are programmed that way but most of us are just simply too shy or too embarrassed to explore it. Everybody dances till they're like seven, then they stop and never do it again. I found dance interesting. When it became a legit art form for me instead of just something I liked to do, it became even more interesting and more varied. That keeps happening to me all the time."

Dance is a better name for what Morris does, but modern dance fits. It is definitely different from ballet. Modern dance started at the beginning of 20th Century. It was inseparable from early feminism, associated with women losing corsets and having a life of their own. On purpose, it was not classical ballet. That schism is long gone. Today, classical ballet is incorporating more and more modern dance. It has to because there are no ballet choreographers who are not modern dancers. They don't exist anymore.

Morris works both worlds. He is a frequent collaborator with the San Francisco Ballet and is the founder and director of a company that creates, produces, and performs nearly 100 times each year all over the world. "I'm good," Morris admits with ease. "I don't think dancing is a joke. I don't think it's just a fun workout." Most people don't see serious dances frequently and so they don't know how to watch them very well. You have to practice that. For most, dance is just something lovely to look at or something that's so impenetrable because it's more modern than they are that they don't understand it and so it becomes high art. Morris has tried to avoid the pitfalls of both. "I'm perfectly unafraid," Morris announces. "I'm totally paranoid as a person but in my work I do exactly what I think should be happening in a piece. And that's what audiences like about my work; it seems inevitable. The music I use is very exciting and the choreography is not show-offy. It's a fully realized work of art in the time it takes to watch it."

Morris started studying dance at nine. He began with flamenco. But he saw himself as a choreographer from the very beginning. "I was making up dances when I was 12 that were totally legit," Morris reports. "In retrospect I was a prodigy. The first dance I made up that was satisfying was at 15." Morris performed his first dance in the inaugural concert of the Mark Morris Dance Group in New York in 1980, years after he created it. Morris is certain he was destined to be a dancer-choreographer and he is equally certain that destiny plays an enormous role in becoming proficient at any craft. "I'm a believer in talent. Some people are more talented than other people at certain things and if you're lucky enough to find out what that is and do that, chances are you'll be really good at it."

Morris works relentlessly at being really good at creating dances out of the music. But he doesn't visualize dances in his head as many assume. "It may happen to people who aren't choreographers," Morris chides, "but I listen to music because I love music and when there's a piece of music I think would make a good dance, I study it. That's what I know. I know music. Then, I make up a dance, lots of them because I like to. I'm a choreographer, so I choreograph. I work to make up a dance that pleases me entirely and if the audience doesn't care about it, that's all right. But chances are if I think it's fabulous, they will as well."

Now some of Morris' dances that he thinks are truly fabulous are not audience favorites. There are those who say they have never seen anything more profound and inspiring and there are others who couldn't care less about the piece. "People who don't like my work don't like it for the same reason that people who like my work, like my work," Morris replies. "They say, 'That's what's supposed to be happening.' What is always true is that people will disagree. So, I don't worry about that."

Morris is not a conductor. And his dances are neither accompaniment nor ornamentation. They are art and Morris, the artist, is nearly militant about making them so. "I was once asked why I use live music. Well, tell me, would you want to see a film of the dancers? Of course not. Then why use a recording? A recording is one studio session of one person's point of view and it's legit but that's not WHAT the music is. In a theater with actual people playing instruments, the music is never the same and yet it's always the same and that's the same with dancing. It has to be re-created each time."

Morris is serious about his craft despite a world in which dance is not taken seriously. "If you fervently believe that your work is important, then you create a piece that's perceived that way and people watch and say, 'That was something,' instead of it just being a fun date to watch people dance. I don't mind a fun date to watch people dance but if it's actually richer than that, it's even better. That's what I do."

Morris is the first to admit that the world should not take dance seriously because most of the dance that is out there is not very good and because dancers have been trained to believe that dancing is not very important. "It doesn't need to be taken seriously but it is nice," says Morris. "But if you're going to make it a legitimate art form you'd better have the credentials and the knowledge and the historical consciousness. You have to know a lot about music, you can't just put it on and dance around. It doesn't work. So much dance is so shitty it's embarrassing. I go to concerts that are so bad that I think, 'Oh thank God I'm better than that and I can make up a beautiful dance in a second,' or I think, 'What a joke to be involved in this pointless pursuit.'"

Pointless or poignant, Morris is involved in his work every second of the day and night. "I work really hard," Morris declares. "I am driven and I'm impatient but I'm not ambitious. I don't want to be, like, president of dance or anything. I am driven by ideas. The music starts me and then I'm taken completely. I'm completely obsessed with the project, with the performance we're doing. There's always something to adjust, to make more or less, to improve."

Morris is thinking about and experimenting with his ideas constantly. But like everything else, he has strong opinions about the point or pointlessness of such a lifestyle. "Look, I have enormous energy because I'm interested in what I do and I have a good time doing it," Morris defends. "I like my life and I like going to work. It's what I do all the time." But lest you think he is a workaholic, beware. "I don't like the structure of the word," Morris retorts. "It's a bad word. Workaholic means you're addicted to workahol. I am a 'workic.' And all that stuff about missing anything because of it? How would I know what I am missing? As corny as this is, my work is a great pleasure to me."

Morris and most of his company have been together for 20 years and they would not be dancing into their 40s unless there is something there that is satisfying. "It's not that you just want to run around and kick your legs like you did when you were 17," jokes Morris. "If I start to hate it, I'll stop. For now, this is what I do. There are people who ask themselves what they will be doing in 10 years. I don't think that way. I'm doing exactly what I want to do. I'm not waiting to be discovered or to become a choreographer, I already am. I am really, really content with my life."

There is a demanding physical requirement to be a dancer but Morris does not consider himself an athlete. In fact, he is not the least bit interested in athletics. Athletics are all about competition. "I am an artist not an athlete," retorts Morris, "for the same reason why figure skating is not art. It's sport. Art cannot have a competitive element to it." As a dance company Morris is competing with other dance groups for the same gig, but that's business and Morris leaves that to his managers. "I don't compete with any other choreographers for recognition. I could be anonymous and I would still be very content," Morris asserts while quickly adding, "although we wouldn't get as much work as we do because I'm a good interview."

Morris is indeed an artist but he is also an entertainer. The same is true of cellist Yo-Yo Ma. The cello concerto is the art and his performance is the entertainment. It's like a poem. If you read it alone, it's art. If you read it out loud, it's entertainment. But, as Morris is quick to point out, "Entertainment doesn't have a good connotation. A tragedy like Tosca is fabulously entertaining. People tend to use the word entertainment to make things seem lighter than they are. But tragedy is entertaining so entertainment does not always equal a good time. Engaging is a better word. I am an engager."

The public tends to regard dancers as fringe individuals, often homosexuals, and rather bizarre. Morris acknowledges the perception but explains that is not a prerequisite to produce great art. "I've thought about living in a different way, but I don't because if you're going to actually do something that's new in that it's combining things in ways that haven't been done before, you tend not to be a particularly conservative thinker. That doesn't mean you're queer or crazy; it means you think differently."

Morris is as passionate about thinking out of the box as he is about creating his dances. He is vociferous about pursuing life and career from the viscera not from the cerebellum. "You don't have to study music to be a choreographer," Morris proposes. "Sure, I am passionately interested in music. That's fascinating to me. I love that, but you don't have to. Paul Taylor is quite a good choreographer and he doesn't read music, he doesn't approach it any way the same way I do and it's fine. It doesn't matter. Merce (Cunningham)'s approach to music and dancing are completely different from what I do. It's very simple. If you have to choreograph, do it. Otherwise, don't."

> "I am definitely comfortable with who I am. Why not? I totally believe in what I do and I do it really, really well. My decisions, my instincts, my abilities as a craftsman are totally reliable."

Sounds simple. Let's take it from the top. It begins with talent. "I am not tinkering. I'm not an amateur. I'm a very skilled musician and I'm a really, really good choreographer," Morris avows. One must have passion. "I'm dead serious about what I do. I am not on the back shelf of art where I hear some music and dance around. If I did that nobody would want to watch that. I wouldn't want to watch that." Can't forget creativity. "I don't like the word inspire too much, but the surprise parts that I don't know I'm coming up with happen fabulously because I know inside out my job." And finally, lots of energy. "I could make up a dance in a minute that would be fabulous. I don't. I slave over it for months but usually I end up with my first idea because it's what I do all the time."

Morris is highly analytical and is perceived as cold because he is not particularly patient. Morris is confident and is perceived as arrogant because he is not particularly shy. "I am definitely comfortable with who I am," Morris agrees. "Why not? I totally believe in what I do and I do it really, really well. My decisions, my instincts, my abilities as a craftsman are totally reliable. If I didn't do good work, I wouldn't have had a company for all of these years and I wouldn't be invited back, and everywhere we go, we're asked back. And I wouldn't have musicians who beg to work with me. It's not an accident. But, I am shy. I'm just shy in a loud way."

Belding Scribner

Physician Whose 1960 Invention
Led to Chronic Kidney Dialysis

For much of the past 50 years, Belding Scribner left his sparsely-decorated, 80-year-old houseboat at dawn, climbed into a canoe, and paddled across Portage Bay to his office at the University of Washington Medical School where he rose from instructor in medicine to head the division of nephrology. Now retired, today he spends more time at home with his wife, Ethel, listening to Beethoven recordings and savoring his extraordinary Bordeaux red wines.

Today, an estimated 920,000 kidney dialysis patients worldwide and the millions who preceded them owe their lives, in part, to Scribner. Before he developed the arteriovenous shunt in 1960, patients with no kidney function were doomed to death. Virtually overnight, with permanent access to the bloodstream made available, lives that were once considered lost could be saved. "I am not famous, or great for that matter," Scribner chuckles. "Maybe I became famous for what I accomplished along the way but I don't feel like I am great. I led a charmed life and I am still leading a charmed life."

Scrib, as he is called by everyone who knows him, has been both the provider and recipient of major advances in medicine. "If I'd been 10 years older than I am, I would have gone blind. Instead, I received one and then a second of the very first corneal transplants ever done and it saved my vision and my career."

Scribner admits that he did not have crystal clear vision about his career either. It was a step-by-step process, each step connected to some serendipitous event. "Irrationally, I wanted to be a doctor because I was very sick as a child," Scribner concedes. "I had asthma. I had hay fever. I had eczema." Scribner's family did not have a great deal of money but managed to get by and with a little bit of luck, Scribner managed to get a scholarship. "And luckily to a private school. I'm one of the people who needed the shelter and protection of that environment. It wasn't the prestige. It was because I was insecure. Ethel knows I don't do well at banquets. I hate banquets and I've had to attend a lot during my lifetime."

After one year at Williams College in northwestern Massachusetts, Scribner's family moved to California, so he transferred to the University of California in Berkeley. After graduating in 1941, Scribner remained on the west coast. "I always liked the west coast. I had the sense there was more freedom there and a lot more chance to be an individual. I had to choose between Harvard and Stanford Medical Schools and I chose Stanford for that reason".

Following his internship and residency at San Francisco Hospital, he did his fellowship at the Mayo Clinic in Rochester, Minnesota. "While I was there, I had my first corneal transplant and I realized that problems with my vision would prevent me from going into medical practice so I sought refuge in an institution."

Hired by Memorial Hospital in New York, Scribner traveled back to the west coast to visit his parents and friends. On a lark he added a northwest excursion. "We stopped in Seattle and it just happened that the University of Washington was starting a medical school and opening the VA part. The head of the VA was my old teacher at Stanford who recognized that I had certain abilities. He talked to the chairman of medicine who called his buddy at Memorial and talked him into letting me give up my commitment and so we came to Seattle."

It was in Seattle, 10 years later, where dialysis literally received a shot in the arm. It began with a man who was flown in from Spokane in eastern Washington dying from kidney failure. Scribner immediately provided acute dialysis, a one-time cleansing of the failing kidneys, the only form of dialysis available at the time. Then, it was a surgical procedure cutting into arteries and veins to insert glass tubes that connected patients to a kidney machine. When finished, the tubes were removed and the blood vessels closed and, hopefully, the patient's kidneys regained normal function.

Scribner's patient responded well but a biopsy revealed the condition was irreversible. "He was walking up and down the hall and everything was looking great, but he wasn't going anywhere because he was going to die," Scribner recalls. The patient returned to Spokane and died. Scribner ruminated about the incident for weeks. "I kept thinking about that and I woke up in the middle of the night and I can still remember writing the idea down of how we could solve the problem: the shunt."

The idea was simple: insert plastic tubes into an artery and a vein and provide constant access to the circulatory system by connecting the tubes together to form a shunt between artery and vein. During dialysis, the gate shunt would be removed and replaced by the lines to the kidney machine. It could have occurred anywhere. In fact, a Swedish colleague of Scribner's, Nils Alwall, published a paper in 1947 that hypothesized the shunt, but with glass, which was impractical. Again, through his charmed life, Scribner found a substance that made it all possible.

By chance, Scribner was walking down the steps at the medical school and ran into a colleague who had learned about his shunt. "He said, 'I heard you and David Dillard were going to put a tube in a patient's arm. Go to central supply and look at this thing called Teflon. We're using it in the dog lab and it works great. It doesn't have any tissue reactivity.' So I went to take a look."

With the help of an engineer, Wayne Quinton, Scribner learned how to bend it and fashioned the necessary tubing. But it was luck again that made it work. "We chose it for the wrong reason," Scribner laughs. "Sure, it had low tissue reactivity, but the real reason it worked is because Teflon is a non-stick substance and the blood just slid off. Pure luck, and it's played such an impor-tant part all the way. I have some abilities and I'm a gadgeteer, but luck transformed my talent and my curiosity into success."

Fortunately for Clyde Shields, a 39-year old machinist who was dying of incurable kidney disease, the research continued. On March 9, 1960, he received the first shunt. Suddenly certain death was trans-formed into a 90 percent survival rate. Shields lived for 11 years on the new procedure called chronic dialysis.

But the early days of chronic dialysis were fraught with new medical complications. During his dialysis, Shields suffered from a string of ailments. For each, Scribner and his colleagues would find a cure only to have Shields attacked by the next. "We made

At home in his wine cellar.

huge mistakes over the years and we learned huge amounts," Scribner reports with obvious sincerity. In the beginning, all of Scribner's patients were getting hard lumps under the skin composed of calcium phosphate deposits. "They were turning to stone until we figured out that their plasma phosphorous was too high and we reduced the phosphorous intake in their diets and the lumps melted away."

Scribner faced each challenge of his medical breakthrough the way he approaches life, highly motivated by an insatiable curiosity and a keenly developed instinct. "I felt tremendous compassion for Shields, but the ulti-mate objective was how to keep him alive. It was curiosity," Scribner admits. "I have a total inability in mathematics. I cannot solve a problem mathemat-ically and I just marvel at people that can start with the mathematical and move to the practical. I can't. It's intuitive, intuitive, intuitive. I built a rabbit trap once when I was a kid and it worked like a charm but it was entirely intuition and that is not something you can teach. The same kind of intuitiveness thing was driving the shunt."

Scribner does not view the human body as just another gadget like his rabbit trap. On the contrary, Scribner is poetically serious about his profession. While Scribner's curiosity drove him to keep dying patients alive, his ethics strongly place limits on the endeavor. "We were asked once to dialyze an 80-year-old man with cancer and I refused," Scribner states unequivocally. "I feel very strongly that compassionate death is a part of the practice of medicine."

The jovial nature of the conversation suddenly shifts. The subject is no longer about the past; it is all about the future. Scribner leans forward across the table like a prosecuting attorney cross-examining a key witness. "The kidney is not a carburetor in the human machine. The human body is infinitely more complex than a car and tweaking it is the basis for mistakes," Scribner charges. "You tweak one thing but you don't know the consequences and that worries me about today's medicine. Things are moving so fast that nobody takes the time to figure out the adverse side effects. We don't want to pace things. The whole world is at a breakneck pace and going in the wrong direction. I'm very pessimistic but I won't be around to see the result."

> "There is a difference between being great and living a great life. I prefer the latter. We've enjoyed what there is to enjoy in life pretty much maximally."

Every generation feels that the generation following it is going the wrong way. But we forget the transformation Scribner's generation has experienced. Only a handful of years before he was born, state-of-the-art flying machines skirted pastures. Today they cross the solar system. "In 1924 my mother called her sister in Paris and everybody in the community listened to her talk because nobody could believe she could talk to someone in Paris," Scribner remembers, recalling the thrill as much as the event.

"Technology is dangerous. I have no right to worry about that but I do. And, maybe we have an obligation to worry about it. Today, four-year-olds are spending their time on the Internet and they're getting all these exciting things so kindergarten and first grade become boring as hell. How are you going to teach people the basics when they've got all this technology? And you've got to have basic knowledge first."

Scribner's original shunt included couplings he obtained from a local plumber. Obviously, the device has undergone a lot of technological enhancement since. Problems associated with the external shunt spurred development of an internal one formed by surgically joining an artery and vein to create the fistula. Although much improved by recent engineering advances, traditional machine-aided dialysis remains very expensive, clumsy and inconvenient.

In response to that, a different dialysis technique called continuous ambulatory peritoneal dialysis (CAPD) has emerged. It involves attaching a plastic bag containing dialysis fluid to the lining of the abdominal cavity. After about 30 minutes, the fluid is withdrawn into the bag and discarded. This process is repeated about three times a day. The evolution owes its progress to Scribner who simply deflects it. "The shunt gets all the attention, and it deserves that because it's the key, but to this day, it's the care of the patient that's the critical thing and it's getting worse all the time."

So passionately convinced that the profession he loves and the patients he values are deteriorating, the 80-year old physician continues to speak out, even writing to *60 Minutes* to air his views. "People have access now. The fistula is much better than the shunt because it is made out of your natural veins and it lasts for a lifetime. So that's no longer the stumbling block. It's the new profit business of medical care that's causing the disaster."

The Bordeaux wine collector is not just positing sour grapes. He could have been a billionaire. The first commercial dialysis company, National Medical Care, sat in his houseboat and asked him to come on their board and share in the profits of his discovery. He turned them down. "That was 20 years ago and I am still fighting them," Scribner avows. "The problem with doctors today is money. That's why a lot of people apparently go into medicine. I thought we went into medicine to provide answers and care."

Ethel nods her approval and reminds her husband they need to go. It is Saturday and — as is their ritual — they will attend the faculty lecture that precedes each Washington Huskies home football game. After the game, they will return home where Scribner will tinker with his radio-controlled model airplanes, enjoy a fine wine, and listen to music. "Ambition is not something that pulsates in my veins," Scribner says as the smile returns to his face.

"There is a difference between being great and living a great life. I prefer the latter. We've enjoyed what there is to enjoy in life pretty much maximally. I'm a good fly fisherman. Ethel is better. If you ever hook a bonefish on Christmas Island that weighs 20 pounds, you'd discover there's nothing quite like it. She did — caught the biggest one. I taught her how to fish but she can out-fish me. Some people seek to become someone but that gets in the way of life."

If you look at Hollywood or Wall Street or inside the Beltway, you would think the driving forces in life are power and money. Think again.

Chapter 5

You Have to be Prepared to Work Very Hard

Sparky Anderson

*Hall of Fame Manager of
the Cincinnati Reds and Detroit Tigers*

The records speak for themselves. With 2,194 regular season victories, Hall of Famer George Lee "Sparky" Anderson stands as the third winningest manager in Major League Baseball history. Only two legends from the early days of the game, Connie Mack (3,731) of the Philadelphia Athletics and John McGraw (2,784) of the New York Giants, won more. From 1970 through 1978, Anderson guided the hard-hitting Cincinnati Reds to five division titles, four pennants and two World Series championships. The "Big Red Machine" World Series victories in 1975 and 1976 were the first back-to-back championships for a National League team since McGraw's Giants did it in 1921-22. The senior circuit hasn't seen a repeat world champion since.

In 1979, Anderson was tapped as a midseason replacement to skipper the underachieving Detroit Tigers in the American League. He would hold the post for 17 seasons and become the greatest manager ever to wear a Tigers uniform. He led Detroit to two division titles and a World Series championship after a dominating 1984 season in which the team finished 104-58. He is the first manager in history to post 100-win seasons in both leagues and the only manager ever to win a World Series in both leagues. He is also the only manager to retire leading two teams in all-time wins. Anderson was named National League Manager of the Year twice, in 1972 and 1975, and received the same honor in the American League in 1984 and 1987. How did he do it all? "Hall of Fame managers had great players," Sparky explains in a gravel-like voice that always sounds a bit hoarse.

Anderson's teams were loaded with talent, but the manager also had a knack of bringing out the best in his players. Like Don Shula of the Miami Dolphins and Red Auerbach of the Boston Celtics, Anderson built his teams on no-nonsense, straightforward, old-fashioned values of hard work and dignity. "I can tell you if a player will be great," Anderson guarantees. "If his work habits are excellent, he controls his own destiny. You have to have the tools but the work ethic is the difference." Hall of Fame coaches and managers have that same kind of work ethic. Anderson repudiates the frequently cited apology, "Don't do as I do, do as I say."

"That is totally wrong," he exhorts. "It should be, 'Don't do as I say, do as I show you.' The great coaches showed people how to have a work ethic and how to have class. You never picked up a paper and read one bad word about former UCLA basketball coach Johnny Wooden, never. He would not allow that of himself because he wanted those young people with him to see how he did it. If you can't discipline yourself to the highest level, you can never be great."

Anderson believed this lesson was good enough to show to current Reds slugger Ken Griffey Jr. He took the future star aside soon after Griffey broke into the majors with the Seattle Mariners in the late 80s. "His daddy played for me (in Cincinnati)," recalls Anderson. "I told him I just wanted him to do one thing. I wanted him to come to the park every night and — whether he got any hits or not — when the people left, I wanted them to say, 'Boy, wasn't he something to watch play?' I told him to leave them with that every night. Don't cheat them."

While it is trite to say that nothing worthwhile comes easily, Anderson does not hesitate to extol the virtue of hard work. He even goes so far as to say hard work can transform the merely good into extraordinary. As an example, he compares Griffey to Pete Rose, a baseball legend and one of Anderson's former players. "The talent's not even close," Anderson states without equivocation. "Griffey will out throw him, outrun him, out field him, and hit with more power. Yet Rose proved beyond a shadow of a doubt he could come from being someone who shouldn't have been a major leaguer to one of the greatest players in the history of the game, all because of his work habits. He had one goal in mind: to please those fans every night. He wanted them to leave the ballpark knowing they'd seen a great player."

That was Rose's obsession. A lot of people would look at driven individuals, at obsessed individuals, and say that they are dysfunctional, that they don't understand the whole of life. Anderson agrees and points to himself as an example. "When I first started out, I used to blame myself for everything," Anderson admits. "I'd blame myself for all the losses. I used to say that you should die a little if you lose. Well, that's crazy. It doesn't have to be that way. You can drive yourself but you don't have to cross that line where the drive becomes an obsession and takes over."

During his days in the Brooklyn Dodgers and Philadelphia Phillies organizations, Anderson was by all accounts a scrappy and resourceful player. His famous nickname — coined by a minor league broadcaster — derives from his trademark determination and spunk. However, a self-described "chronic minor league infielder," Sparky spent most of his 11-year playing career away from the big show. He played only one season in the majors, batting .218 for the Phillies in 1959 as their regular second baseman.

But when he began managing it was clear that he found his niche. "I was a young, wild bull in a china shop that had no idea whatsoever how to go about this. I just took off in it," said Anderson, who in his first managerial position heading up a minor league team in Toronto was known more for his on-field outbursts than anything else.

In 1965, Sheldon "Chief" Bender, then the assistant general manager of the St. Louis Cardinals, reluctantly offered Anderson a position skippering a Cards farm team on the condition he had to learn to "control himself." Anderson did, and four years later, after Bender and general manager Bob Howsam had moved into the Reds front office, Anderson became the National League's newest manager. But the chronic minor leaguer soon found he had his work cut out for him. The day after Anderson formally became Reds manager in October 1969, the *Cincinnati Post* ran a headline that simply said, "Sparky Who?" Anderson himself initially had very serious doubts in his new position.

Then Sparky's tenacity kicked in. He started learning. Like for many of us, much of what he learned came from loss. It wasn't until later in life that he finally came to understand it. "I was into every one of these kids and I always knew somewhere down the road they would come back either to haunt me or to bless me. I didn't want them to come back to haunt me. I didn't want to lose any kids. But I lost Bobby Tolan and I'll never forget that as long as I live."

Tolan was a talented outfielder and first baseman on the Reds roster in the early 70s who went through emotional problems that Anderson ignored. Although voted Comeback Player of the Year by *The Sporting News* in 1972 after returning from an injury, by 1973 he found himself in a slump and a bitter feud with Reds management, resulting in a suspension and ultimately a trade. Afterwards Tolan drifted from team to team, played a season in Japan, and finally retired a broken man at decade's end. "I am not sure yet what the total problem was because I never took the time to dig into it. That's the one that will haunt me always. He was the lamb I had to sacrifice to understand you can't lose players. That was a great lesson to me. I lost him in 1973 and I never lost another one since then. There's a way to help them. Had I known my first years of managing what I knew over my last, I would have even been able to help more players."

Anderson helped a lot of players in his 26 years as big league manager (only Connie Mack, John McGraw and Stanley "Bucky" Harris managed longer). He did it by admonishing his young players relentlessly with his ideas about living that became his principles for coaching. "I always told them, you don't have to like me and you don't have to respect me, but I'm going to win

> "Money will never make you a good player. Only you can do that. What you give from inside of you will be what you end up with, not the money. If money is the goal, you're going to falter."

both," Anderson avows. "First, because I'll never lie to you. You'll get the truth from me. It might hurt sometimes but you're going to get the truth. Second, because I'm going to treat you the same as every guy in this room. The only favor a star has in this room is the paycheck. He ain't got no more favors than you got. And when you become a star you'll have no more favors than the guy that took over your spot, except in the paycheck."

But don't mistake his gruff challenges as coldness. They are part of a tough love. Anderson truly loved his players. "I'll tell you why," he offers, eager to share his world view. "They come from all different walks of life, all different nationalities. They're floating on clouds and they don't understand the real goal they're trying to reach because they have been so confused with what I call green flies buzzing around them." The flies are agents and the green is greed. Anderson tried to get his players to forget the money and let matters take care of themselves. "Money will never make you a good player. Only you can do that. What you give from inside of you will be what you end up with, not the money. If money is the goal, you're going to falter. How many suits can you wear? You want a Rolls Royce or a yacht? That's the problem. All I want is for every one of my children and grandchildren to be healthy. Money is not going to buy you happiness; it's how you treat others and how they treat you that does."

> "You're going to have one thing in your whole lifetime that's going to be free. It will never cost you a dime, and that's to be nice. ... There shouldn't be a penalty for being nice; that's a gift you have to give to other people."

Treating others with care is Anderson's personal trademark and he demanded nothing less of his players. Near the end of his career, as athletes became icons and dignified demeanor gave way to self-indulgence, Anderson again challenged his men to remember their obligation to the fans. "Why do you want to show kids that you're a jerk so now they can be jerks? You owe it to the mothers and fathers to show them a good example, to help them out."

Don't try to obfuscate the issue by taking the Charles Barkley route and argue athletes do not choose to be role models and thus do not need to be role models. "It's a lie," Anderson says. "You've got to be a role model if you are in a sport, because more children will come and listen to Michael Jordan talk than to the president. You put the President of the United States over here and you put Michael Jordan over there and announce they're going to talk, and me and everybody else are going to be with Michael Jordan. Sport is something big in our society and we owe it to the kids to show them that you can be good at this game, but you don't got to be a jerk to do it."

The late Tom Landry held the same philosophy during his nearly three decades as head coach of the NFL Dallas Cowboys. In the eyes of the public he was a legend, but he never considered himself a legend. Confident but never smug, he was able to live with his achievements and retain the qualities of a gentleman. Anderson believes the absence of those qualities has ravaged sport. "Look what happened to UCLA ever since Wooden left," Anderson challenges, referring to a series of highly publicized incidents following the departure of his lifelong coaching friend. "Wooden would never allow that behavior. With him, turmoil never came in. Some guys are not capable to stop turmoil, but he stopped it. And you stop it by not letting it start. It's done by and through you. If you're a yeller, yell. If you're quiet, be quiet. Whoever you are, you be, because if you're not you there's no chance in hell."

For more than a quarter of a century the one and only, very real Sparky Anderson walked the dugouts of Major League Baseball. Then, his own philosophy about pleasing the fans and one of the biggest lessons of his life brought him home for good. By the mid 90s, the Tigers were no longer contenders. "I knew it was time to hang it up when I knew I had no chance to win, not a chance in hell," Anderson says with disappointment. "It wasn't right. You're taking money knowing you can't possibly do it. I'd done it 26 years and I'm working for some club for money because you ain't going to do nothing with them to make a difference."

But there was another factor that ultimately convinced Anderson to hang it up. He realized it while he was in Chicago with the Tigers waiting to play the White Sox following the All-Star break. "I had 12 grandkids and I said, 'What am I doing in Chicago?' I wasted my children's lives being away. Now I'm going to waste my grandchildren's lives? No way." So in 1995, Anderson said goodbye to baseball and his legions of fans and quietly walked away. In February 2000, the Committee on Baseball Veterans elected him to the National Baseball Hall of Fame in his first year of eligibility.

Anderson credits his values and philosophy and, indirectly, his personality to a handful of men who shaped his outlook on baseball and life. In his acceptance speech into the National Baseball Hall of Fame, his remarks acknowledged, as he so sweetly put it, "what my father started" and what Los Angeles youth baseball coach Benny LeFebvre, his Dorsey High School coach Bud Brubaker, USC coach Rod Dedeaux, Brooklyn Dodger scout Lefty Phillips, Cardinal coach George Kissell, and his first pro manager George Scherger completed.

"I was so fortunate because each one of those men are a part of my life. I never copied any of them but I know that they are there." And the only man ever to win World Series rings in both leagues never wears one to honor that. "I never wear a World Series ring, never. That's out of respect to Lefty Phillips who raised me as a second father and passed away before I won my first ring. I decided I'd never wear one. Having him inside of me is more important than having the ring on the outside of me."

Not only does Anderson refrain from wearing one of his three world championship rings, there are no plaques or certificates or trophies in his home to attest to his success. In addition, despite his long association with the game, he never set foot inside the National Baseball Hall of Fame in Cooperstown, New York, until after he was elected. "I always made myself a promise that I would never go inside the Hall of Fame unless I made it," he said shortly before his election.

Instead, Anderson's shelves, walls and mantel are covered with photographs of his children and 14 grandchildren. Baseball and the men who played it — with him, for him, and even against him — are stored in a tender heart that belies the tough exterior.

But when he talks about the players on his dream team — all Hall of Famers in their own right — you come to know as much about Anderson as you do about them. "No man will ever play better than (catcher) Johnny Bench. And he really grew up. He won the MVP at 22 and he was a little chesty but we had discussions and he came back into the fold. Tony Pérez at first base. I've never found a gentleman more professional than him," Anderson said of his former player, who joined him as a 2000 inductee in Cooperstown.

"Joe Morgan at second. They can't even come close to him for intelligence or ability and his smile was great. I had fun with him. I loved the little man. I called him little man and I can honestly say I truly love him. Brooks Robinson at third because of his ability as a player as his character as a man."

Not a bad nucleus for an infield. And the Anderson All-Star Team doesn't lack for an outfield either. "Frank Robinson was something else in left. He was a good person, a tough person, but he was a good one. He and Roberto Clemente are the most underrated players I've ever seen. Clemente was the best player I saw in my time and a true humanitarian. My pride and joy would be Willie Stargell in right: big, strong and gentle as a lamb."

The common thread among those men is decency. They possess the same old-fashioned values Anderson encourages and uses every day. "They all have faults, don't get me wrong, just like I have them," Anderson qualifies. "That's the one thing that has to be put in front of kids. We all have faults, but we can overcome our faults. None of us are perfect, that's impossible. But you can overcome them if you work at it. Know your faults. Know yourself. If you know yourself you know what's inside you and if you start to cheat on what's right you can pause and say hey, this won't cut it."

Anderson has indeed been hard at work at what his father started. But he worked on much more than building baseball teams. He also worked hard at building men. For Anderson, it is a matter of duty. "Don't we have an obligation to be nice to people?" Anderson challenges. "When I was 11, my father told the three of us kids, 'You're going to have one thing in your whole lifetime that's going to be free. It will never cost you a dime, and that's to be nice.' I never forgot that and we must make young people understand there shouldn't be a penalty for being nice; that's a gift you have to give to other people."

In an age when young people are focused on making a buck, Anderson is an old buck focused on making people. While his career has made him a walking encyclopedia on baseball, his people have shaped his own lexicon on life. "There's a word in the dictionary called 'better' and that word should not be in there," Anderson counsels gently and compassionately. "It's impossible for you to be better than me and it's impossible for me to be better than that man in Ethiopia who's starving. It's impossible. It's impossible for you to be better than any one. If that were so, then we've been lied to for 2,000 years. There's no god. There cannot be a god if a human being can be better than another human being."

Before you have time to absorb the profound truth of the Anderson doxology, Anderson provides his own amen. "There is another word in the dictionary, should be number one, and that's 'fortunate.' That's where those people I told you about come in. How fortunate I was to have a father like that and have the people I named in line like that to take care of me. That's the part that we must never forget. Johnny Wooden was fortunate. Every guy down the line you want to name was fortunate, not better. Once you truly know in your heart and have accepted how fortunate you have been, then you are able to put it out on you. See I've never been better than any single human being, but I have been a hell of a lot more fortunate."

> "It's impossible for you to be better than me and it's impossible for me to be better than that man in Ethiopia who's starving."

Anderson, visibly moved by his own remarks and memories, gets up from the table and begins a slow, easy walk through the house. It's the same house in Ventura County, California, he bought when still a minor league manager. He's lived there happily for 33 years. It bears the accoutrements of the times, including a volcanic rock fireplace. "Look here," a rejuvenated Anderson exclaims. "There are leaves stamped in the rock. It all came from Colorado." Like many people, Anderson and his wife could not afford to buy the home. His father-in-law provided $8,000 for the down payment. "He's passed away, but he gave us an opportunity and I will never forget that."

Anderson continues through the living room, sharing stories about his grandchildren, and out the front door. "We've been here 33 years and people say to me, 'You ought to move.'" There are two new sections nearby with larger, more attractive, more contemporary homes in North Ranch and Wood Ranch. Anderson points to the foothills where the developments are located. "You know, 'You're a famous baseball manager' and money and all that stuff." Anderson pauses and looks at me with the same intensity he used when he talked to one of his pitchers in a discussion on the mound. "They don't know how I got in this home. My children were raised in this home. I'll never leave this home, because I don't need North Ranch or Wood Ranch to make me George Anderson, see? I don't need that. This is my home. I like it here. People don't understand. But all that other stuff, well, that isn't George Anderson. You are who you are. Don't be somebody else."

Revered and treasured by his players for his work ethic, humility, humanity, and eternal optimism, George "Sparky" Anderson was inducted into the National Baseball Hall of Fame on July 23, 2000. Joining him as new members of the Hall were the heroes of Anderson's amazing 1975 World Series triumph, Carlton Fisk of the Boston Red Sox and Tony Perez of the Cincinnati Reds.

Harry W. Brooks

Retired Major General and Former Commander,
25th Infantry Division, U.S. Army

The offices of Brooks International are unassuming. The street-front, stucco and wood complex looks like the Allstate Insurance suite you find in every small town in America. Visitors enter a modestly decorated reception area, guarded by a lean, gentle, soft-spoken middle-aged man in casual attire who leaves to ask if his boss is ready. When he reappears, he is followed by a small, equally gentle, dignified man dressed impeccably in a suit, a Major General Harry S. Brooks, retired commander of the 25th Infantry Division of the United States Army.

Fifty years ago, he was an enlistee. "I beat such incredible odds," Brooks remarks, leaning back in his desk chair. "I came out of a segregated neighborhood, segregated school, with a high school diploma. I was a private in a segregated army where I couldn't even go on some parts of the post. Time passed and I ended up commanding a division." Brooks pauses to let the enormity of it all sink in. What happened in between is a story of luck and will that Brooks dearly loves to retell.

Luck always enters into these things. Unlike many, Brooks has no difficulty in admitting it. For Brooks, luck always means the love of a good friend. The first bit of luck opened doors for him to Officers Candidate School. He was a sergeant at the time, stationed at Fort Dix, New Jersey. "I was hitting .500 on the baseball team and I had a lot of visibility and a white Lieutenant Colonel said, 'I really like this kid; we're going to send him to OCS.' I hadn't even thought about OCS," Brooks smiles. While Brooks was tearing up the military league that year, Dodger rookie Jackie Robinson was breaking the color line in the major leagues. Call it luck or timing, Brooks was admitted to OCS during a period when the Army was experiencing a shortage of officers and welcomed a few non-college candidates. The door for such applicants closed shortly thereafter. Although OCS was integrated, the army was still segregated, a position that would not change until the Korean War. In 1949, when Brooks was commissioned, there were only three black colonels in the entire United States Army. One was a chaplain, one was a doctor, and one was in infantry. "The idea of reaching general, well, I mean, it was just not something you even thought about," Brooks laughs.

That did not stop Brooks from attempting to become the finest military man in the Army. And the one and only attribute that Brooks can identify that made him so was his work ethic. "If you want to compete against me, you have to be prepared to work very hard. You dare not sleep. I will outwork you," Brooks announces with a twinkle in his eye that suggests he still can. "I've never met anyone I couldn't outwork. Any shortage in ability, I made up with energy." Brooks would work twenty-two hours a day to do something right, even if it was the demeaning task of laundry detail. "I was just determined to do it right, to spend the time. So I had one attribute that followed me throughout my career and that was the ability to apply the energy to the task."

There are certain fundamental requirements to achieve the rank of general in the army. Academic education is one. There are no general officers without a college degree. Not to be viewed as a deficient officer, Brooks applied his energy to pursuing a college degree during and after his studies at OCS. "It took me from 1949 to 1962 to get my bachelor's degree, all of it at night-school, except for four months. It took another ten years to get my Master's degree," Brooks says with unabashed pride.

> "Obstacles have great advantage. They harden you, they make you tough, and they make a survivor out of you."

Military education is another prerequisite. There are two key military schools, the Command and General Staff College at Fort Leavenworth and the War College at Carlisle Barracks, which Brooks attended. The name is misleading. The War College is not a program about how to kill people. It offers a curriculum in subjects like economics and world affairs and serves as a post-graduate educational institution where officers meet those who are commanding the army and where officers are groomed to be commanders in the years ahead. To be selected for the encounter, officers must finish in the upper third of their earlier army education.

While working at the Pentagon and continuing his studies toward a Master's Degree, Brooks would spend weekends "writing papers, papers, papers, and when the War College list came out, lo and behold, I was in the top three percent among all the army colonels. But it still never occurred to me — never occurred to me — that I might be a general officer some day."

Good assignments and performance in combat are the final two resume building criteria. As a major, Brooks survived an early and rather benign reserved officer training assignment in Syracuse, New York, with the help of a little more of that good fortune that only human kindness can provide. "I got stuck up there for a couple years and some very influential people got me out of there." The key assignment for Brooks that would change his career and his life occurred when he was transferred to artillery. There, he found his destiny and met his life-long good luck charm and most beloved friend. Brooks leans to the right and faces a gallery of photographs that decorate the wall including one of Brooks and President Gerald Ford and one of Brooks and General Colin Powell, former Chairman of the Joint Chiefs of Staff and one of Brooks' protégés, signed, "To Major General Harry Brooks, friend, mentor, inspiration."

He points to his photo with Colonel Ernest Frazier. "This man right here was my best friend for forty-four years. We entered into a pact where he taught me everything he knew and I taught him everything I knew. What he knew was the basics of artillery. He was the best I've ever seen, and he taught me that. I taught him nuclear weapons. We were assigned together many times and he was always there opening the way."

After completing artillery school, Captain Brooks served several assignments in artillery battalions and ten years later was given command of an artillery battalion of six hundred men and eighteen large artillery pieces. "I had the opportunity to train those men from scratch and take them to Vietnam. The battalion was absolutely outstanding: hardworking, fundamentally sound, great guys. We arrived in Vietnam with 85 expert gunners and I had become one hell of an artilleryman. Still am today. People feared me when I walked in their area talking about artillery," Brooks boasts and with good reason. In short order, Brooks was promoted to lieutenant colonel supervised by three different general officers. "Even then I couldn't imagine becoming a general officer. It was 1967, and we had no black general officers. There were no role models. So, I just didn't think about it."

When Brooks returned from Vietnam, he served on the Army Staff and attended the War College. After his promotion to colonel, he was reassigned to an artillery corps in Germany that had ten battalions under the command of two men. "I had five and the poor guy that was competing against me had five," Brooks says with glee. "Based on a complex set of activities — inspections, field exercise, and so forth — my units came out one, two, three, four and six. I should have fired the battalion commander who ended up sixth but I had mercy on him and instead of firing him, I trained him and he went on to do OK." So did Brooks.

In 1972, there was a great deal of racial unrest in the army. Unknown to the public, there were riots and racial disturbances in Okinawa, Hawaii, Korea, Europe and the United States. The army was literally imploding. Not so with the units Brooks commanded. He had few incarcerations and no desertions. As Brooks recalls, the army staff looked at the "high morale of my men and said, 'What the hell is this man doing over there in Germany?' So they pulled me back to Washington and made me Director of Equal Opportunity and Race Relations, a new military position. Career-wise this is like putting a blindfold on and lining up in front of a firing squad." But Brooks had some strong credentials. He and a white classmate, Jim Miller, had written their thesis at the War College on *Racial Instability in the Army, the*

Gathering Storm. Their paper discussed in depth what was happening in the military, and what might happen in the future if things did not change.

"Most general officers refused to admit there was a problem," Brooks criticizes angrily. "They'd say, 'There's nothing wrong with the army; put those damn people in jail. Just build more stockades.' They didn't want anybody coming up with programs to address the problem." But the Secretary of the Army felt otherwise, and Brooks had to make one of the most important decisions of his life. "I felt there was only one way for me to play it, and that was to call it like I saw it, regardless of the impact on my career. If I stopped as a colonel, well, that was so far from what I ever could have expected from where I came, it would still be a good career."

Through Brooks' leadership, an affirmative-action plan was born, but painfully. Ironically, the two greatest enemies for race relations and gender equality in the army were the Chief of Chaplains and the head of the Women's Army Corps. "The chaplain was a bigot and the lady didn't want to expand women's roles at all," Brooks tells it like it was. "I had to fight hard to get that done. We did pretty well." Again, luck was behind the scenes. There was a three-star general protecting Brooks from his detractors. "He kept me from those people who were saying I was losing my mind, and who were asking what the hell I was doing. Critical, absolutely critical."

Brooks, who was reared and honed by difficulty, was as tough on blacks as he was on whites. "The obstacles for minorities were so great then, the ones that survived were super people. Obstacles have great advantages. They harden you, they make you tough, and they make a survivor out of you," Brooks states. It is not at all contradictory to his efforts in affirmative action. If you want to make people better, the struggle must be profound, but one must at least be in the arena to engage in the struggle. Brooks continues to expound that philosophy today, committed to increasing the numbers of minority officers lest the army become an institution with white officers and black enlisted men.

One of the ways he helped change that is by giving scholarships to minority candidates to the Reserve Officers Training Corps (ROTC) and increasing minority attendance at the U.S. Military Academy at West Point. Brooks justified reducing the entrance requirements to place minorities in the stadium but refused to play with the graduation requirements to keep the struggle intense. "Who in the hell can object if what comes out on the other end is as good as it is intended to be," Brooks argues. "There are guys out there with the potential, like I had, but somebody has to find them and get them up here to play. Just like finding in the old Negro Leagues the great ball players of the future. I get angry when I hear arguments against affirmative action plans. If we hadn't done those things, God knows what would have happened."

In the Pentagon, if you want to get something done, you need to write it up and then get a dozen or more agencies to concur in the action, and there's an art to that. Whenever Brooks would find he could not get an action traveling up through the army staff, he would go up to a friend who was Deputy Assistant Secretary of Defense and have him send it the other way, in accordance with the old idiom that successful people make their own luck. "I would address him most respectfully, 'Mr. Secretary,' and I'd go in the office and close the door and I'd tell him I can't get this thing through the army staff. I know I can't, I'm not even going to try. I would ask him to direct the army to do it. And I'd write it all up and he'd look at it and agree." Then Brooks would go back to his office and wait for the order to come down. As soon as it came in "I'd pick it up and shout, 'Goddamn it! Who wrote that stupid thing? Who in the hell is going to do all that work? You tell that Defense Department to kiss my butt, I'm not doing it!' Of course, I had to do it and it got done."

Photo credit: Oscar E. Porter
U.S. Army Audio-Visual

Brooks got a lot done that way, and it benefited the army. A lot of general officers started lining up on his side when they saw the results. When the Promotion Board met to examine the file of Colonel Brooks for brigadier general, the results made the headlines. "Five black guys came out of that board. Unheard of, made every newspaper in the country," Brooks notes with delight. And I was the second one on that list." Whether it was luck or work or the affirmative action that emerged from Brooks' luck and work, as time continued to pass it was also assistant division commander and major general and commander. "Then it was time to split."

It is simplistic to state that Brooks had something to prove, but at every turn in his military career, his ideas and his identity were on the line. And Brooks did not like losing much. "I have an ego," he acknowledges, "but not a large one. It's enough to keep me driven so if somebody comes out against me I'm going to try to prove them wrong. That's a very positive thing." There are some people who allow their ego to carry them over the lines of appropriate or sensible behavior. They just run over people in their zeal to be proven correct or worthy. "We have some of those in the army. Their ego is so big that they can't see things or understand things. That is destructive."

Seeing things is essential. On the road to the top, you have to have an instinct about the right move to make. Brooks was uncanny. "As I look back, I reached a lot of little crossroads. I could have gone this way or that way, and something told me to go that way. That's instinct," Brooks proposes. In a tennis match, there is no time to think consciously about where to place a shot. A top player reacts out of the viscera, out of the bowels, and the decision is right time after time. The reaction may be subconscious but a lot of training has occurred to create it. Brooks uses an analogy that is closer to home. "A boxer doesn't think to himself, 'Oh, now he's throwing that right cross I watched him do on film so now I'm going to throw my left cross.' Nope, the guy throws a right and the boxer comes with a left instinctively but only because he's studied this guy first. We're born with instinct, but if it's not developed, it's not useful."

But more than drive and instinct, Brooks is certain the most important ingredient for his success and the success of those around him is luck. The opportunity has to come along. He uses his former subordinate and friend Colin Powell as the best example of all. "Over the years, I saw people as good or better than Colin, but they never had the opportunity. If Colin had been born ten years earlier, he wouldn't have had the opportunity to reach the level he did. There was just no way it could happen. The system would not have let it happen. The opportunity has to be there whether you call it timing or luck."

> "I live by the motto, 'You say to me it can't be done and I say to you, not true, you mean to say it can be done but it cannot be done by you.' The pen is mightier than the sword. The pen is the sword."

Becoming a general officer is not a simple task. When Brooks was on a board to select brigadier generals, there were 4,700 colonels, and the Board was allowed to promote only fifty-five to general. There were five general officers on the board and they had thirty days to make the decision. They all read through the files and, working in five separate groups, three weeks later whittled the list down to two hundred. "It was so hard to differentiate those final 200 by record," Brooks laments. "They'd all been in combat, all had master's degrees, all been to War College, all were heavily decorated, and most had worked on the army staff." They attempted to rank the candidates. Any colonel that was ranked in the top fifty-five on all five lists was in. Only eighteen were and so it was time to pick up the phone. "There's so much luck here because we call their superior officers and ask if there is anything wrong. 'Was he a heavy drinker? What is the meaning of this remark you made in his efficiency report?' When you get down to those questions, it's like trying to get a colonel through the eye of a needle. There's just a lot of luck. Some of the finest officers I've known retired as colonels."

Brooks found his way through the needle and retired as a major general. While his tour of duty did not include a world war and his combat record, despite numerous decorations such as two Bronze Stars and the Legion of Merit, did not garner him public notoriety, he nevertheless was made of the same stuff that oozed from the likes of George Marshall, Douglas MacArthur, Dwight Eisenhower, Omar Bradley, and George Patton. With very few exceptions, most of the great military leaders really cared about their soldiers, even Patton. Pointing to the photograph of his long-time friend, Colonel Frazier, "He was the meanest man that ever lived," Brooks recalls. "He was always number one to his soldiers because soldiers love to be on a winning team. He would come in there and huff and puff and they'd groan and complain, 'I hate this son of a bitch,' but inspections or exercises would occur and they'd come up number one and all of a sudden it was, 'but I love him too,' because they were winners." When morale is high, people work harder. Brooks understood that and turned on his mean streak when his people were not doing their job. "I had this little streak of meanness and Frazier had this big streak of meanness. It was a little known fact but I fired people quicker than him. He had all this loudness but his heart was gigantic. I had all this quietness and my heart was sometimes puny. But I did love my soldiers." Brooks made sure they knew, too, by placing a sign on his door that read, "I give a damn!"

There are a lot of men who served under Brooks that would agree. Among the mementos of his military career, Brooks is most proud of a certificate presented to him by the State of Hawaii, during his tenure as Division Commander. During Brooks' assignment in Korea, he found his men catching venereal disease as fast as they could from the 3,500 call girls operating outside the gates. When he assumed command of the 25th Infantry Division in Honolulu, Brooks was determined to prevent that from happening again and he decided to divert the attention of his soldiers to education. Brooks ordered his Chief of Staff to put his men to work on their high school diplomas and college degrees. "When I told him that I wanted 10,000 soldiers in education programs, he thought I was crazy," Brooks howls. He said, 'Sir we can't do that, we don't have the classrooms, we don't have the teachers.' Ten thousand people, signed, passed on, that's it, brief me in a week."

Brooks held classes in the day room and on the field, between exercises, during lunch, and late at night. The certificate honors Brooks for enabling 1,500 men to become high school graduates and 600 more to obtain associate and university degrees. "As those soldiers were coming across that stage, the look on their face told you they could finally see that they could do something. I live by the motto, 'You say to me it can't be done and I say to you, not true, you mean to say it can be done but it cannot be done by you.' The pen is mightier than the sword. The pen is the sword." Over the years, Brooks has run across a number of those graduates, one recently at the VA Hospital in San Francisco. "He came up to me and hugged me. He said, 'Sir, I was in your division and because of you I got my degree and it changed my life.' I felt so good about that. I had touched that man. And so the momentum picked up and before I left I got a great amount of personal satisfaction out of touching that many people."

Throughout his career, Brooks found himself in situations where he easily could have been derailed. Brooks will tell you without any hesitation, the most wonderful part of his life in the Army was the soldiers who served under him and the soldiers who stood by him. "I always came out of difficulty or moved another step forward because of key people," Brooks remembers fondly. "I worked for a Southern colonel once who loved me. He couldn't even pronounce Negro. 'Negra' was the closest he could get. I ended up giving him blood when he had bleeding ulcers. He really, really liked me and he always protected me." The memory tugs at Brooks. He sits silently, the only noise in the room the panting of his dog nuzzled at his feet. Eyes moistening from his reflections, Brooks points again to the photograph of Frazier. "He was my guide. When I came to the Pentagon he went around and protected me, he lobbied for me, and this thing went on and on and on and had a lot to do with my success. See, it's all about chance, opportunity, that this particular man came along in my life. This friendship lasted until he died. The biggest sorrow in my life was losing him." Brooks cries freely for his lost comrade.

Brooks rises. So does his dog. As we walk toward the exit, Brooks offers a brief postscript. "The army is a lot like football," Brooks says as he puts a hand on my shoulder. "You have to know the basics. If you are a signalman, you become the best you can become. If you are an artilleryman, you have to know fire direction. In either case, if you work your ass off, with a little luck, you'll move through the system."

The receptionist -- the general's son, Wayne — escorts me to my car and thanks me for coming.

The pleasure was actually all mine.

Paul Ehrlich

Biologist and Author
of the 1968 Best-Seller, The Population Bomb

Biologist and activist Paul Ehrlich sees the world in a desperate situation. More than 30 years ago, he characterized the dire circumstances of the planet in his earth-shaking book, *The Population Bomb* (1968). The problems haven't changed much. Ehrlich hasn't stop voicing his opinions. "I'm a born loudmouth," Ehrlich bellows and then modestly acknowledges that all the attention cast his way is rather serendipitous. "I got interested in these issues when I was in high school and I had the good luck of being too young to be killed in the Second World War and the additional good luck to teach at Stanford."

Ehrlich's prestigious achievements did begin as a teenager filling his room with butterfly and tropical fish collections. He later donated his collection of butterflies, numbering in the thousands, to the American Museum of Natural History, where he had worked with its curator of entomology, Dr. Charles Michener, mounting collections in exchange for duplicate specimens. Ehrlich followed Michener to the University of Kansas, where he studied evolutionary biology and the process of natural selection by which insects developed resistance to DDT. He joined the faculty at Stanford University in 1959, where he began his 40-year study of local butterfly populations, the most thorough research ever done on their ecology and evolution.

Ehrlich's specialty is evolution. He taught a course at Stanford in which the first nine weeks were devoted to where humankind came from and the last week was left to discuss where it was going. The last series of lectures got to be very popular. "Students told their parents, and I began to get invitations to speak. After a talk at the Commonwealth Club, I began getting radio and TV requests and I said to myself, 'Why harangue 50 students at a time if you can harangue 50,000 people at a time?' So I started doing that."

At the request of David Brower of the Sierra Club, Ehrlich put down his remarks in a brief book with the intention of influencing local or national elections. He wrote it in about three weeks of evenings. It had very little impact at first, although it did help Ehrlich and his associates to start the activist organization Zero Population Growth. Then Arthur Godfrey, who had interviewed Ehrlich, gave *The Population Bomb* to Johnny Carson who put Ehrlich on his show, eventually more than 25 times. "He had me on three times in three months," Ehrlich notes with amazement. "After the first *Tonight Show*, we had the biggest mail delivery ever, and in about a year ZPG went from six chapters and 600 members to about 600 chapters and about 60,000 members. Basically, that was the end of my private life. So it was a matter of chance more than anything else."

The basic facts of *The Population Bomb* and the basic message of Ehrlich's public work suggest that the scale of the human enterprise is much too large and cannot be properly supported by the environmental systems of the planet. Ehrlich is notorious for his efforts to focus attention on the connection between human population, resource exploitation, and the deterioration of the environment. Ehrlich contends that all competent scientists understand this and, 30 years later, he reiterated the problem in a book he wrote with his wife, Ann, called *Betrayal of Science and Reason*. In it are the warnings to humanity by the world's leading scientists and by 58 academies of science.

> "Only fools steer their research towards prizes because the fun of being a scientist is to do what interests you, not what's going to get you a prize."

By and large, scientists are not celebrities, though Stephen Hawking, Rachael Carson and — to a degree — Carl Sagan and Paul Ehrlich have had their measure of attention. Limited appeal does not bother Ehrlich, who is the first to admit public acclaim is not the hallmark of great science. "We're in a scientifically illiterate society," Ehrlich proclaims. "Most folks don't have a clue what's involved in science. Partly, it's the responsibility of scientists who don't care to inform the public of what science is all about, and partly just due to our culture. It turns out economists feel the same way. They believe the average person is clueless about how the world of economics works, just as the average person is clueless about their utter dependence on the functioning of natural ecosystems for their lives. The level of illiteracy is absolutely horrendous. So, having the public think you're a great scientist would not do much for the ego of most scientists."

There is, of course, enormous ego involved among scientists. "You show me a good scientist without an ego and I'll show you a liar," notes Ehrlich in his classic no-holds-barred style. "But you can aggrandize yourself in your field or with the public. Aggrandizement with the public is more of a pain than a benefit because it interferes with the things that I really love to do, namely biology." Despite hundreds of public appearances, Ehrlich says the only time he is nervous is speaking before his former professor now in his 80s.

"Scientists live on the approval of their peers," Ehrlich explains. "So there is gigantic ego involved and it certainly helps you in the public domain because you get all kinds of shit all the time. I just had a vicious attack on me in a business newspaper. You've got to let it go off your back. It's easy to do when your colleagues are behind you."

Ehrlich's colleagues have backed him. His many honors include the Crafoord Prize in Population Biology and the Conservation of Biological Diversity from the Royal Swedish Academy of Sciences (1993), the World Ecology Medal from the International Center for Tropical Ecology (1993), the United Nations Environment Program Sasakawa Environment Prize (1994), and a MacArthur Prize Fellowship from 1990-1995. But while the public may not know the scientists or science, they know the Nobel Prize, a distinction Ehrlich's career to save the world has not accrued. Again, Ehrlich is caustic about the value of the Nobel Prize. "There are lots of prizes but the Nobel gets all the prominence," Ehrlich asserts. "It's just another form of recognition. Nobel laureates vary all over the map. Some have saved the earth and there are others that are relatively small scale, where someone worked out this or worked out that and somebody else would have worked it out later on and it wouldn't have made all that much difference. Besides, only fools steer their research towards prizes because the fun of being a scientist is to do what interests you, not what's going to get you a prize."

Now you can package what you do in a way that everybody ignores it or you can package what you do in a way that's likely to draw attention to it. As Ehrlich adds, "only fools would do all the work involved in scientific research and then not seek the most advantageous publication you can get" which may explain his constant effort to influence the public marketplace of ideas through 37 books, 800 technical and popular articles, and a position on the Audubon Society board of directors.

But Ehrlich reminds his critics that while there is a lot of politics in such venues, the thing that distinguishes science from being political is that it's an adversary game and it's transparent. "You can't pretend to be a world class scientist any more than you can pretend to be a world class pitcher or pretend to be a world class violinist. You're always performing," Ehrlich suggests. "You're always being judged by your peers and they all know how you do it; so it's just not published unless it's clear how you did it and other people can repeat it or check it. You have to pay a lot of attention to trying to be objective, because if you're not, they'll catch you."

That doesn't prohibit scientists from being ambitious. They care about their reputations, want to be valued by their colleagues, want to be asked to participate in symposia and to be told their papers are valuable. "Show me an unambitious scientist," Ehrlich challenges, "and I'll show you one that's not very good. The notion that circulated among the public that Einstein was so unassuming and that he really didn't care is full of crap."

Ehrlich is in his medium. Animated and full of fury he tells a wonderful story about Albert Einstein that demonstrates the point. "Einstein was waiting for results from astronomical observations of whether or not a star's light would be displaced when it went by the sun. When the results came in, the observations absolutely matched his prediction. Einstein started whooping and dancing around the room and his sister said, 'Albert, what would you have done if you were wrong?' and Einstein said, 'I would have felt sorry for the deity; the theory is correct.'" Einstein was human after all. There is nothing that distinguishes scientists from other people in that regard.

Contrary to the cartoon image, scientists are not different from the rest of us. There are over 200,000 scientists by some definition in the United States and while there are some odd ones among them, there is no higher density of eccentrics among scientists than anywhere else. "Forget the TV representation of the crazed scientist running around in his white suit, trying to get the brain stuck back into Dracula's head," Ehrlich jokes. "We are the same as any well-educated, successful people where success involves a fair amount of hard work."

Like their corporate counterparts, noted scientists define hard work at a higher threshold than eight hours a day. There may be some who are so smart or so lucky that they acquired their reputations without being obsessed, but Ehrlich says, "I don't know any. I'm not sure obsession is the exact term. It isn't that we do science 24 hours a day. I may easily spend four nights a week drinking wine with my friends. But when my students ask me how I manage to get so much done, my answer is I don't screw around."

Ehrlich works while waiting for a medical exam or traveling on a plane. If he has any secret to success, it's time management, learning how to work in 10 or 15 minute bites. "There are those who have persuaded themselves they can't do anything creative unless they have four uninterrupted hours," Ehrlich scoffs, "but somebody in a position of reasonable responsibility that has four uninterrupted hours is unlikely to be doing his job."

Ehrlich has been doing his job close to 24 hours a day for close to 40 years and he shows no signs of slowing down. "I'll quit when I drop," Ehrlich predicts. But it is not entirely altruism that drives him. "It's not that I feel I must crusade until the end of my life in order to save the world," Ehrlich hints. "I'd like to save the world for my grandchildren; but if it can't be done, it can't be done. I just enjoy my work enormously and there's a lot of evidence that people who retire just fade away. I don't want to fade away so I have no interest in retiring, at least intellectually."

There is the maxim that the longer you use it the less likely you are to lose it. But there are limits to its truth. Most scientific advances are made by young people. "One of the great advantages of my position is that I can gather around me a group of brilliant young people who not only can do the things that I can't do, but will tell me when I'm out of it. That's really important because I don't want to end up with people saying, 'Ehrlich was a pretty good scientist for the first sixty-five years of his life, but then he gradually turned into a blithering fool.'"

There are costs for life quests whether you are building a corporate empire or saving the planet. By his own admission, Ehrlich is not a contented man. "I have led a happy life," Ehrlich says softly. "I have been a lucky man and I've learned to live more for the moment than I used to. I am contented in some areas and not contented in others. I'm certainly contented with my scientific career. I'm not contented with the impact I have had on the course of society."

Ehrlich is loathe to talk about the uglier costs. His daughter wouldn't sleep in their house because there were so many threats made on him when she was growing up. "Sure, there are costs," Ehrlich muses and grinds to a halt to think. "You can't let them stop you. There are enormous benefits. I've done work in parts of the world where I never would have been because I became prominent and I got on TV. People wanted me to lecture on cruise ships, wanted me to come to different countries and give lectures. I get to see things and do things that I never would have had access to if I had been just doing straight science. It's a mixed bag. There are costs and benefits." He is quiet again.

Sorting samples of butterflies.

Ehrlich is a living example that you should never go into this business unless you love it. It is highly unlikely you'll ever be a real success at anything you do unless it is a huge chunk of your life and you really enjoy it. As Ehrlich himself puts it, "Leave it before you get into it if you don't love it and as soon as you feel you don't love it, leave it. And that's especially true of science because a lot of science isn't cruise ships. It's just dull, sloggy work."

Even at 67 Ehrlich is still doing the sloggy work. He recently returned from Costa Rica where he awakened at four every morning to observe details of bird behavior he has seen hundreds of times and record it into computers. A year or so ago he was "in a half-baked, half-finished inn on a tributary where we only had water part of the day," Ehrlich recounts and the energy begins to enliven him. "Even though we were sleeping on cots and being eaten alive by insects, we all had a hell of a good time. If you didn't really love what you were doing and believe in it, you wouldn't have a hell of a good time."

Becoming extraordinary isn't easy. In fact, it's downright difficult. "Someone doesn't just touch you on the shoulder with a sword," Ehrlich decrees. "It's a process."

Edgar Martinez

*Seattle Mariners Two-Time
American League Batting Champion*

Seattle Mariners designated hitter Edgar Martinez is the best right-handed hitter in the American League in the last 50 years. During that time, he is the only righty to win more than one batting title. Martinez did it in 1992 when he hit .343 and again in 1995 with a .356, the highest average by a right-handed hitter in the American League since "Joltin'" Joe DiMaggio hit .381 in 1939.

Martinez's philosophy is simple. Like legendary Dodgers manager Leo Durocher once said, "He hits it where they ain't." It obviously works. After 1,387 major league games over 13 seasons — all with the Mariners — Martinez entered the 2000 season holding a .320 career batting average. Major league hitting coaches agree that to be an All-Star hitter one has to study the opposing pitchers and be able to hit the ball to all fields. But those skills only come from being an All-Star person with the desire to be the best, the pride to correct your mistakes, and the work ethic to do it every day.

Martinez is the poster boy for those ideals. "You have to have a desire to be the best you can be," says Martinez in his soft-spoken Puerto Rican accent. "That motivates you to create good work habits. You get better by working out and learning. Those are the ingredients that helped me. The desire leads to hard work and discipline."

Martinez's work begins long before game time and deep in the bowels of the stadium, where he sweats through a conditioning and weightlifting program that is unmatched by other players in the league. On a typical game day, Martinez arrives at the ballpark more than four hours before the first pitch to ride a stationary bicycle and warm up his legs. From the bleachers, fans may not realize how strong he is, but sitting with him at his locker, the impression is unforgettable: he looks more like a running back than a DH. Weighing about 185 pounds when he started in the big leagues, he now tips the scales at a remarkably lean 205, all muscle.

After the game, Martinez frequently stays until well past midnight lifting weights. His car is usually the last to leave Seattle's Safeco Field parking lot. The routine is no less arduous when the Mariners are on the road; his workouts often force him to miss the team bus and hail a taxi to get back to the hotel. "It helps me know mentally that I'm ready," Martinez explains, "that I've done everything that I can. When my body and my mind is ready for the competition, I have a better chance to do good."

Martinez earns the respect of his teammates and opponents for the way he approaches the game and how he hits. The key to both is his preparation. Even when he is on the bench (which as a designated hitter is most of the time) Martinez is studying and planning for his next at bat. Opposing pitchers say the result is Martinez doesn't have a weakness to exploit. Unlike most players who can't hit a certain pitch — outside, inside, low, high –- Martinez can hit any ball. Despite arguably being the best player at his position and a perennial All-Star selection, Martinez continues to analyze other hitters. "I keep watching hitters and try to learn something I can use," Martinez says, clearly eager to find one more clue to success. "I might see something I like that might work for me. So I keep looking."

> "You get better by working out and learning. Those are the ingredients that helped me. The desire leads to hard work and discipline."

Like the aging Roy Hobbs in the mystic baseball film *The Natural*, Martinez loves the game so much, he just wants to play ball and play it every day. "It's draining to be at this level because it's a business," Martinez allows. Teammate Jay Buhner jokingly bumps into Martinez, nearly knocking him off his chair, but Martinez continues as though the moment never occurred. "It's a game for the fans but for the people inside here, if you don't do the job, it's like a business and you no longer have your job. You have to really love the game and enjoy it day after day after day with that pressure."

Martinez leans back and rubs his hands across the stubble of his beard, thinking. There is only the slightest hint of a smile on his face but his eyes burn with intensity. "For me, I am very naturally compelled. It's the desire inside of me to be the best, the desire of winning, the desire of victory. The adrenaline, the rush, I feel when I play this game, when I'm hitting; I can't find that anywhere else, in anything else that I do. It's the bullpen phone that keeps calling me. I need that. I have to have that rush and the desire to compete and win just comes out. I don't have to push myself."

Although born in New York City, Martinez grew up in Dorado, Puerto Rico. As a young boy he dreamed about wearing a big league uniform but the dream almost ended before it began. After signing with the Mariners as a free agent in December, 1982, Martinez was assigned to Bellingham, Washington, in the single-A Northwest League. Because that team had an abundance of third basemen, Martinez played in just 32 games and his batting average was a woeful .173. "I hit just terrible and I thought I was going home," Martinez recalls. But instead, the Mariners sent him to another single-A team in Wausau, Wisconsin, where in 1984 he hit 15 home runs, drove in 66 RBIs and batted .303, good for seventh in the Midwest League and a promotion to double-A Chattanooga, Tennessee, for the next season. By 1988, Martinez was a standout for the triple-A Calgary Cannons, and was getting called up to the Mariners several times a season. He was on his way.

At the time Martinez signed with the Mariners, he was attending American College in Puerto Rico. If Bellingham had been the end of the road, Martinez believes he would have finished college and would be working today in a management position for a small business. "But I would not be the same person. It's this game. It has something special, and I love it so much."

But then and now, nothing about Martinez suggests his dream ever included millions of dollars or fame. You may have noticed that some truly remarkable athletes are not truly remarkable human beings. Martinez, however, is definitely both. He makes a special effort to give back to his home community of Seattle. Among his civic activities, Martinez serves as an honorary Big Brother and raises money and awareness for the Boys and Girls Clubs. On a global front, Martinez donates his financial support to Esperanza, an organization that addresses the concerns of the poor in the Dominican Republic, the homeland of many major leaguers, and is a member of the Caring Team of Athletes that generates money for children badly in need of health care. "People have different personalities," Martinez notes, staring across the locker room at his teammates. "Some are outspoken, some shy, and some reserve everything for themselves. I'm on the shy side, pretty reserved because I was raised with my grandmother and grandfather and they taught me respect and to always work with people."

It explains why Martinez is one of the most popular players in baseball among the fans and why he is not a frequent media headliner. "The media like people who are outspoken. If they see some people get in trouble, that's what the media grabs and the more those people will stay around in the papers, in the news, and the more fans become familiar with their faces and recognize them everywhere. The media is always looking for them because news sell papers."

In a world where extreme is the dominant virtue for success, Martinez is the master of equilibrium. To balance the intensity of his quest for baseball excellence, Martinez embraces the joys of personal happiness. "Baseball will be part of my life forever, but the most important thing will be my family and life after baseball," he says, relaxing for the first time in our conversation. "Life in baseball, it's hard because you travel a lot and work hard and it's draining. If you look from outside it looks easy because you make a great living. But once you leave baseball you have another life. It's more important to have a personal life that is sound and without problems and grow a relationship with your family members than be all the time in baseball. That really gives you happiness."

Martinez always assigns credit for those values to those who raised him. His extended family was large and very close. "They always helped each other, and I was raised in the middle of it so I was able to learn good qualities," Martinez says, pleased with the results. He is also troubled about the absence of such values in today's children. "Today a lot of people become independent at a young age very easily and the family goes, that closeness goes. They are on their own and there's not much comfort with family anymore."

Relationships are very important for Martinez but they are not easy to find or develop in the world of travel and training his love for the game requires. "It's really easy to get cut off because you spend so much time in this clubhouse," Martinez explains. By now the room is buzzing with noise as players are making last minute preparations to go out to the field. Catcher Dan Wilson is finishing a pre-game televised interview. Outfielder Ken Griffey Jr., who would soon announce his decision to leave the Mariner organization, leans his chair back against the wall and talks on the phone, animated and laughing throughout.

"You spend more time here than in your house. We come here at 2:30 for a 7:00 p.m. game and we get out of here near midnight. It is like that for six months of the season plus spring training, for so many years." The intense publicity-centered world of professional sports does not make relationships easy either. "This sounds bad," Martinez qualifies, "but you always ask if the person is truly taking my friendship because I'm a sport player or because I'm me. You get suspicious. It's very easy to get suspicious. So, you have to be open-minded and give people a chance to show themselves and know them better."

If fans had the chance to get to know Martinez, they would find a man who sees himself as "quiet, intense, and disciplined. This shows up in my life," Martinez reports and then adds, "but sometimes I'm also a little anxious when things are not the way I want to have them." Martinez has come out of his shell in recent years. While he prefers staying at home or going to dinner with his family and typically shuns the spotlight, he has actually enjoyed filming his popular television commercials for Eagle Hardware. Of course, it was no surprise to see him film one with his son by his side.

Amid the fanfare and energy and routine and pressure, it is easy to see why few take time to think about the future, about their lives after baseball. Martinez won't let the introspection rest. "Thinking about what happens when you are done is more important than what happens today. The family you live with, the kids, the relationship with all the people, that's what's going to be more important. But it's easy to lose that thinking here when you are in the clubhouse 10 hours a day. It's very easy to forget about what's going on outside."

Players do think about that, but they usually reserve it for a time when they are close to the end of their careers. Martinez is approaching his. In 1997, when expansion required an American League team to move to the National League, there was speculation the Mariners might be that team. Since the National League does not utilize the designated hitter, Martinez was forced to do some speculating of his own. He is too slow and worn down from injuries to play third base. (Martinez still

makes rare infield appearances, but he has not played third base regularly since 1994 — and not at all since 1997.) Fortunately for him, he was not forced to make that decision as the Milwaukee Brewers made the switch instead. "I don't know what I would have done. One of my options was to quit playing but I really wanted to keep playing with the Mariners since I'd been with them my whole career. You don't see that very often anymore. And it's a perfect situation because my wife is from here and Seattle is home to me."

At 37 and the second-oldest player on the Mariners roster, Martinez is not sure how much longer he will perform even though he remains one of the most feared hitters in base-ball. "I don't really feel old. I just feel like one of the guys who's been around a long time," Martinez says with a hint of humor.

Martinez says he will know when it is time to call it quits. "If I can't perform at the level I'm still happy with, it's time to get out. I want to know I've done my best. That I've given everything I have. And I want to feel very sat-isfied with what I did so that I can be happy and not regret what happened. That would make me be a better person later if I have no regrets about what I did with the game. So far, I'm happy with what's going on."

Whenever it is, Martinez will bow out with class and live out his sweeter dream, a lifetime of joy with his wife, Holli, and their son, Alexander. "She completes me," Martinez says, beaming. "She completes that part that I was needing, a person that you share everything with. She's there for me for everything. She's my friend and that part is what I was needing for years. Once I met her I have fulfilled my goals. I am a very lucky man." All his life Martinez has just wanted to play ball and to have a healthy family and com-fortable home. "I didn't expect it to happen, really," Martinez says, sitting forward and staring between his legs at the floor. "But things have turned out really well for me. It's been a good dream."

Martinez grabs his glove and heads out to warm up. He is unquestionably a hero back in Puerto Rico. People there admire the way he has worked to become all that he has become. They admire him here too. He is a first-class ballplayer and a first-class person. As he disappears through the clubhouse door onto the field, you wonder if you could possibly meet a nicer person in baseball or anywhere else.

Chapter 6

You Can't Let Anything Stop You

James DePreist
Renowned Conductor and
Director of the Oregon Symphony

While he is by no means a household name, the *Chicago Sun-Times* views James DePreist as "one of the most important American conductors of the day," and the *Chicago Tribune* hails him as "one of the finest conductors this nation has ever produced." Not bad acclaim considering DePreist does not even reside in Chicago. DePreist is Music Director of the Oregon Symphony in Portland, Oregon, and, for four years, music director of the Monte Carlo Philharmonic in, yes, Monte Carlo.

In addition to his two resident positions, DePreist is one of the most highly solicited guest conductors in the world with appearances in Amsterdam, Tokyo, Helsinki, Prague, Vienna, England, and France, to name a few. When he is not traveling, he is creating. His discography includes 35 recordings, with several more scheduled for release, and he is the author of two books of poetry. His accomplishments have earned him, among many awards, 15 honorary doctorate degrees. "I don't think much about the achievements," DePreist says in a smooth, articulate voice. "If you spend your time looking over your shoulder to see how many people are noticing what you do, you really don't have time to do what you should be doing. Assessments of achievement are really only useful in an internal way, examining how effective you've been against the yardstick you've set for yourself."

The yardstick is enormous and was set by his aunt, opera singer Marian Anderson, three years after DePreist was born. In 1939, Anderson's agent tried to book her into Washington D.C.'s Constitution Hall, owned by the Daughters of the American Revolution. The DAR denied her request because they had a policy of white artists only. First Lady Eleanor Roosevelt resigned from the DAR in protest and a concert at the Lincoln Memorial was arranged instead, attended by 75,000 people, the largest turnout to date. Four years after the Lincoln Memorial concert, the DAR invited Anderson to sing at a Constitution Hall concert to benefit relief programs in China. Anderson's most triumphant moment came on January 7, 1955, when she made what many critics called her long overdue debut at the Metropolitan Opera on a stage that had been closed to all black performers. At 57, an age considered long past prime, Anderson became the first African-American to perform at the Met and received ovation after ovation.

"When I think about real achievement, I think about my Aunt Marian," DePreist offers immediately and genuinely. "She dealt with bigotry in a way that was self-effacing, and she did not gloat later in the face of obvious chances to be exploitative. She had a charismatic personality that was incredibly powerful and the power came from within. It had nothing to do with what she'd achieved — singing for kings and Presidents — it was not that. It was an inner strength and dignity. That's impressive and rare."

DePreist is likewise made with rare inner strength and dignity. After completing his music study at the Philadelphia Conservatory and obtaining his Bachelor of Science and Master of Arts degrees at the University of Pennsylvania, DePreist served in the army. On a musical tour for the State Department in Bangkok in 1962, he contracted polio. "The contrast between the way I'd gone there with silk suits made in Hong Kong and coming back on a stretcher made it clear to me that we must come to understand constructs of happenstance and, in spite of bad ones, recognize good things can happen too," DePreist says poetically from his wheel chair. "The tour enabled me to discover conducting was what I wanted to do. So, if I could buy into the good that came from it, I had to buy the downside. I can't demand that happenstance be good all the time." The big question was whether he could still conduct. There was no frame of reference for conductors sitting down. But, there were not many references for African-Americans as conductors either so he forged ahead. One can engineer the future by trying to be in the right place at the right time with the right people doing the right things or one can concentrate on being prepared. DePreist chose the latter. "It has been unfailing that if it's going to happen it happens and if it's not going to happen it doesn't happen. Lo and behold it did."

Two years later, seated, DePreist won the Dimitri Mitropoulos International Conducting Competition, named after the famed conductor whose amazing memory allowed him to conduct without a score and who guided the New York Philharmonic from 1949-1957. "The chances of winning that having just decided you want to conduct were not great, but it happened," DePreist states. It also influenced Leonard Bernstein to select DePreist as his assistant conductor of the New York Philharmonic for the 1965-1966 season. But happenstance has a way of reminding you it is only happenstance and DePreist quickly adds, "Despite the Mitropoulos and a year with Lenny, absolutely nothing happened in the United States."

In 1966, DePreist was a conductor without an orchestra, hoping for a European debut. Serendipitously, it happened, but not until 1969. Renowned conductor Lorin Maazel of the Berlin Radio Symphony Orchestra was slated to lead the Rotterdam Philharmonic, with which he had made his European debut, but fell ill and needed someone to lead rehearsals. DePreist's agent was Maazel's agent and she asked DePreist to step in. Maazel was so impressed with the readiness of the orchestra he invited DePreist to conduct in Berlin and later in Cleveland. Concerts followed throughout Europe including Sweden where DePreist developed his friendship with Antal Dorati, conductor of the National Symphony who, in 1971, chose DePreist to become his Associate Conductor with the National Symphony Orchestra in Washington, D.C. "It was the last season of the National Symphony in Constitution Hall, so my debut with them was in the same place where my aunt couldn't sing," DePreist shares with a smile. There is something poetically just about that.

After five successful years in Washington, D.C., DePreist became the Music Director of the Quebec Symphony, Canada's oldest orchestra where he remained until 1983. In 1980, he was named Music Director and Conductor of the Oregon Symphony, a contract that runs through 2005. Now among the top names in the business, DePreist sits at his desk surrounded by easily a thousand musical scores shelved systematically in his tastefully fashionable apartment and studio. The journey has made him as much an expert on career as he is on music. "Dorati told me, 'Don't be concerned if others have faster or more exciting careers. Concentrate on music making and let the career take care of itself.' And that's been my byword."

Career is important in that it gives you the opportunity to work with better colleagues and the better the colleagues, the more likely you are to realize your vision. But, everyone wants career to happen quickly, including DePreist. In 1966, after Mitropoulos and Bernstein, DePreist had one concert and that was canceled. He wrote to Dorati asking for advice and Dorati repeated his earlier counsel. "He wrote back, 'Your job is to make certain that you

"My family taught me if I was prepared, anything I wanted to do, I could do. So I was never afraid of stepping forward."

have what is necessary when you're called. Don't worry about when you're going to be called. Your job is to bring your brick to the edifice, not to tell the grand architect you want it over the center door with a spotlight. Just bring your brick. Your only concern should be making certain your brick is whole and the best you can bring.' I set out to build my brick." DePreist used the time to study all the scores in the repertoire, the concerti, everything he hoped someday to conduct. "You can't imagine anything more depressing than looking at this great music you are so far away from doing. But it was very useful time and I tell young conductors to take advantage of the times when nothing is happening, because later, if you have ten weeks in a row of concerts, you can't study then. You have to have absorbed it earlier."

Whether you regard it as a calling, a personal imperative, or a desire to call attention to oneself, DePreist recognized early that once you get the spotlight, there had better be something there. Thus, it is no surprise that DePreist views his place on the podium as more than having a career. It is having something to say. It is also no surprise that to be eloquent in his execution, DePreist has spent his whole life making his brick. "When I was a little kid I would play the part of the drum major on the street as a parade was coming," DePreist remembers with a broad gentle grin. "I would be strutting around at five years old leading the parade and making the sounds of the band. Whether it was a need to be noticed or not wanting to be just one of the guys, I liked leading the parade." It often happened that way. While in college, DePreist organized concerts that mixed jazz and classical music which had never been done before. "I didn't do it because it was unheard of. It was something I wanted to do, something I loved, that was a passion such that rather than wishing somebody would do this so I could participate, my inclination was to do it. And the confidence to do so was there from my family who taught me if I was prepared, anything I wanted to do, I could do. So I was never afraid of stepping forward."

Those who achieve have the ability to step forward and convince others they are prepared, that they know what they are doing in a way that will work. As conductor, DePreist spends most of his days trying to convince people, very often wordlessly, with instructions at rehearsals. And often, as guest conductor, he must convince people whom he is meeting for the first and only time. "Nearly all musicians believe themselves to be conductors, so conducting can easily be a gold mine for charlatans where nothing comes out of the stick. Incompetence and ineptitude are more easily merchandised in conducting than practically any other area of the arts," DePreist divulges. "You really can be almost a non-talent and survive. I don't know any people with major careers who are, but one can get around. True conductors are remarkably skilled. If a musician makes a false move, they immediately are aware of it."

> "It's best to use criticism as an incentive to do better."

Like many occupations, within five minutes, the workgroup either believes in the leader or it doesn't. To get the workgroup actually doing what you want requires establishing a rapport. "I have no idea how that happens," DePreist admits. "It becomes a matter of the musicians saying, 'We really felt like playing that way.' So there's an element of motivation or inspiration that accompanies an element of music making for which the musicians are responsible, and you are the catalyst." It is an awkward paradox. Conductors are at the front of the stage yet totally dependent on the musicians who are making the music. DePreist thinks the incongruity fosters strength and dignity. "Despite the hype, you cannot put yourself at the level of the composer who starts with a blank page and fills it with music so transcendent you can't imagine a human mind could conceive it. You are not on the level of the musician. With humbleness in the face of the music you're doing, and the musicians who are preparing it, conductors should have a certain regard for where they really stand in all of this. A child once said, conductors hear music and tell it where to go. Not bad."

Nevertheless, life on the stage and behind it is constructed so that most everybody around the conductor adds to the hype. Very seldom does anybody backstage say the performance stunk. There is applause in front of the stage and agents in the wings. Perhaps all of that is needed since conductors risk their private vision of a piece of music by placing it into the mainstream of life. But it is fair that there is some objective or even non-objective opposition. That opposition comes in the form of musical criticism. "We must have confidence, not pride," DePreist stresses, "in the vision and in our technique to get it across. That confidence can be bent by someone who says you weren't so great. But that's really important because it helps you discover that maybe there's more that you have to do. It's best to use criticism as an incentive to do better." It does not always happen, especially when you see it in print. But achieving does require you to be far more critical than a critic. "You have obligations to yourself, to the integrity of your work; to the composers, for their creations; to the musicians for what they are producing; to your public, so they have positive feelings about the experience. But there are no obligations to the critic. It's a peripheral element in what we do, not at all central to how we operate."

Attending to those obligations, DePreist has transformed his regional orchestra into one of national attention. In fact, unknown to most, the Oregon Symphony has the largest subscription per capita of any orchestra in the country. DePreist is not upset by the anonymity of his success. In fact, he is a bit self-effacing about the dichotomy of private meaning and public location. "One of the difficulties of conducting is that one could find oneself languishing in the boondocks. I'm sure there are people who are doing outstanding work in Wichita. Their brick is ready but the serendipity hasn't happened so nobody is going to know about it except people in Wichita, which is fine in terms of being a whole with yourself. But if you're in Wichita and you want to conduct the Chicago Symphony, that probably won't happen, so you'd better find meaning in your work there, all the while sad that the orchestra and the audience in Chicago do not have the opportunity to hear how wonderful you are." DePreist is acutely aware his career has been in the boondocks. Oregon is off the orchestral beaten track, so is Monte Carlo, more so Quebec. "True," DePreist replies, "but there was something to be done there, and we're still in the process of doing it here. And I am fortunate that I can make recordings so people can recognize the importance of what goes on here while I have the opportunity to go to Chicago and Philadelphia and Boston and New York. I am very, very fortunate."

The fortunate happenstance today emerged through a labyrinth DePreist gamely followed. Like his Aunt Marian, people who hear him conduct now and sing his praises are often the same people who passed on him earlier. Despite his global success, DePreist only recently made his debut with the Boston Symphony in their subscription series. One could argue he should have been there years ago. But DePreist is not bitter about then or now. "That's the nature of the business. It is ruthless," DePreist explains. "The assumption is if you're going to survive in this business you have to perform at increasingly higher levels of ability. So if it's not for fifteen years that the call comes, when it does come, everyone is expecting phenomenal things, so you had better be busy for those fifteen years. The implication is, if you deserve to be in the highest company, somebody somewhere has seen you. And if it's to be, the stars have been right and things have happened. And that's fair." DePreist can say that because he is working all the time. Others are not and may not embrace the capricious nature of the system or DePreist's explanation. "If they're not working it is not that they're any less talented. Serendipity plays such a big role I can't tell you."

The look on DePreist's face is sublime. His life is equally so — paid rather well to select the music he wants to conduct, doing what he wants to do, rehearsing with musicians to ensure he gets exactly what he wants done and performing it before an audience that applauds. "People tell me they can't wait to have a vacation. I don't see it," DePreist counters. "My work is my life." Both of which he shares intimately with his wife, Ginette, who travels with him almost everywhere he goes. "Each time I think I'm burnt out, I am inspired by a performance or find a new piece of music and I am turned on in the same way I always have been." There is also poetry and jazz and his orchestra. "I am kaleidoscopically varied. I'm drawn to so many different things and I am constantly enriched by my work. I don't feel that I'm missing anything in life." At 63, DePreist is still traveling around the world doing what he wants to do and has the unique satisfaction of saying there is not a piece of great music that he hasn't conducted. "That's saying a lot. I am very fortunate to be in a position to say that. I'm just endlessly challenged and I would not have predicted any of the things that have really happened."

There are few people who deserve the adulation of the public. If one looks at yardsticks in the world of classical music, there are only a handful of household names. "Greatness implies that there is substance, but the substance may or may not result in fame or stardom," DePreist expounds. "Fame and stardom are ephemeral and may or may not relate to any substance. But if there has been some substance to the achievement one would not be surprised if there was some recognition." That seems fitting for DePreist but he does not agree. "My wife and I chuckle about that," DePreist begins and offers a story from his days jointly conducting the Minnesota Orchestra and the Saint Paul Chamber Orchestra in the early 1990s. One afternoon, DePreist and his wife were sitting in the restaurant of a hotel. Throughout lunch, two men across from them would look over at DePreist and then talk to each other and nod. "For those of us who are before the public, there is a reflex within us that presumes that it is not unlikely that they have recognized you," DePreist reports. "And as they were leaving, one of the gentlemen comes over and says, 'Excuse me for interrupting, but both my friend and I had the feeling that we were in the presence of a great man. What is your name?' I said, 'James DePreist,' to which he replied, 'Oh, we thought you were James Earl Jones.' It was properly deflating for both of us. You need to have a good sense of humor about such things."

What you really need is the good sense of James DePreist about all things.

Vladimir Feltsman
Renowned Concert Pianist
Who Defected to the U.S. in 1987

Photo credit: Al Nowak

Born in Moscow in 1952, Vladimir Feltsman made his concerto debut at the age of 12 with the Moscow Philharmonic Orchestra. At 15, he won first prize in the Concertina International Competition in Prague and immediately began study at the Moscow Conservatory. Another first prize followed at the prestigious Marguerite Long Competition in Paris in 1971.

"I knew I would be a pianist early: 11 years old," Feltsman remarks. "When it clicks you have to give it all you have, otherwise it will not work. When doesn't matter much, it could be early or later. With people in my field it's usually earlier." For 15 years, Feltsman toured extensively through Russia and eastern Europe and studied conducting at conservatories in Moscow and Leningrad (now St. Petersburg). But when he applied to emigrate in 1986, Soviet authorities responded by severely limiting his performances, effectively throwing his career into limbo.

Feltsman was living *persona non grata*, consigned to playing in elementary schools and factories in remote areas. After considerable support from the West — especially from President Ronald Reagan — Feltsman was finally granted permission to leave the USSR in 1987.

"At that time in Russia, it was a totalitarian society, which is not good and conducive to anything," Feltsman suggests in his thick accent. "But in a very odd way, they created an atmosphere for special boutique schools, like music or gymnastics or ballet. This would never fly here, because it will be terrible politics and CNN and the *New York Times* will ruin it in five seconds. But in Russia it was not so and they gave very small elite groups of kids unbelievable conditions in which to grow and to succeed." At the school Feltsman attended there were 10 to 12 prodigies per grade, creating an extremely intense and competitive atmosphere.

Feltsman developed his extraordinary gift under the watchful eye of a master teacher, without whom, he believes, his talents would have come to nothing. "You need a teacher for whatever aspirations you have. Very few have such clarity of vision that they can see without assistance." Feltsman believes the role of the teacher is indispensable and crucial but he also believes there comes a time when the pupil must seize the day. "Real teachers are hard to find. A teacher can open the door for you, can bring you to the lake, but he cannot drink instead of you. He can tell you, 'That is a lake, that is water, partake of it,' but if you cannot swallow it, too bad." When the relationship between the teacher and pupil is sound, the transformation of pupil into teacher comes naturally.

Feltsman spent nine years with his teacher, but didn't even play for him after the sixth year. "We just talk about music, have a dinner; it was friendship. In the beginning it was lessons on weekly basis, sometimes twice a week, then once a month. But that has to happen."

Feltsman, now himself a teacher, realizes that teaching is all about not being needed anymore. "This is why you're doing it, that they would not need you one day. You bring them towards being their own teacher because if they cannot teach themselves it's hopeless."

It is possible that his pedagogical philosophy may explain why Feltsman never needs to memorize any piece of music. He just plays it, rehearsing it, over and over, until it resides in his head. "It's just volume, it's there after you play it enough times," Feltsman notes. But with his characteristic sense of humor he adds, "I use music only when I play Bach. I use a score and get a nice looking girl next to me with a short skirt for inspiration and that's it."

It is more likely that determination accounts for both his memory and his accomplishment. "You can't let anything stop you. I became recognized from one thing: stubbornness." Feltsman emphasizes. "I was a pretty diligent guy. Narrow-mindedness. I was really fixated on getting there and nothing would stop me, not even communism."

Feltsman's arrival provided him with the opportunity for immediate success and matching notoriety. Despite the fanfare, Feltsman prefers living in rural New Paltz, New York –- one hour north of New York City --diligently perfecting his beloved Bach repertoire and teaching his students, the rewards for his resolute quest for personal and creative freedom. "I actually never wanted fame for fame's sake," Feltsman explains, "because I would not be comfortable with it." But in 1987, Feltsman arrived with a lot of exposure, not only musically but also politically.

He was interviewed on *60 Minutes* and on *Good Morning America*. He performed at the White House. But those were not his objectives. Prior to entering the country, Feltsman secured his job as a Distinguished Chair in music at the State University of New York campus in New Paltz. "I don't like big cities and that tells you something about me. I could live on Fifth Avenue in a penthouse but I live very modestly here. It suits me better. I like my work to practice and to teach. It's not right or wrong. Different people like different things."

It isn't that Feltsman believes success is unimportant. It is more that he approaches it with caution. "To have admiration, love from public, the glamour, you have to have a head on your shoulders," Feltsman warns. "If you don't and you start to believe your own publicity it is a terrible thing. You get self-obsessed. It's happened to some of my colleagues and they're ruined by that."

Some of Feltsman's friends and colleagues with whom he studied in Russia were so obsessed with success, they ended up in mental institutions. One girl he knew killed herself. "I was mentally pretty strong from the beginning. I was very competitive but never jealous in my life. When I saw somebody who played technically better than me, I was never upset. I just said, 'So that's how we should be,' and then I try to get it. You have to be competitive, but you cannot be concerned with success and fame."

There is a difference between the excellence and mastery that draw Feltsman onward and the celebrity that accompanies him. In fact, Feltsman believes they have nothing to do with each other, that "greatness and fame demands very different, sometimes opposite, qualities in your character." Fame demands a shrewd comprehension of the public and the mechanics of winning their admiration. To achieve great artistry "these qualities are not required," Feltsman asserts. "It takes devotion to your goal; it takes purity of heart. It is very important that whatever you do you do it sincerely not because you will get fame and success. "I'm not in the bracket of Placido Domingo. I'm not a superstar. I'm just being recognized in classical music. That's all and I am happy with that."

> "You need a teacher for whatever aspirations you have. Very few have such clarity of vision that they can see without assistance."

Recognition is a very delicate line to walk. It helps if you take it right and if you're not working for that end. Feltsman's path to America and his artistic exploration of music, ranging from his favorite composer, Johann Sebastian Bach, to the contemporary Alfred Schnittke, suggest the pianist is more interested in finding out who he really is rather than who others think he is. According to Feltsman, the most important thing one can be is "being yourself. Nothing else."

The path to self-discovery is Feltsman's approach to music. "There is a reason a certain piece of music has been written," Feltsman argues. "You can play the piece, do it very well, or through that piece you can go somewhere else and then it becomes an expression of something bigger." The audience is usually unaware of the grander place Feltsman is going but he is not at all dismayed. "They have no idea. They're looking for experience. They want to have a good time and they are totally entitled to be merely entertained. They paid $40 for the ticket."

Appreciation for classical music, like all art, is a matter of perception. It is like a mirror. What you perceive depends on the way you look at it. If you look from one angle, you see one image and there is a different image from every angle of view. But essentially, it is the same mirror. Feltsman is not concerned about his audience's point of view. "You cannot reach whatever degree of perfection you are trying to reach if you're trying to play for them and to please them. It will never happen." He is equally disinterested in the views of critics and he has instructed his publicist not to send him copies of their remarks. "No critics made me," Feltsman proclaims. "Critics did not make Yo-Yo Ma. You are not made by critics. You are made by yourself. They didn't make me and they will not break me down. You get dates with orchestras or recitals not because you have a good critic in the *New York Times* but because people want you to play and you can sell the hall. And people still want me to play and I still can sell."

Feltsman continues to dazzle audiences with his energy and his remarkable technique, but nothing sells the house more than his unrivaled sense of self that bursts forward in his music and his presence on stage. "If people had blindfolds on and listened to several pianists, they would hear my quality of sound," Feltsman claims. "I don't want to be self-aggrandizing, I really don't, but you can say that about very few people. It's obvious with Itzhak Perlman. Without looking to him, you recognize his sound immediately. It's magical." And the magic is not something Feltsman copied from another artist nor is it something any one can copy from him. For Feltsman, it is simply incomprehensible for people to be anything but themselves. "Somebody can inspire you, they can give you something to think about, but you cannot copy it. It has to be unique. It's got to be your own. You cannot even copy your own signature totally. You will sign it millions of times, and you cannot copy. So why copy anyone else?"

Feltsman puts down his spoon and takes the final bite of the sandwich he has been enjoying for the past half hour, completely satisfied with his lunch and with his commentary. "Mmmmm, I love it! Portabella mushrooms are great. Good bread, good cheese. Mmmmm! Am I great? Yeah. I'm sorry, I am. Terrible, huh?"

There is an ageless idea that whatever you can lose or that can fade away is not worth having. It follows, then, that one who has greatness always has it, not on a good day, not on a bad day, not just playing the piano but in one's sleep, in life and in death. It just goes on. Perhaps that idea was on the minds of Russian leaders when they invited Feltsman to return to Moscow to play triumphantly where he once had been banned.

Kathy Johnson Clarke

U.S. Gymnastics Medallist
in the 1984 Olympic Games

In 1977, 18-year-old Kathy Johnson was named Gymnast of the Year by the United States Gymnastics Federation (now USA Gymnastics). Eight years later, after what may be one of the most motivational stories of perseverance on record, she received the honor a second time. At 25, nearly double the age of many world-class competitors, the award was a marvelous tribute to a career that defied logic and the foibles of the human body.

Unlike today's athletes who are placed in training programs while in pre-school and groomed for stardom, Johnson did not even join her first gymnastics class until she was 12, an age at which many gymnasts are vying for an Olympic medal. Johnson discovered the Olympics as a little girl when her grandmother gave to her an Olympic coin collection. It was love at first sight. Only she was in love with everything. "My first hero was Jesse Owens, based on what I read about him in the coin collection," Johnson reports with as much exuberance today as she must have experienced as a child. "I became completely infatuated with the Olympic Games. I wanted to be an Olympian."

A natural athlete, Johnson's first romance was with track. During the 1968 Olympic Games, she watched long distance runners on television while running around the living room in an imaginary competition. "They just showed this courage and nobility and passion for what they did as they were running, and I drove my family crazy, running in circles while the race was going on, thinking that I was running with them. I had no idea how fast they were going, but I figured I would just ran as long as they did."

During the course of the broadcast, Johnson also saw her first gymnastics competition. "It took my breath away," Johnson exclaims. "I was ridiculously small in school. I had every nickname you can imagine from 'Peanut' to 'Atom' to 'Molecule.' All of a sudden, here's a sport with little people flipping and twisting and turning and I just sat mesmerized as I watched." Among those she watched was 15-year-old Cathy Rigby, who burst on to the gymnastics scene with original moves like her trademark needle scale on beam. Johnson saw it and figured, "I can do that." She immediately got in a doorway, slid one leg up the side of the doorway so she was in a vertical split, reached above her head and grabbed the extended leg with both hands and hopped out of the doorway to show her parents. "Funny, but once I got into gymnastics I ended up having that move in my routine for years, and it was the first gymnastic thing I ever learned."

Johnson's parents could see that she had fallen in love with gymnastics but discovered there was no team in her home town of Indialantic, Florida, a small hamlet on an island off the coast of Melbourne. She would have to wait until junior high. As a sixth grader, Johnson was seated on the floor of the gym watching practice while waiting for her ride home. The coach of the team invited her onto the floor to try some moves. "He taught me a backwards walkover, which is not the first thing you're supposed to learn. There's a progression of other things that lead up to that, but that is the way my career went at first. It just sky-rocketed. He asked me if I wanted to join the team when I started seventh grade, and I was thrilled."

Looking back at it, Johnson does not believe training in a program coached by volunteers put her at any disadvantage. In fact, she reports the opposite. "I was very fortunate to start that way because it was pure passion, pure joy," Johnson says. "It was never work. Never, 'Oh I've got to go train.' It was the ultimate thrill and I couldn't get enough of it. They had to physically take me off the equipment and get me out of the gym so they could close the doors."

Johnson was so fearless in the beginning she was often described as foolish. She would simply launch into the air and try whatever her coaches asked. But beyond the rapidly developing skills, in the first years of gymnastics, Johnson developed something that would sustain her through her whole career. "I had no idea how difficult my career was going to be, no idea how long it was going to be, no idea there were going to be extended periods of time where I questioned whether I could do it, whether I was too old, whether I enjoyed it anymore. The thing that I developed most in those first few years was a love so deep for being a gymnast that it would last through hell."

By the time she was 14, Johnson was drawing attention. She skipped the beginner and intermediate levels of competition, going straight to the elite division at state, regional, and national meets. In order to find the coaching she needed to press onward and upward, Johnson left home to live and train with professional coaches eight and one-half hours away in Atlanta. After one year of their tutelage, Johnson qualified for the 1976 Olympic Trials. She finished 12th overall, only a half of a point away from making the Olympic team and only a tenth of a point from making the official training squad. Recognizing her potential, the Olympic coach requested that she be allowed to train with the team. The request was denied.

Following the trials, an even more determined Johnson moved to Shreveport, Louisiana, and began an intense training program for the 1980 Olympic Games in Moscow, realizing she would be the oldest athlete attempting to make the team. In the fall of 1976, she made her first US National Team and by winter of 1977 she leaped to the top of the list by winning the country's most prestigious meet, the *American Cup*, and Gymnast of the Year honors. After finishing high school, Johnson entered Shreveport's Centenary College and started their gymnastics team with three fellow athletes from her Atlanta training experience. Early in her first college season, she severely broke her elbow and was informed by the doctors she would most likely never compete again.

"It was the first time in my life that gymnastics was hard," Johnson explains and shifts uneasily in her chair. "As a beginner it was easy and I learned things really fast. After my elbow, I couldn't do anything. I'd lost three and a half inches across my back, had no strength, no power, nothing. My first reaction was to quit so I wouldn't have to face it."

"I was very fortunate to start that way because it was pure passion, pure joy. It was never work...It was the ultimate thrill and I couldn't get enough of it."

Johnson overcame her initial feelings and began to strengthen her back. But she avoided practicing her routines. She stuck to individual passes and dance moves. When her father asked why she refrained from her routines, Johnson went ballistic. "I just lashed out at him. 'You want to see me fall on my butt? Fine!' I marched over and turned on the music and I did my routine and I fell on every single pass. I was dying. I was so tired at the end of the routine and I was in tears and feeling so ashamed because nobody in this gym had ever seen me falter. Nobody had ever seen me have trouble." After she calmed down, her teammates congratulated her for trying the routine and for getting up after every fall and completing it. "Almost everybody in the gym was so proud of me," Johnson says in amazement.

The road back was not any smoother. A few weeks later, before her first meet since the injury, Johnson became ill with the flu. Feverish and wearing her pajamas, she traveled to Memphis. The tiny gym was draped with signs welcoming the *American Cup* champion. On the opening move of her bars routine, the champion fell, started again, struggled through to her handstand dismount and fell again, smashing her mid-section against the lower bar. "I was lying on the ground, my leg up in the air, gasping desperately for a breath. They had to be wondering, 'This is the best we've got?'"

Once she caught her breath, Johnson had every intention of heading home. "I'm throwing my clothes in my bag and I'm pouting and my coach came up to me and said, 'Why don't you stand up and tell this audience how good you used to be and quit?' Steam was coming out of my ears — that infuriated me so much. It got me mad, it hurt me, but it did something in me and I decided to stay." On her next event, Johnson fell on the beam but recovered before tumbling to the ground. "That was somehow a victory to not touch the ground," Johnson proclaims. "I climbed back up, did my dismount, and walked away ashamed because it wasn't what I used to do, but really proud in a weird way that I stayed on the beam. My coach came up with tears in his eyes and said, 'That's the first glimpse of the old Kathy I've see in a long time'."

Rejuvenated, Johnson continued on floor exercise and danced with all her heart. As she walked off the floor, the coach of the other team told her he was proud of her. "I realized there's something else to strive for. There is another reason to be an athlete than just winning and just being the best," Johnson expounds. "I was fortunate to learn that because that gave me inner strength and inner peace that no matter what, if I continued to try, there would be personal victories I could achieve every day that didn't come with a medal, with a score of 10, with media articles, and television interviews. That definitely defined things for me and started me on a search for developing character instead of just the need to win, the need to be the best at all costs as though that was the only thing of true value. It changed the course of my career."

Kathy (on the right) displaying the bronze medal for the balance beam at the 1984 Olympic Games

Johnson was never as strong and never as powerful again. But she became a dancer and that would become her trademark. Later that year, Johnson, the eldest 1978 US team member, competed in her first World Championships finishing eighth in the all-around competition, the highest American finish ever. In one of the most dramatic moments of the meet, Johnson scored 9.75 for her floor routine immediately following the 9.8 of Romanian Nadia Comaneci. But the crowd was so moved by Johnson's performance they demonstrated repeatedly until the judges raised her score to 9.9. With that score she qualified for the finals and she finished with a bronze medal. Two years later, in 1980, despite being seven years older than Olympic Trials winner 14-year-old Tracee Talavara, Johnson made the Olympic team with a second-place finish only to wake up from her Olympic dream to the reality of the 1980 boycott.

"I always wanted to run a marathon," Johnson says about her Olympic odyssey. "I loved the thought of going the distance, of being able to overcome anything that could happen in that 26.2 miles. I knew instinctively I had that in me. My career was a marathon but they kept moving the finish line. That was the hardest part about it. I never knew where my finish line was, so I was very scared of quitting, of not knowing the difference between quitting and retiring. That was a driving force for me." That was also a debilitating force because Johnson spent a lot of emotional energy struggling for the answer. "I wanted more than anything to finish my career with no regrets and the biggest regret I could see was quitting too soon, not finishing my race, not getting to my finish line, but getting to someone else's." Johnson pushed on toward 1984.

Hampered by another injury, this time a stress fracture in her foot, Johnson's career again appeared to be finished. "The elbow was dramatic. The damn little stress fracture just snuck up on me and would not heal," Johnson mutters in disgust. She was out eight months. Every time she tried to return the pain was so horrible she would have to stop. The doctors finally forced her into a cast. It still did not heal and surgery appeared to be the only option. "That would've been the end of my career so I took mega doses of vitamin C, B-15, calcium and everything else I had heard or read about and said, 'It's OK' and ran out there and did a double twisting summersault." During her disability, Johnson kept busy coaching a group of young children. But when the foot healed, an internal alarm clock signaled it was time to make a move. She called the national team coach, Don Peters, in California and told him she wanted another shot. "I was out of shape and overweight. Everybody had written me off and I looked like I should be written off. On the spot, without even knowing where I'd stay, he said 'If anybody deserves another shot it's you and I'd like to give that to you.'"

At 24 and allegedly washed up, Johnson pulled together her team of nine- and ten-year-olds to explain her departure. She sat with her teary-eyed team and began sensibly enough. "You're not going to understand right now, but when you get older this is going to make sense to you. I've got one last shot in my life to do something I've dreamed about since I was your age and to do that I need to go someplace where I can train with other people trying to do what I'm doing, and with a coach who can push me through a very difficult time. You would not want me to be your coach if I don't do this, if I don't fulfill this in me and try. There's no guarantee I will make the Olympic team again but I need to find out, because if I don't I wouldn't be a good coach, I wouldn't be fulfilled, I wouldn't be whole." The youngest child came up after with tears running down her cheeks and sanctioned Johnson's homily. "I understand," she announced. "You need to do this so you can go on with the rest of your life and know you did everything."

Johnson packed and left a comfortable place with wonderful people and walked into a gym clear across the United States and came face-to-face with 13-year-old and Olympian-to-be Michelle Dusserre, performing moves Johnson had never even tried. The coaches explained the conditioning program and Johnson realized, "They were doing three sets of 10, I couldn't even do one. In my head I'm panicking, but I just decided to put one foot in front of the other and keep trying, trying, trying." There were horrible days where she looked like she had never been a gymnast, and there were days where she could see a light at the end of the tunnel. "Eight months later I competed well at the World Championships doing tricks I never thought I would ever be able to do, but to get there I never worked harder or struggled more. And I never felt better at the end of any journey." Johnson finished as the top American in the meet, the best she had ever performed and surprisingly at 24 years of age. "I shocked myself, my coach, and people on the other side of the world, whose opinion of my gymnastics mattered to me most. The Soviets and Romanians were my heroes, my idols in gymnastics. I had lived for that moment."

Photo credit: Dave Black

After the World Championships, Johnson and her coach began talking once again about the Olympic Games. "He was talking to me like I was 13, talking about adding things to my routines, dreaming of these possibilities for me." The psychic drain of the World Championships and the long road to her dream took a heavy toll. Johnson returned to the US from France and became very ill. Every morning she would rise and get ready for the gym but she never went. She never left the house. Instead, she sat in the house with the windows drawn entombed in her fear. "I knew what it was like coming back and I was on borrowed time," Johnson reports sadly. "I had trained so hard and put myself out on a limb to so far. I had already stretched my talents and stretched my determination to the max."

Johnson had lost time at the very beginning because she started so late. Now time was running out. "It was the biggest fear of my life," Johnson says, literally in pain as she issues the words. "Do you know what it feels like to work so hard to get someone to believe in you and now they do and you doubt yourself?" The Games were practically on the horizon, 10 months away, which may not seem like a long time to most people, but for an old gymnast it was an eternity. "I knew what it was going to take and I just wasn't sure that I could do it one more time. I wanted to be at the Olympic Games but there was real pain in knowing that the dreams I had about the Olympic Games were most likely not feasible. But the real pain was the thought I didn't love it anymore. That you could love something so dearly and so deeply and with every ounce of your being and all of a sudden question that was very scary for me because I did not want to ever leave this sport not loving it. It was too important."

> "I wanted more than anything to finish my career with no regrets and the biggest regret I could see was quitting too soon, not finishing my race, not getting to my finish line, but getting to someone else's."

She made a very conscious decision to try one more time. "I needed to risk that dream. There was absolute pain in making that decision then and there's pain now even looking back on it." Tears stream down Johnson's face and we sit silently. Our table at the sidewalk café becomes a remote island in a tumultuous Los Angeles sea.

At the Olympic Trials in Florida, before hundreds of hometown and nearby Atlanta and Shreveport supporters, Johnson opened up the competition with a devastating 7.1 compulsory bar routine. Her chances of making the Olympic team were now nearly mathematically impossible. With her former little athletes waving banners and yelling with every move she made, Johnson threw herself into overcoming the numbers. "I kicked ass the rest of the meet. I just hit everything," Johnson rejoices. She made the eighth and final spot on the team. The first four athletes were guaranteed Olympic competition, but the next four would fight it out for six weeks at training camp for the final two spots. The two eliminated would become alternates. When the battle was over Johnson was not only among the six, she was named team captain.

Nearly 25, and 13 years after she started, Johnson was finally at the Olympic Games. With Pam Bileck, Michelle Dusserre, Julianne McNamara, Tracee Talavera, and Mary Lou Retton, the team won the silver medal. Energized by the team medal performance, Johnson set her sights on winning an individual medal on the beam as she competed in the all-around portion of the meet. She opened the individual competition with a 9.9 on the bars, normally her weakest event. "I am like a kid again feeling fully capable of doing it, and I need someone to calm me down," Johnson says, switching to present tense and reliving every minute.

During her next event, beam, she fell. She fell again on floor. "I am too excited. Trying to do a 10, trying to do the highest triple I've ever done in my life," she analyzes. "I have two falls in the Olympics. I am in shock. My heart is smashed to smithereens. It might as well stop beating."

Emotionally broken, Johnson wanted to just stop. It was not until years later that she even bothered to discover where she finished in the all-around. Qualified for finals in the beam, she had one more day as an Olympian but "I was broken-hearted, devastated, and had given up finally for the first time in my life. The feeling horrified me and it shamed me," Johnson states with disdain and then plays the scene for real. 'You little brat, you've qualified for event finals in the Olympic Games. Do you know how many people would like to be in that position? Do you know how many of your teammates didn't make an event finals? And you're feeling sorry for yourself.' I couldn't look at anybody."

Olympic coach Don Peters pressed on with business as usual and approached Johnson with training plans for the final. When he saw the resignation on her face he started yelling. After the scolding, Johnson turned to assistant coach Roe Kreutzer. "I asked, 'Why is he doing that?' She said, 'Because his heart is broken too.' I instantly forgave him. He wasn't trying to hurt me. He didn't want to see me give up, and neither did I." While teammate Mary Lou Retton became an international celebrity thanks to her performance, Johnson's heroic path to the Olympics and her bronze medal on the beam convinced gymnastics officials to once again name her Gymnast of the Year.

Johnson takes a deep breath and exhales slowly. She stares at the passersby. The café is empty but for the two of us. Three hours have passed since lunch began; 16 years since her marathon ended. "I am very emotional about it," Johnson sniffles out the obvious and offers a brief smile. "Finally being at the Olympics at almost 25, final performance of my life, knowing it was going to be the last time I am going to put on these grips, the last time I am going to try. I was very emotionally attached to being a gymnast, emotionally attached to going the distance, to having a career that I could look back on that was rich, that was full, not just one big meet, a gold medal here, a 10 there. I wanted more than that. I needed fulfillment."

Johnson's look, posture and voice are reminiscent of British sprinter Harold Abrahams, who won the gold medal in the 100-meter dash at the 1924 Olympic Games in Paris. A subject of the classic 1981 film *Chariots of Fire*, Abrahams' character, played by Ben Cross, admits that he has known victory and defeat, but has never known contentment. "That's what I was searching for, that point when I could say, 'I am fulfilled now, that's the end of my career,' and not have this nagging feeling of 'I could have, I should have, if only I would have.' Not knowing that drove me." Then, as if occupied by

Abrahams' ghost, Johnson describes her last routine by quoting the Olympic hero. "What'd Abrahams say? 'My entire existence lies in the next 10 seconds.' I thought about that right before my final routine at the Olympic Games. Then I had the most amazing experience, bitter and sweet, but in the end just so sweet it hurt."

You often hear achievers say if you dream it, if you believe it, if you work hard enough, if you persevere, you can become it. But there really is no guarantee. "I dreamed huge dreams for myself," Johnson says. "I dreamed of being the best gymnast ever in the history of gymnastics. I would never want to deny a child the big dreams that I dreamed. They were incredible to have every day."

Despite the pain she suffered and endured and continues to feel for trying to make those dreams come true, and despite the fact she did not quite fulfill them, Johnson talks positively about the process. "Success is really becoming the best you can possibly be. That's the real success — not the definition we are bombarded with on a daily basis by the media about who won, who's the best. I was a bronze medalist on balance beam and I found the Nike ads during the Atlanta Olympic Games so offensive. 'You don't win a silver medal, you lose the gold.' How offensive." In addition to being totally contradictory to their 'Just do it' ads, we should remember that athletes can win gold medals without doing their best.

"I would rather be the one who won the silver or the bronze knowing I'd done the performance of my life," Johnson counters. "I wish we would truly value becoming the best you can, that is really the most important." Johnson is not rebuking victory. She won many times and loved every one of them. "It's a thrill to win, but it's a bigger thrill for me to have accomplished what I did considering the circumstances. Even though the big dreams aren't going to happen, more important ones are."

Johnson is married to actor Brian Clarke, best known for his dual role as Grant Putnam and Grant Andrews on the daytime soap, "General Hospital." They met in 1986 while she was on assignment for ESPN. Their son, Brian, was born in 1999. Now those are important dreams.

Dawn Riley

First Female Captain (1995)
and CEO (1999) of an America's Cup Boat

As CEO and captain of *America True*, the coed challenge for the America's Cup 2000, Dawn Riley is the first woman in the world to manage an America's Cup team. Her leadership role is the result of a remarkable history as a big boat and match race sailor. Riley served as pitperson and the only female on Bill Koch's *America³* team in their successful America's Cup Defender trials in 1992. The following year she was skipper of *Heineken*, the all-woman team in the 1993-1994 Whitbread Round the World race. In 1994-1995, she was the team captain of the historic all-woman America's Cup team, also called *America³*. Her journey to sailing's top spot began on a sailing trip with her family at 13 when the Rileys sailed for a year from Detroit to Maine to Grenada and back and came across the Cup trials during their cruise. "We weren't close enough to the boats to realize that there weren't girls on the team," Riley remembers, "but I said I want to do that."

While the Riley children saw the year at sea as a vacation, their father forced them to sail the boat hard and fast. "He was obsessed with it," Riley recalls. "It was always, 'Put down your book and trim the sail. You can read later.' That really developed my skills." When Riley returned, she began racing for the first time and realized that she was pretty good. In a story that appeared in *Sports Illustrated* years later, Riley's first public pronouncement of her America's Cup intentions occurred at a race in Detroit. "I was in a bikini contest after the race. It was like a fake Miss America and each contestant was asked 'What do you want to do with the rest of your life?' I said to myself, 'I want to steer in the America's Cup.' They all laughed and I said to myself, 'You can laugh but I'm going to do it.' It just made me more determined."

At the time, there was absolutely no place for women in the America's Cup but Riley followed the traditional path to the helm, which was sail and work on boats. "If you can dream it, do it. That's my personal motto," Riley asserts. "Maybe it's stubbornness or stupidity, but if somebody laughs and says 'no way,' that makes me ten times more determined." Riley operates out of an enormous sense of justice. Life may be cruel but it should be fair. "If someone told me I suck at sailing and could prove it, then I would believe it. But if they just said 'You are not allowed to do this,' there's no way I'm going to believe that." But sheer determination isn't all it takes. There are a lot of people out there who have tried real hard to steer the Cup and failed. And Riley could demand a spot on a boat in the name of gender equity but there was no equal opportunity because sailing was the hobby and pastime of men. "Why did they have to let a woman on the boat?" Riley asks rhetorically. "They didn't. You had to prove that you were good enough or better to be on that boat."

That is just what Riley did, race after race, month after month. And the male sailing establishment was not too pleased. One well-known skipper announced at a sailing party that women didn't belong in boats and Riley went on the attack. "This other girl and I challenged him to a race, girls against men and whatever boat he wanted to pick. He got so mad he had to leave the party," Riley grins. The hostility was not always amusing. Riley has heard her share of female slurs. At one regatta, the owner of the boat didn't realize Riley was on the crew because somebody else had organized his team. "When he found out, he said, 'I don't have to have any cunts on my boat if I don't want to.' What do you do?" Riley demands. "A lot of people heard it. So I got on another boat in another class and won. Eventually I ended up sailing with him."

Riley admits that for every man she encountered who didn't want any "damn women" on his boat, she ran across someone that was supportive. But she also admits that to cross the hard lines of history and tradition, you have to be on your toes and handle each situation as it comes up. "You don't grovel. You don't beg. You have to keep your dignity," Riley proclaims. "But, I did punch a guy one time."

People who don't know sailing characterize it as fluff. Captains sit and call out "steer left, steer right, all engines ahead full." But contrary to the image, sailing is quite physical. "It is damn hard," Riley retorts, "and if you whine, you're out of here." Everyone is involved fully in a weight program. The crew must have explosive strength to perform their tasks and guard against injuries. And in big boat sailing, you are going to have plenty of injuries just by being tossed around on the boat or getting fingers caught in ropes and cranks. The crew also works diligently on being flexible. "If you haven't done enough stretching you're going to tear your shoulder off," Riley reports. "This is a contact sport between you and the boat. It's like being on a football field but the waves are the ones that you are up against."

Any sailor knows that when you are on the water, there are certain things outside of your control. You can do everything perfectly, be coming up to the finish line in the lead, and the wind can shift and all of a sudden the spinnaker backs and your opponent sails around you. Sailing can be cruel because no matter how good you are you can still lose. There were a lot of losses for Riley in her quest to sail the Cup. "You need to be very strong emotionally," Riley suggests. "You've got to have confidence in yourself and get back up on the horse. You've got to make yourself available and you have to have the balls to ask." Indeed, that is how Riley finally got involved with the America's Cup in 1992. She and another female sailor called up skipper Dennis Conner and asked to try out for the America's Cup. He agreed only to meet with them. "We flew to San Diego to interview with him and he didn't grace us with his presence. All of a sudden I'm there and heard about $America^3$ and ended sailing with them. Until that moment, I didn't even know $America^3$ was happening."

Riley is obsessed with the sport and with her dream. From the time she captained the Michigan State sailing team to her current role as syndicate chief, she has set aside her social life for her quest. "You always have your foul weather gear in the back of the car just in case there's a regatta. In college, I never went to football games because I was sailing every weekend. Like everything I did in my life, whether I was conscious of it or not, I was pushing to this point. If that's your goal, you forsake all others and drop everything else you're doing." To that end, Riley lived in a van for a year and a half in Florida fixing boats and obtained a diver's certificate so she could clean boat bottoms. She did whatever it took to get know boats and the business of sailing.

The skills Riley learned from steering big boats serve her well in her leadership role with *America True*. The only American to sail the Whitbread Round the World twice, the 8-month, 31,000 mile race provided value lessons on how to handle time and risk. Whether it is sailing down 50-foot waves at 30 mph on a remote sea or leading a syndicate for four years against ten other challengers, Riley notes such adventures are "not really that risky when you're prepared."

"Maybe it's stubbornness or stupidity, but if somebody laughs and says 'no way,' that makes me ten times more determined."

Being prepared to lead has never been her problem. "I've always been bossy," Riley acknowledges. "I am always the captain of the sailing team, I was editor of the school paper and squad leader in the band and all that kind of stuff." Lest those credentials appear to disqualify Riley as CEO, her role as skipper of *Heineken* in the Whitbread of 1993-94 more than compensates. "I had to manage women who had mutinied against the previous skipper before and who thought they should be in charge," Riley explains. "But I was in charge. I was literally brought in by the sponsor and the owner to manage a hostile team in the middle of the Southern Ocean. That was true management training on the job."

Sailing, like any specialized skill, requires natural talent, but Riley believes the most valuable tool for the endeavor is the one that lets you connect well with the other people on the boat. After all, there are sixteen people aboard. You have to be able to do your job well and you have to be able to "interact with the people that are attached to the other end of the line you're pulling on," says Riley. Team cohesion is the most important factor. Individuals have to want to make their teammates look good. "At the last try-out we had a bow person we thought was pretty good," Riley remembers. "Then we put a different person in the pit and we realized the pit person was really good and he was making the bow person look pretty good. If we can all make each other look good then we're there."

For Riley, the goal is to win the Cup back and bring it back to the U.S. To do so, she has assembled a team of people who believe in her corporately and personally and have come to San Francisco despite very limited resources. "We're not the well-funded, you're-going-to-get-rich kind of syndicate," Riley accepts. "Our budget is $28 million. Only $3.2 million of that goes to the sailing team and that includes operations, travel, housing, and salaries for four years." Compare those numbers to the annual salary of one player in the NBA or any other professional sport and you understand her difficulty. "You go someplace else if you're looking for a paycheck. If you're looking for passion to play, you come here."

> "You don't grovel. You don't beg. You have to keep your dignity ... But, I did punch a guy one time."

Like any CEO, Riley must size up the competition to be successful. And there is plenty of competition to size up. The New York Yacht Club clearly has more money than anybody else, nearly all of it procured through private fundraising. But Riley counters that her San Francisco-based operation has a "better marketing base because we are truly American and we are truly accessible. We are coed and we represent diversity so we have a lot that corporate America wants to associate with." Riley's sponsors are definitely diverse, including an online broker, a law firm, an architect, a tool manufacturer, a luggage maker, a microbrewery and Australia's Qantas Airlines, among others.

"Probably overall the challenge that's going to be the toughest is New Zealand," Riley predicted before the champions defended their title. "They're doing it as that culture does, very methodically, very thoroughly."

Riley has been methodical and thorough herself. The very name *America True* was chosen to symbolize Riley's life long quest for accessibility. In her mind, everybody can come in. "We have a true youth program where at-risk kids get out on the water with people who sail to mentor them," Riley is proud to report. "And we have open tryouts. It might be a horrible experience for some because they might realize that they're never going to be at this level, but at least they know that and they can move on with their lives." The skeptic might ask whether *America True* is so true that even the boss has to try out for the team. "Let me put it this way," Riley replies, "I don't think there'll be a tryout, but if I'm not the best person for the job I won't be on the boat. If I'm not physically able or if all this takes too much time and energy, I've got to pull the plug out of one or the other. I would rather pull the plug on the management."

There is a depressing phenomenon that happens when a project is done or a play has closed or a goal has been achieved. You start wondering what you are going to do next. "After the first Whitbread," Riley allows, "I was exhausted and I didn't have anything else to go to so I took naps in the afternoon. I'd never done that before in my life. I was just overwhelmed with 'what am I going to do now?'" Not this time around. Riley has already begun to think about the options. "A lot of people would say I'll never quit because sailing is my life. No, it's time to live another life. Maybe a teacher." But after 20 years of steering the gender issue into the winds of sailing and one enormous effort to cap it with the Cup, can she walk away with no regrets if she doesn't win? "No regrets. Success is doing something that's bigger than you are and being comfortable and happy with just doing that. You have to be satisfied with what you've done that day. And I am very satisfied."

Riley is comfortable, relaxed, content, antithetical in many ways to what you would stereotypically expect of captain and syndicate chief. "I made a pact to myself that I'm going to be happy," Riley explains. "I'm doing what I like to do and I'm not obsessed with money or fame or any of that kind of stuff. I'd like to win, but losing wouldn't be a destructive result. It can't be." In her journey from fun sailing to the business of sailing, Riley has had her share of losses. She continues full steam ahead to win but she knows the winds are unpredictable. "If we lost I don't want people to say, damn it, I wasted four years of my life. This sucked. I want them to be crushed and heart-broken that we lost, but I want them to realize that they had still done something worthwhile."

In late 1999, 11 boats (five American) from seven nations battled each other for the Louis Vuitton Cup and the right to challenge *Team New Zealand*, winners of the previous America's Cup in 1995. Following three round robin competitions, six boats, including Riley's, won enough races to reach a semifinal round. Although Riley and her crew picked up wins against other American semifinalists, *AmericaOne* of the St. Francis Yacht Club and Dennis Conner's boat *Stars and Stripes*, Riley's team went 0-6 against the French, Italian, and Japanese entries and was eliminated with the fifth-place finish. Despite the final standing, two *America True* members were selected by *Sailing World* magazine to its "Dream Team."

AmericaOne and *Prada Challenge* from Italy faced each other in a best-of-9 series that the Italian boat narrowly won 5-4, and earned the right to take on defending *Team New Zealand*. The Kiwis won the 30th America's Cup with a 5-0 shut out over Italy, and were hailed as "intuitive, purposeful, aggressive, focused, and dominant."

On their return to San Francisco on May 11, 2000, Riley, helmsperson John Cutler, and COO G. Christopher Coffin were presented with plaques from SFYC members. The inscription reads: "You have touched us with your determination, you have awed us with your seamanship, and you have humbled us with your dedication and achievement."

In accepting the award, Riley then announced, "We still have unfinished business, because we are going back in 2003," making it clear that Dawn Riley will continue her quest for the America's Cup.

Chapter 7

It's Ultimately About Perseverance

Mark Allen

Six-Time Winner of the
Hawaii Ironman Championships

Mark Allen swam competitively from the time he was 10 until he graduated from college in 1980. But like most of us, he was mediocre. Two years later he was sitting in his apartment near the beach wondering what he was going to do with his life. He tried several careers. Life guarding was enjoyable, but didn't feel right.

One Saturday, he turned on the television to watch ABC's *Wide World of Sports*. The program was covering an event that Allen knew absolutely nothing about.

"I had never even heard of a triathlon before," Allen recalls. The visuals were of a young woman riding a bike in Hawaii. The announcer spoke of an "iron man" competition. As he watched, Allen was drawn into the beauty and athleticism of the woman's performance.

The event was the 1982 Hawaii Ironman Triathlon, a race in which an emotionally and physically exhausted Julie Moss stunned the world by crawling on her hands and knees across the finish line. The exploit has been named one of the top five visual images in sport. "There I was in my living room by myself having this private sob moment. It was very emotional watching that and I wondered why anybody would do that."

Ruminating on what he had seen, Allen decided to go to Hawaii and try the race once himself. "I thought Julie was the most amazing person I had ever seen. Her performance was truly inspiring. I also figured if I had to train for a 2.4-mile swim, a 112-mile bike ride and a 26.2-mile run, I wouldn't have time to think about what I was going to do with my life for at least nine months."

Allen had some old running shoes, a swimsuit and a pair of goggles. To round out the necessary equipment, he bought a used bike and began. During that year he did well enough in regional triathlons to obtain a sponsorship from local companies. At the end of the competitive season, a La Jolla, California, investment firm invited him to compete for their triathlon team and offered to pay him a salary. "I said, 'That's for me.' One attempt turned into a 15-year career."

Allen made his Ironman debut in 1983, but for six years he never seriously contended for the title. "I had six races in Hawaii where my results ranged from OK to totally disastrous." The breakthrough came in 1989. Allen outran Ironman legend Dave Scott in the closing minutes of the 140.6-mile event. It was a victory Allen and Julie Moss celebrated together with a wedding. Allen went on to win the next five Ironman Triathlon World Championships in which he competed between 1990 and 1995 (he took 1994 off to focus on his family and recharge himself). He also won 10 consecutive Nice Triathlon titles in France as well as many others around the world.

Allen won his final Ironman in 1995 in a dramatic and awesome fashion. Behind by nearly 13 minutes at the start of the marathon, Allen began to tick off the minutes and the competitors in front of him to pull off one of the greatest victories in Ironman history. "I knew in my mind that this would be my last race in Hawaii," Allen remembers. "I trained as hard as I ever had and knew that I would have to give this race everything I had left in order to win. It proved to be the perfect bookend finish to my career."

Allen announced his retirement during a press conference at the 1996 Ironman. He went on to serve as a commentator for NBC Sports' coverage of the event and later appeared on the cover of *Outside* magazine, which named him "The World's Fittest Man." In 1997, Allen was inducted into the Ironman Hall of Fame, joining his wife, who was enshrined three years earlier. "It's pretty wild when I think about it," Allen says. "It's not surprising to me that she is in the hall of fame. She inspired a lot of people with her performance, including me. But back in 1982, if someone would have said I might someday be in the hall of fame, I would have laughed."

Still living near the beach with Julie and their son, Mats, Allen is once again thinking about what to do with the rest of his life. His strongest interest is motivational speaking, which his fame gives him opportunity to do and through which his insights give listeners opportunity to explore. "To win the Ironman, you have to have patience," Allen advises. "There's no one part of the race that is the key. It looks like the run is because that's the last part, but it's not. It's really a swim, a bike, and a run, three separate sports. It's a triathlon, one sport with three different elements. It's definitely a waiting game, having the patience to be first across the finish line and not first out of the water or first at the end of the bike or first halfway through the run. You can lead the race all day but unless you cross the line first, you haven't won it."

Allen knew the truth of such a statement first hand. Before his seventh Ironman appearance in 1989, and his first win, he was totally intimidated by the event. "It's a tough event under tough conditions. It's long and I don't care who you are, it's a daunting task and a huge part of me was afraid of it." He was afraid of the distance, afraid of falling apart, and the more races he had where he did fall apart, the bigger the fear became. Like for so many of us, there was nothing to support the fact that it was possible, that he had the ability to win. There was plenty to remind him of his weaknesses, frailties, insecurity, doubt, and fear.

So before that fateful 1989 race, Allen made a change. "I decided just to go over there as who I am," Allen explains. Before, I was trying to imitate the aura of the guys that had won. I was trying to be something I wasn't."

Maybe it was the attitude shift that opened Allen's mind to discovery. But to this day he considers a pre-race experience transformational. Allen was flipping through a magazine trying to keep his mind off his race when he came across an advertisement for a workshop in Mexico. The ad showed an old Indian man with a big smile, totally happy, speaking to the participants. No big deal. In the race, Allen was stroke for stroke with defending champion Dave Scott on the swim, with him on the bike, and with him half way through the run when his energy started to go. "He was going to do it to me again," remembers Allen. "Then right at that moment I saw out of the corner of my eye the image of the old Indian floating near me and I felt like he was giving me this energy and then, wham, he was gone. From that moment on I just got stronger and stronger and won the race."

"You have to enjoy the people that you're around when you do whatever it is you do because if you don't, you're going to be an unhappy person."

The apparition was the face of Don Jose Matsuwa, a shaman of the Huichol tribe in Mexico. A year later, Allen attended the workshop he had seen advertised. Matsuwa died in 1990, but his hand-picked successor, an American named Brant Secunda, enlightened Allen. He taught Allen how to develop a relationship with an energy that's much greater than his own. Interestingly, "God" in the Huichol language also translates as "energy." The training gave Allen insight into his purpose in life.

Many native cultures contend we are all meant to have that kind of a connection. "It's part of life, not something you do on the weekends," Allen explains. "It's wrapped into everything that you do. Making a conscious connection with that empowers us as human beings and simplifies our lives."

Allen believes the mental shift separated him from the other competitors. "We all do the physical work and a lot of guys do more than me," Allen admits. "In fact, if I had to do the training that those guys do to get second or third I wouldn't have done it, I couldn't have done it. I realized that there's more to reaching your potential than just doing the physical work, even if it's a physical event."

The transformation was not something Allen had studied to enhance his ability to race the Ironman. It was the other way around. He made a change in his worldview and it affected everything in his life, including his performance. "The most humbling thing about the Ironman," Allen now understands from a distance, "is that it forces you to let go of your ego. When you're out there for eight hours and your body is so tired, you can't imagine how you're going to take another step, that ego is long gone. My ego, that pride, that desire had enabled me to the point where I was within an inch of being able to win it. But that last inch always stayed ahead of me until my ego finally died and I was just there doing the race and it didn't matter whether I won or not. It became more the proverbial journey, just being with it and giving it everything I had, regardless of whether I came up short or not. I realized that in the earlier Ironman races I was trying to satisfy that ego and after that it felt like there was a switch."

As Allen sits at the beach contemplating his extraordinary achievement and his future, he has discovered lessons from his career in triathlon that are important parallels to life. The motivational speaking provides the platform to share those with his audience. "When I was racing, so many things were second nature to me that I now see people need to know beforehand. The most important is how to be quiet, how to be patient, to ride it out, and to take it all the way to the finish."

If you look at really basic greatness, it is about people who have consistency in their lives, people who say one thing and live what they are saying. Allen clearly operates that way. "You have to enjoy the people that you're around when you do whatever it is you do because if you don't, you're going to be an unhappy person. What you get out of your endeavor and what you give by doing it is only going to be a half a thing. The people who are at the top didn't do it that way. They did what they did because it was something that they enjoyed and they enjoyed those around them in the process."

Allen's story points out that even in the most grueling of endeavors, it is not about doing a lot of work. It is about doing the right kind of work. The rest of the time he let it go. "I took two months off every year after Hawaii and about two and a half months before Hawaii, I would take a week off. People would look at me like I was nuts wondering how I could possibly take off a week in the height of the season. But, it's really simple. Achieving requires doing the right kind of work at the right time. Just because you're busy doesn't mean you're going to achieve what you want to achieve. Being busy does not equate to effectiveness. Life and achievement are best approached one day at a time."

Craig Breedlove
Six-Time Holder of the
World Land Speed Record

On December 18, 1898, Frenchman Gaston Chasseloup-Laubat drove his Jeantaud electric automobile 39.245 miles per hour to set the first recognized world land speed record. Just over 100 years later, British driver Andy Green and American designer/driver Craig Breedlove are engaged in a head-to-head battle to push their jet-powered cars past the unthinkable speed of sound, which varies according to weather and altitude but is approximately 748.111 miles per hour. When accomplished, it would be the 50th time the world land speed record had been exceeded. Breedlove, the first man to drive 400, 500 and 600 miles per hour, set the standard five of those times.

Photo credit: Peter Brock

"From the conception of the automobile, some guy has asked, 'How fast will it go?' So, there has always been an automobile speed record. From that standpoint my achievement is historical and credible," Breedlove articulates loudly to be heard above the noise in the ramshackle diner. "As to the significance? One criterion for significance today is that the achievement has to be global. The land speed record has that. But who knows if 2,000 years from now any of this will really even exist? So foremost, it is something that I can do, that I am interested in, and that has credibility to it. Whether it's significant, I'm not sure."

It's nearly noon and the Black Rock Café is buzzing with activity. A handful of locals are downing their grub and coffee at the counter. Seated at two small tables are a half dozen of Breedlove's racing team. All the men in the room look dirty and tired save Breedlove. Attired in his Nomex fire-resistant red, white, and blue racing suit, he has only recently awakened and he is primed, impatient, and preoccupied by the details of the forthcoming events.

While the rest of the desert is empty and silent, Breedlove and his men are still hard at work to accomplish their supersonic mission. "I don't seek the fame, I am just pursuing a goal," Breedlove states between bites of eggs and potatoes. "When I was younger I had a real strong desire to leave some kind of mark. I was 20 at the time, had three children, was working on the fire department, and wondered why I was on the planet. What am I going to do? Was I just going to be here and leave, and no one will know I was ever here?

I tried to assess what talents I had and what I could do that would be meaningful, or important. And you can't pick some goal like brain surgery where there is no possible way to get there from here."

"Here" was Costa Mesa, California. Breedlove's father was a special effects engineer in the film industry. His mother was a dancer who had performed with Fred Astaire. Breedlove bought his first car at 13 and was racing by 16 in timed speed trials along the dry lakes of the Mojave Desert. After graduating from Venice High School, Breedlove worked as a technician in the structural engineering division of Douglas Aircraft before becoming a Costa Mesa firefighter. "At that time, I had been in speed racing and drag racing and I was interested in motor sports but I was not in a position financially to pursue things like Indianapolis. I knew people in the land speed thing and one of them said there were three ingredients to setting speed records: ingenious design ability, a huge bank account and far more desire than common sense. I was plentifully endowed with two of the three." He was also enormously impressed with driver Mickey Thompson. Known as "Mr. Speed," Thompson set 295 records on the Bonneville Salt Flats in Utah and was the first American to unofficially break the 400 mph barrier. "He really showed people like me that you can do anything if you quit listening to everybody who says you can't and just start. That's really the big thing, you know."

> "People are very understanding if you lay out to them the situation you're up against. If you're candid about everything, you build respect."

It is no small thing to keep going against circumstances that knock you down along the way. In 1958 at the Bonneville Salt Flats, Breedlove used a supercharged Oldsmobile engine on a streamlined car to hit 236 mph. It was a far cry from the existing record of 364.196 mph set by Britain's John Cobb in 1947 on the same desert, but Breedlove was making a name for himself, and sponsors started to fill in the missing second ingredient. Fate played a more dramatic role. "We were involved in an American Motors-sponsored project for the Wheel Driven Record and we had just come back from Bonneville and set the engines on the shop floor," Breedlove reports. "I had gone to Seattle for a car show so the car was actually in Seattle but the engines were back in the shop. While I was in Seattle I got a call from my crew that the shop had been flooded. I had just gotten a divorce and had moved all my furniture to the shop. Everything was destroyed. The financial loss was so great, American Motors withdrew its sponsorship. Those things are not cool. There are circumstances that occur in life that you can't control, and that's one of them."

Without an automobile engine, Breedlove did what any red-blooded, American adventurer would do. "I decided to turn the car into a rocket car because we didn't have any engines." With rocket power, Breedlove's car set a quarter-mile speed record of 377 mph that still stands today.

Breedlove paid $500 for a surplus military J47 jet engine and set a new goal to design and build the first *Spirit of America* land speed record vehicle. For three years, with help from Shell and Goodyear, Breedlove labored on his revolutionary concept. "If you look at the whole thing you'll never start because it's so overwhelming," extols Breedlove. "You've got to break it down into a beginning, middle, and end, and break those three into segments. Then you start and you don't worry about how you're going to get there. You just pick off things and get those done. You build up to your worst problems last, knowing that you have solutions to all of them and you just need the wherewithal to get there." In 1962, he took the car to Bonneville to attack Cobb's record but handling problems prevented him from accomplishing the task.

Photo credit: Peter Brock

As people accomplish things, those accomplishments often build their own momentum. The fact that you have accomplished one thing inspires others to join in and participate because they sense the commitment and the energy, and begin to see the dream. But, equally often, you run into realities that clog the path to the ultimate achievement. Breedlove says, "No problem. You simply differentiate the things you can do and the things you have no control over. In this business you run into many weather and mechanical problems. But people are very understanding if you lay out to them the situation you're up against. If you're candid about everything, you build respect. If something is your fault and you acknowledge it, you build credibility. And if you get down stream, and you're literally against the wall, and you say, 'Look, we need this thing,' they know from dealing with you, they can take it to the bank." The sponsors remained aboard.

The following year, Breedlove returned to Bonneville with a stable vehicle and was able to set a new official speed record of 407.447 mph and return the record to America for the first time in 35 years. During the next two years, Breedlove pushed the record higher four times battling against four land speed rivals. In October 1964, he eclipsed the 500 mph barrier, scorching the salt flats at 526.277 mph. "When you're zooming along, it's exhilarating," Breedlove says with a sparkle in his eyes. "It's incredible, the ultimate sensation of speed. You can't find that in aircraft because you're not related to things. You're definitely related to your environment in the car. You have to have precise control because it has to go down a 50-foot wide lane and you're six inches off the ground, so you can see all your markers and desert stuff coming at you."

The new record came at a high price. After surpassing the mark, Breedlove's wheel brakes failed. In addition, he lost both of his parachutes trying to bring the vehicle to a stop. The car slammed through a row of telephone poles at 400 mph and dove into an 18-foot deep salt brine pond at 200 mph. Breedlove was miraculously unhurt and swam to safety, but it was the final run for the original *Spirit of America*. The car has been on display at the Museum of Science and Industry in Chicago ever since.

It takes a different kind of individual to sit in a rocket car and hurtle along the earth at such speeds. "It's really simple," Breedlove suggests. "If a negative thought enters your mind, you get it out of there fast. It's really all about positive thinking. You simply regard the vehicle and the whole endeavor in a very positive mental frame of mind, and you don't allow negative thoughts to persevere."

Like buying stocks, speed racing is a very risky thing. But there is clearly a different ethic in the people who are involved with NASCAR than those involved with NASDAQ. "I've run across individuals in business that would literally sell their grandmother for 20 grand." Breedlove says. "In motor sports, individuals will simply put their life on the line whether they get paid or not."

The accident also placed Breedlove in a financial quagmire. "The cash flow thing got to be big. You have $200,000 worth of balls in the air that are going to all come down, and you're going to have to hang onto them. To keep yourself from going crazy you can't get emotionally involved. You just pay it off at $35 a month if you have to. But a certain amount of credibility comes from that and it's nice when you get it behind you. It isn't much fun to go through, but that's life."

Ah yes, life. Life is very fragile. We don't even know whether we will be here tomorrow. And the thing that stops people dead in their tracks is that unknown, a fear of what the future might bring. It does not stop Breedlove. "People tell me 'What if you do this and you fail and you end up flat broke and you're 65 years old, what are you going to do then?' Well, I might not make it to 65, so I better get off the couch."

Breedlove not only got off the couch, he built a new car. The *Spirit of America Sonic 1*, equipped with a more powerful J79 jet engine, set a new speed standard of 600.601 mph in November 1965. The record stood five years until American Gary Gabelich took his rocket-powered *Blue Flame* to 622.407 mph.

Over the next 25 years, Bonneville deteriorated from years of salt removal and drainage for commercial projects, and government restrictions on the use of rocket engines and fuels curtailed American efforts to raise the record. In 1983, Richard Noble brought the record back to England as his *Thrust 2* roared across the Black Rock Desert in Nevada at 633.470 mph.

During that same 25-year period, Breedlove and his team toiled with new designs and new fuels to regain the record and carry them past the next two grand plateaus: 700 mph and the sound barrier. For Breedlove, his team was and is his life support. Its cohesion and camaraderie evolved slowly but thoroughly. "The hard task is to get a synergy of people who can be together day in and day out like any championship sports team," Breedlove explains. "Deion Sanders might be the best defensive back going, but he might not work with his team because, for whatever reason, he doesn't fit with the organization. Happens in motor sports too."

The problems are compounded with Breedlove's organization. Breedlove lives and works on his car in Rio Vista, a town of 3,000 people in central California, and, unlike an NFL team, he has limited financial resources. "This is not a government project, so we have to be very cost effective. Our funding comes from my personal wealth or by what I get from sponsors. It's not like the government ghost in Northrop when they wanted an advanced tactical fighter. No $20 billion and no 20,000 people so a big bureaucracy can churn out the product."

Photo credit: Peter Brock

But like a tactical fighter, Breedlove needs people with specialized talents, particularly metal workers. They have to be willing to sacrifice income and move to Rio Vista. "There aren't many aluminum people in the United States anymore like 20 years ago," Breedlove expounds. "We had to go to England to find them. And then, they have to be willing to come over here and you have to be able to afford them and live a pretty tough existence." Most live next to the shop in RV trailers. Sometimes there is an apartment. But, more often than not, they crash after a hard and long day's work on mattresses on the floor in a warehouse while their home is halfway around the world.

Sometimes they just don't work out. Most frequently, their temperament was not suitable. Occasionally, the task was more than they bargained for. The project and the demands were unreasonable. Breedlove did a lot of searching and selecting and changing before he found the team that stands beside him every day. "Sometimes you've got to kiss a lot of frogs to find your princes," Breedlove laughs. "And turnover and change are really hard because usually folks get very emotionally involved. And if they don't work out it's very difficult to make the change because they don't want to acknowledge it's not working out. But you do these things with the most ethics and the most love that you can."

It's late fall 1997. Another day of the Duel in the Desert is about to begin. The locals have long gone from the café. Designer Richard Noble and his new driver, Andy Green, the British entrants in the two-nation contest have long since departed from Gerlach, Nevada, a sleepy desert town two hours north of Reno. Eight weeks earlier, Green ignored the threat of rain showers and powered the 10-ton, twin engine *Thrust SSC* to 700.661 mph on the first of two timed runs down the 13-mile course. He then turned around within the allotted one hour for a 728.008 mph blast. The 714.144 mph average shattered the 14-year-old record Noble had set in 1983. Four weeks ago, Green broke the sound barrier twice but failed to enter the record books because the second run came a minute later than the allotted hour. A few days later, October 15, one day before the 50-year anniversary of Chuck Yeager's historic first jet flight through the sound barrier, the error was muted. Green again broke the sound barrier twice, rocketing through the course at 759.333 mph on his first run and 30 minutes later set the record when he was clocked at 766.609 mph on his second attempt. That mark would stand as the record going into the new millennium.

> "Success teaches you absolutely nothing. It's the hardships in life you learn from. They make the indelible impressions. I've never learned a damn thing from success."

For months Breedlove and his crew awakened every day with promise in the air and headed back to camp unrequited. Today, he and his crew are eager and determined. "I don't know where thoughts come from exactly, but a thought has power, and a thought is the beginning of creation," Breedlove philosophizes. "The goal defines me to a certain degree. It's basically all that I do. It's certainly my most passionate interest." Breedlove steps in the truck that will take him out to the course. For the next 15 minutes he is just like any other commuter, heading to work, looking at the jagged landscape, chatting. "The pursuit of the land speed record has made my life very interesting. There are problems that arise but there are problems that arise out of everything. Life is a series of solving problems. There are problem makers and there are problem solvers. I consider myself one of the latter. You could pick things to do that are destructive and there have been people throughout history who have done that. It's really important that what you do is constructive."

As he approaches the course, Breedlove sees the lone reporter who has stayed with the story following Green's triumphant run and departure. He also sees two spectators. "I know that some people react to what I do as though I am a hero," Breedlove says softly, staring at the two figures in the wind. "That gentleman out there has been extremely moved by the thing. He was in tears and he had his son with him and it just struck him that to sit out of the front in that little plastic thing was beyond his comprehension. That's nice but I don't do it for the public interest. It's my passion. By and large, we don't have much of an audience out here."

Breedlove steps from the truck and offers a kind word to the three gathered in his name and then visits with the crew. The report is not very good. Weather and mechanical problems scuttle the effort. "You learn to respect yourself through all of this," Breedlove responds. "There is a great amount of personal satisfaction in going out and doing what you gave your word you would do. You honor that. The fulfillment of that promise is very, very satisfying. So, I'll keep trying. The only thing that I would like to gain is people's respect for what we've done. That's all; to have them look and say a lot of positive accomplishments resulted from the effort."

For more than 40 years, Breedlove has been preparing for one unforgettable, unbeatable blast across the sand. "If it were easy, everybody would be doing it," he jokes. "Success teaches you absolutely nothing. It's the hardships in life you learn from. They make the indelible impressions. I've never learned a damn thing from success."

The record did not happen in that fall of 1999. It hasn't since. But Breedlove and his crew will try again. Rest assured.

Ken Burns
Two-Time Emmy Award-Winning Filmmaker

Photo credit: Pam Tubridy
Baucom/Florentine Films

Ken Burns produced his first film for public television, *Brooklyn Bridge*, in 1981 and received an Academy Award nomination in 1982. He followed with another Academy Award nomination in 1986 for *The Statue of Liberty*, and then grabbed gold with back-to-back Emmy Awards for Outstanding Informational Series with *The Civil War* (1991) and *Baseball* (1994). While each film offered an exquisite portrait of American history, Burns did not begin his career as a historian or as a documentarian.

"Right from high school, I wanted to be a filmmaker," Burns begins with his customary articulate and meticulous manner of speaking. "I wanted to be John Ford. It was a way to connect with my family. My father and mother liked old movies and foreign movies, so to be a filmmaker was to honor some sense of tradition in my family." Right after high school, Burns enrolled at Hampshire College in Amherst, Massachusetts, only to discover there was no program in dramatic filmmaking. The focus was social documentary still photography, with documentary filmmaking as a companion subject. The error proved to be an opportunity. "I thrived there," Burns reports, "because I saw how much drama there is in real events, both past and present."

Burns sees life through powerful introspective lenses. He is moved profoundly by those elements of life that for most people seem disconnected. "We are all beneficiaries of fortuitous happenstance that can come in unrecognizable packages," Burns proposes. "My mother died when I was 11 years old. I wouldn't be here talking to you if she hadn't died because the alchemy of responses that I had to that event created who I am now. So, in that tragedy was a certain amount of luck."

Burns brings the same probing viewpoint to his never-ending analysis of human behavior and he offers a historical illustration to reiterate that luck often does not appear as luck. "Franklin Roosevelt was essentially a rich man born to privilege and power who breezed his way through government service and extramarital affairs. Suddenly he is brought up short by infantile paralysis and transforms himself — without abandoning the frivolous — into one of the most compelling political figures in the 20th Century. One wonders whether that was in store for him without this impairment that rocked the foundations of who he was. It is much more likely that it took this intervention to provide the final impetus towards greatness."

Few people look at the intricacies of life with such laser precision as does Burns. Most individuals are preoccupied with their search for comfort, companionship, shelter, and occupation. Burns even dares to slice into them. "Within each human being there is a grain of possibility and spirituality. I believe that firmly," Burns whispers. "The human organism has a responsibility to evolve: not physically, but spiritually or rationally."

Burns says we are duty-bound to develop our spiritual or rational faculties. He views life as an inescapable imperative. "The gift of human life is the gift of consciousness, not just life," he expounds. "Consciousness implies a responsibility. A responsibility to the past, a responsibility to the present, and a responsibility to the future." Burns cites Abraham Lincoln who in the Gettysburg Address cast his audience back to Thomas Jefferson's framework of equality and described a better future by challenging America at that moment to live up to its words.

Whether the subject is sport or war or urbanization, Burns weaves compelling narration and marvelous visual images into a message. By his own admission, it is the same message every time. "I am driven," Burns admits enthusiastically. "I love my country and have a fairly complex sense of what real patriotism is. I feel there are movements and tendencies and disruptions in the fabric of who we are right now that require someone to sing epic Homeric verses operatically before this electronic campfire that might remind people why we agreed to cohere as a people."

Historian Arthur Schlesinger Jr. once borrowed the Latin motto imprinted on US money — *E Pluribus Unum* (out of many, one) — and suggested that there was "too much *pluribus* and not enough *unum*." Burns is driven to articulate that *unum*. "It's not a candy-coated morning-in-America vision," Burns challenges. "It is a true, honest, complicated one that's unafraid of controversy and tragedy but equally drawn to those stories and moments that suggest an abiding faith in the human spirit, and the unique role this remarkable republic has in the positive progress of mankind."

He must be succeeding. Forty-five million people watched his Emmy-winning films, *The Civil War* and *Baseball*. Few books sell that many copies; a bestseller may sell one million and be considered a huge success. The result is surely due to Burns' style, which seems more like an emotional archeologist than a historian, as he excavates out of the dates and facts a narrative story that has meaning and feeling.

We learn best about who we are by the way we relate to past behaviors or events. In that context, Burns views history as our national mirror with the life of the country developing along a path similar to the life of a human being. "*The Civil War* was the traumatic event in the childhood of our nation, just like mine was my mother's death," Burns explains. "We tried to struggle out of adolescence in Vietnam and into adulthood. And we are right now striving towards aware maturity. And one of the ways in which you have an aware maturity is to have a past and to involve yourself in it."

Burns' films serve as national discussions, water-cooler engagements. By the time he finishes his current project on the history of jazz, he will have placed three seminal topics on the table for our consideration. "*Jazz* is the final panel of a triptych with *Civil War* and *Baseball*," Burns identifies. "They are big, nine-part series that are about race and the soul of the country."

> "Within each human being there is a grain of possibility and spirituality… The human organism has a responsibility to evolve: not physically, but spiritually or rationally."

They are also no easy matter to produce. All of Burns' films take between five and six years to complete. To accomplish the task, Burns founded Florentine Films and has assembled a talented company of researchers, writers, editors, and technicians for whom he is director. "I succeed first because I have the ability to chose the people who work with me. This is a collaborative medium. The phrase 'Ken Burns' film' is like referring only to the conductor of a symphony. It's an easy shorthand but there are virtuoso instrumentalists who contribute to making it happen."

While Burns appreciates the creative input of his chosen, he relies on their tenacity for the output. "It's ultimately about perseverance," Burns advises. "Thomas Edison had the famous line that 'Success is 98 percent perspiration and only two percent inspiration,' and that is utterly true. There is a sense of doggedness to it all. You just do your job. You get up every morning and it's no different from making a highway or building a bridge. If you think it is going to be anything less, you can lose your way pretty quickly."

Burns literally makes countless numbers of decisions in the course of making one film: type of shot, background color, sequence, music, narrator voice, and a mind-boggling list of others. "The real joy is focusing, being attentive, and thinking of solutions to problems. Getting better is really a relative term," Burns suggests. "It's an evolution of style." Style is how you approach problems. Learning when and how to approach problems successfully is one of the landmarks of a well-lived career. Burns applies the litmus test to his career as well. "I'm glad I didn't do Jefferson, a topic I had wanted to do from the beginning of my professional life, until 1997, because the film required some sophistication to portray the interior, the intellectual ideas and complicated psychology of the man. If I had tried it earlier it might not have been as successful for me."

Burns does not mean success by standards imposed from the world at large. In fact, that success doesn't really matter to him. Burns judges success by a complex set of standards that arise from within and begin with self-satisfaction. "I used to be defined by anxiety. Actually thought it was an important ingredient to success," Burns confesses. "To some extent it is because anxiety is the acknowledgment of the critical importance this action is to you and you always want to have your work invested with that. But as I've grown older, I've absorbed the body blows of external criticism so I am much more calm. I'm not free of anxiety because I realize that adrenaline is a necessary part of achieving, but it's absolutely erroneous to believe that someone else's opinion is important for success. It's not, and freeing yourself from those mental traps allows you to grow."

Photo credit: Lisa Berg

Success is not about money or power either. In fact, too often, Burns finds the two as impediments to understanding success. "Money and power are huge forces," Burns begins, repeating the word "huge" several times. "They are the source of a great number of positive things and, unfortunately, an equal if not greater amount of negative things. We see the damage that money does and the way money has come to define success when it just isn't true."

For Burns, finding success requires going past the accomplishments, past the money and power the accomplishments may bring, and into the person. "As we select heroes today, we forget to look in places where money is not the definition," Burns continues. "Bill Gates is not a hero. Neither is Michael Jordan. Not until they do something beyond their wealth and talent. Hero is a narrative situation in which somebody struggles and negotiates with both positive and negative qualities and it is the fascinating outcome of the struggle that tells the story."

That is not the definition for most of teenage America. In survey after survey, when teens are asked to name their heroes, money-drenched athletes and entertainers top the list. Burns has yet to complete *Jazz*, but he can talk at length about baseball.

"Jackie Robinson is a hero because he not only negotiated the complicated world of athletics in the most difficult sport there is, and did it magnificently, but he overcame in almost biblical dimensions, the resistance, the inertia, of an entire nation, if not an entire world. So it's a great story. Babe Ruth is not a hero but Ted Williams made himself a hero when in his first nanosecond as a Hall of Famer, he asked in his induction speech where were Satchel

Page and Josh Gibson and the other great Negro League players who were not in the Hall of Fame at the time. He took a moment that could have been entirely his own and gave it over to something else. That is heroic character."

When pressed to identify the top three heroes of America, Burns pulls the figures out from his own films: Abraham Lincoln, Jackie Robinson, Louis Armstrong. The common among them? "Love," Burns nearly sings. "It's the oldest force and as far as I can tell, that's what it's all about. They were gifts to us all. That's the other thing. We're so egocentric today. We live in an age in which the 'I' is so big that we all do everything from the big 'I.' These people gave themselves to us."

It is not that Burns fails to take pleasure when people ask him to sign an autograph or tell him how much they enjoy his films. It is not that Burns rejects the revenues from his films and their syndication or regrets the commanding place he holds in the cinema world. He accepts all of the accoutrements of his achievements, but only briefly and then moves on. "I haven't really changed the habits of my life," Burns emphasizes. "I haven't changed the way I dress, which, strangely enough, is one of the ways people manifest that. I haven't bought a lot of suits. I haven't bought a new car. I have been blessed with a great deal of money and I've been fairly judicious about it. I haven't moved. I live in the same small house in the same little town where all of my fame and celebrity, plus 50 cents, get me a cup of coffee. And that's the only way it should be."

Burns has not changed his work habits either. He continues to get up every morning and build his highway through history. While the amount of time that he spends perspiring in the edit room has been costly on his personal life, he is proud to report that he is a single father. "My relationship with my children has been strengthened through all of it, which is exactly what most people who have achieved these sort of things tell you that they don't have. It's the one thing I've insisted not change. But as a single father who does a lot of cooking and cleaning and homework, which I love, and because I live in a remote area in New Hampshire, set apart, I don't have much of a social life. I miss that connection."

As Burns continues his work on the final film in his trilogy, he takes a moment to assess what it is he has done. "The best you could hope for is that you created something that was creating in its own right, that it continued to affect in a positive way, even if it made someone uncomfortable but woke them up, even if it disturbed somebody but changed their molecular structure and that someone did something as a result of that." As if to answer his own analysis, Burns points to his first film as a source for contentment. The story of building the Brooklyn Bridge literally marked its centennial, occurring 18 months after he finished the film. When the bridge was 100 years old, the front page of the *New York Times* showed a couple from Twin Falls, Idaho, walking across the bridge and Burns realized the real power of his work. "I knew they were there because of my film," Burns recalls excitedly. "And I turned to the article and sure enough, they said they'd seen a documentary on television about the building of the bridge and decided to take their vacation in New York and to show their kids the Brooklyn Bridge. And I just went, yes! There's a lot of black holes, lots of places and people and happenstance that suck light out of things and I just want to bring light into some corner. I want to be considered a patriot, a good American, and a good father. That's all."

For 25 years, Burns has continued his dogged quest to sing the Homeric story that would revitalize the America that lives within his soul. The impending final act in his opera causes deep reflection. "There is this pathology, a horrible sense of, 'Well we're done now, what do I do next?' I'm not particularly pleased about that. I've been a person who's been merciless on my own self. I haven't taken an extended time off since I began this in the mid seventies. It's time to take stock, to perhaps go back and collect the old dream of dramatic films, though I don't see that as a step up on a career ladder. In fact Robert Penn Warren tells me careerism is death, and I absolutely believe him. You can't do this into your 80s at the pace that I maintain."

Burns may actually never die. One of the measures of immortality in our current culture is becoming the subject of an editorial cartoon. After *The Civil War* there were a half dozen and after *Baseball* maybe 50 more. Some illuminated the content. Others shed some light on Burns. One summed it up pretty well. It showed this bleary-eyed couple sitting on a couch with the TV set blaring and out of the TV was a bubble with the announcer saying, "Coming soon to PBS, *O.J.*, a 2,750 hour documentary." The old man on the couch says, "Ken Burns has to be stopped."

No way.

Bob Dole

Former U.S. Senator and
1996 Republican Candidate for President

Had he been elected in 1996, Bob Dole would have been 73 in his first year as President of the United States. That would have made him four years older than Ronald Reagan when he ascended to the White House 16 years earlier. But with his defeat, Dole very likely became the last World War II veteran to run for the nation's highest office. He continues to evoke an America fast fading into history.

Dole is a traditional conservative and a man skilled at bare-knuckles politics. He is a legislative pragmatist and a deal maker. He is all about getting things done and getting them done appropriately. "There are only very few truly great people in the world in each generation," Dole muses. "It's not what you are. You could be poor and still be great. It's what you've accomplished, what you have done to make a difference. And, it's who you are." And when historians shine the light of examination on Bob Dole he hopes he will be "perceived as somebody of integrity and honesty who had some barriers in life and overcame the barriers and got certain things done."

Although Dole spent most of his professional life as a legislator, representing Kansas in the United States Senate for nearly three decades, the presidency was the focus of his ambition for 20 years. He was the running mate of President Gerald Ford in 1976, but lost to the Democratic ticket of Jimmy Carter and Walter Mondale. He sought the nomination outright in 1980, only to make an early exit in the primaries. In 1988, he briefly campaigned as an alternative to George Bush.

With the defeat of Bush by Bill Clinton in 1992, Dole effectively became the commander-in-chief of the opposition, a rank he assumed in name after the election when he claimed a mandate from the nearly 57 percent who did not vote for Clinton that year. Dole finally won the GOP nomination on his third try in 1996. Of course, he and his running mate, former Congressman Jack Kemp, lost the general election to Clinton and Al Gore despite Dole taking the drastic step of resigning his Senate seat to concentrate on the campaign. However, Dole's legacy of leadership in the upper house endures.

Thwarted but not alienated, Dole always seemed to be in his element in Congress, preferring the back room to the pressroom. "There are those who may be celebrities only for their allotted 15 minutes," Dole notes. "Celebrity status doesn't mean that you accomplish that much. You can, but it's the exception rather than the rule." Indeed, because media powerfully shape the way the public views individuals, we are at times duped into identifying exceptional leaders who may be merely attractive. Dole continues. "I've always felt there were a lot of outstanding House members who were never fully recognized because the press focused on Senators, inviting them on the talk shows more than House members. It wasn't that they had any more legislative skills or any more wisdom, but the media shape who gets the attention. But if you're going to really leave some footprints behind, it's not one month, one year, one term. It's a whole lifetime."

Dole sees himself as the personification of the American ideal, proof that hard work and determination can lift a man from humble roots and carry him through adversity to success. His belief in that ethic guided him through a political career that began in the chambers of the Kansas Legislature in Topeka and ended in the office of the Senate Majority Leader in Washington.

Much has been said about the impact on Dole of his handicap: the result of being hit by machine gun fire in Italy during the closing weeks of World War II while trying to save a fellow soldier. Dole's right arm was mangled and rendered permanently useless; initially he was not expected to survive. The future senator would spend the next three years rehabilitating his shattered body. Clearly his character was indelibly marked.

"My life was pretty uneventful until World War II," Dole acknowledges. "My leadership began in the platoon and was developed by overcoming a pretty serious disability. I just got off the phone with a woman who used to visit me in the hospital and she said, 'I remember when I first saw you; you were so determined.' There is really nothing exceptional about my life except I am determined."

No longer able to pursue his dream of becoming a doctor after the injury, Dole instead entered law school, earning his degree from Washburn Municipal University in Topeka, Kansas, in 1952. Before finishing his law degree, Dole won a term as a Republican in the Kansas House. Two years later, he became Russell County prosecutor. In 1960, he won the Republican primary for an open House seat and was an easy winner in the fall. "Everything that happened to me was rather serendipitous," Dole reports genuinely, seated on an expensive and tasteful sofa tucked neatly in a small alcove of his spacious and elegant Washington, D.C., law office. On either side of the sofa are large framed black and white photographs of his parents. "My parents were poor. My dad wore his overalls to work every day for 42 years. He didn't have any money or have any political influence, and I thought when I got elected to Congress I'd died and gone to heaven making $22,500 in 1961."

In 1962, the two western Kansas congressional districts were combined by reapportionment, pitting Dole against a Democratic incumbent. Dole won. He won again in 1964 and 1966. Then, in 1968, Dole competed for the GOP nomination for an open seat in the US Senate against former Gov. William H. Avery. Dole defeated Avery in the primary and had an easy time winning the election in the fall. "I wasn't being brought along by my parents or somebody with an agenda that this young man's going to be president or a candidate for president. One thing just led to another," Dole maintains. "I never knew I would be a leader. In fact, I'd been asked in the House to run for leadership. I didn't do it then and I was a little reluctant to do it in the Senate. But I did and I was elected."

"There are only very few truly great people in the world in each generation. It's not what you are ... It's what you've accomplished, what you have done to make a difference."

One of President Richard Nixon's staunchest backers in Congress, Dole was rewarded for his loyalty in 1971 by being named chairman of the Republican National Committee. Dole never got along with the White House staff, however, and was replaced as party head in January 1973. It was serendipity indeed, because as a result he largely escaped implication in the Watergate scandal that 19 months later would push Nixon out of office. Although he had been GOP chair in June 1972 when the infamous burglary occurred, Dole never knew what was going on. "Watergate happened on my night off," he later said.

But Dole was burdened by his Nixon connection and was attacked gruffly on the matter when running for re-election in Kansas in 1974. Dole struck back with an ad in which a mud-splattered poster of him was gradually wiped clean as he insisted on his honesty. Dole came from behind to win in what was otherwise a devastating year for Republicans at the polls nationwide. From then on he never looked back, facing only token opposition in his three subsequent re-election campaigns.

The Kansan re-emerged two years later as the running mate of Nixon's successor, Gerald Ford. However, many believe his negative debating style may have cost Ford a full term in the White House. While he never agreed with the analysis, Dole has rarely sounded as harsh since.

Dole was elected majority leader in 1984 and would remain the top Republican in the upper house for over a decade. In 1986, even as the defeats of several Senate GOP colleagues relegated him to a minority leadership role, Dole coasted and returned to the majority with his party eight years later. For Dole, the career was "something I thoroughly enjoyed. Right now I'm going back to Kansas on a monthly basis for a thank you tour, just going to all these little places and having coffee and cookies and sitting around visiting, saying thanks for 35 years of support."

You have to hold tight reigns on self-esteem and ambition and ego that can be so easily aggrandized with achievement and success. That is a hard task to accomplish in itself. Maybe it's his farm upbringing, but Dole seems to have his hands on the straps at all times. "It's always my view," Dole attests, "that when you think you're pretty important you need to take a trip back home because to people there you're Bob, not Senator Dole. You go to a town meeting and you get tough questions whereas around Capitol Hill everybody is saying, 'Oh yes, sir' and 'You're wonderful.' You have to keep your perspective and remember where you're from and how you got there. If you forget how you got there and forget who got you there, just ordinary people for the most part, you lose touch with the folks back home, which is fatal in our business."

Dole seldom forgets his roots. His image, more now than ever, is as a man with enormous integrity and a tremendous sense of virtue. It is not something one sees in most of the public and it seems to appear even less in public officials. But Dole disagrees. "You see a lot of it around. People shortchange those of us in politics," Dole asserts. "One thing I learned very quickly, in the business of politics, particularly if you're a leader in the Senate, you have your word and whether you're dealing with a Democrat or Republican, liberal or conservative, if you make an arrangement with some person verbally and say, 'OK I'll see that this gets done,' you follow through. I think my Democratic and Republican colleagues — without exception — would say that Bob Dole always kept his word."

America has an image by many standards as a great country, and people like my immigrant parents come from all over the world hoping to take part somehow in the American dream. For Dole, the essence of the dream is in the virtues, not in the commodities. "I talked to people who came to my office after the Berlin Wall and the Soviet Union collapsed. They all gave the same message, many times with tears streaming down their cheeks, 'We want to be like America.'" Dole is ready for the rebuttal that the message is about economic power and foreign aid. "Sure, they'd like some technology. They want some help," Dole admits. "But they were here because they wanted to see the freest country in the world, who we were, and what we did to get there."

Historians and sociologists will argue the answer to that question forever. Dole has his answer already. It is the underpinnings of the right to vote and the right to travel, to religious freedom and access to education. When you look at these ideals you begin to understand why people look to America for leadership. You can't put your finger on any one thing. Rather, for Dole, it is a set of qualities that have been instilled by Dole's kind of people. "It's values you ought to get from your parents and your grandparents whether they're poor, rich, white, black," Dole states. "They were a generation of God-fearing, honest men and women of integrity and accountability. Of course our parents weren't unwilling to use the rod now and then, not often, but discipline was very important."

Photo credit: Sigrid Estrada

Dole and that generation not only survived World War II, they survived the aftermath. "We got out of the service, many of us with no money, and passed the GI Bill of Rights that changed America with one law because it gave millions of young men and women an opportunity they wouldn't have otherwise. We've got to do the same thing today for inner-city kids."

Some say America is on the threshold of seizing defeat from the jaws of victory because we possess the technology to solve many problems but we are unwilling to solve them because of self-interest. Dole is not among them; he is the supreme optimist. "We've got technology," Dole assents. "Just look at what the computer and the Internet are doing. On my flight back from the Letterman Show, a young lady was talking about her four-and-a-half-year-old son and the things this kid does on the computer. I wondered what is he going to be doing when he's six? It's just an explosion. Our problem today is not technology. It's values. It's honesty, integrity, courage, and accountability. It's not rocket science. The values are not outdated, just unused."

No longer in Congress, no longer seeking the presidency, Dole can stand at a bit of a distance and give advice comfortably and freely. One of his platforms has been a series of Success Seminars sponsored by Peter Lowe International. "I always kid the audience that the organizers wanted one failure with the rest of the success stories," Dole chides. "Once you're out of politics, if you conducted yourself as you should have, people suddenly see something they hadn't seen or they had forgotten. You have a certain added credibility and the integrity quotient goes up so people listen."

But at some point, even credible politicians have to bring the accomplishing to a close. Maybe it was the fatigue from his trip to Korea and Taiwan. Maybe it was realizing Mexico was next. Dole travels extensively as Chairman of the International Commission on Missing Persons. Whatever it is, Dole is finally giving retirement some thought, sort of. "I spent four days in the Balkans speaking to the presidents of Serbia and Croatia and Bosnia," Dole reports as the gleam in his eyes grows brighter. "About 30,000 people there disappeared. They're all dead. You go to these meetings and the mothers are there with their little buttons with pictures of their sons. That's important to me so I've agreed to help the Clinton administration."

He is also helping to raise $100 million for the World War II memorial. And then there are the requests from those ordinary people who got him there in the first place. "I've got that big pile of paper right there and half of them are requests to do something and you hate to say no, but you can't say yes. I like people, I like to go out and try to be helpful, and I get these great letters from young people, 'Please come to my graduation. You've been chosen unanimously to be our speaker.' It really makes you feel bad when you have to finally say no, but it can't go on forever."

But with his determination, he may just try to do so. After all, while you can appreciate the good in America today, there are still those problems that need to be solved. "It's time for folks to have some conviction and to believe in value-based leadership and to be committed," Dole extols. "It's still all about wanting to make a difference. There's no magic about it. If you really want to get in a position where you can make that happen in the world, you've got to determine what you want to do with your life."

Some people decide that when they're 18, some in their 20s or mid-50s. For Dole, it doesn't matter. "Whenever, go give it a try," Dole prods. "And if it doesn't work but you believe in what you're doing, try it again. It's like the president of South Korea, Kim Dae Jung. He tried four times and he finally made it at 74 years old. Act on your heart and do it no matter when or where you have to but don't wait for someone else to get it done. There are folks who have everything but the motivation. It's not great things that should move you. It's doing the right things. And be determined enough to survive defeat so you can celebrate the victory."

If anyone knows about surviving defeat and celebrating victory, it is Bob Dole, who enjoys more respect today than at any time in his career.

Chapter 8

Risk Is An
Essential Constituent

Paul Brainerd

Inventor of Desktop Publishing
and Founder of Aldus, Inc.

The Brainerd Foundation is tucked quietly in an unobtrusive building near Seattle's Pike Place Market. The foundation is dedicated to protecting the environmental quality of the Pacific Northwest by supporting grassroots projects that involve citizens in small communities. The clean, simple but attractive offices also serve as the headquarters for Social Venture Partners, a program through which high-tech professionals can give back time, money, and expertise to their communities.

The founder and president of both philanthropic organizations is Paul Brainerd. In 1984, Brainerd founded Aldus Corporation and coined the phrase "desktop publishing" for his software, Aldus PageMaker. The software allowed amateurs to perform creative layout and design functions on the computer for the first time, effectively revolutionizing how the printed word was produced. "I never associate myself with terms like exceptional," says the entrepreneur-turned-philanthropist. "People view what I accomplished as success and I would have to agree with that. We were very successful in what we did, but we had a good idea at the right time and some luck."

If you are fortunate to be in the right place and have the right people around you, extraordinary things can happen. Call it luck or timing, but that is exactly what happened to Brainerd. In order to create desktop publishing, Brainerd needed the processing power to display graphics on a screen so people could see an electronic pasteboard. In 1984, Apple released the first mass-produced computer with such a capability, the Macintosh. He also needed to print high-quality output at low cost, and about the same time Adobe developed the Postscript printing protocol that made laser printers practical. But that was just the beginning. "The biggest piece of timing or luck is I found myself without a job," Brainerd says with a smile. "Suddenly in 1984, I found myself at that point in life when if ever I was going to start up a software company, it was now."

Prior to finding himself unemployed, Brainerd was vice president of customer service and product management for Atex Inc., which manufactured dedicated publishing systems for newspapers and magazines. Before that, he worked in operations for the Minneapolis Star and Tribune Company where he was responsible for planning and implementing prepress computer systems for its two newspapers. During his undergraduate years at the University of Oregon, where he received a BS in business administration and during his graduate studies at the University of Minnesota where he obtained an MS in journalism, Brainerd was editor-in-chief for both school daily papers.

Brainerd knew from personal experience — from having done the work himself — that there was a need to control the process of publishing. Specifically, to become more efficient, publishing had to free itself from its dependence on outside typesetters. "Every publishing project I'd ever been associated with went past deadline," Brainerd recalls. "The frustration of dealing with an outside third party that did not share your sense of urgency, that introduced errors into the process, and required you to send people back and forth with proof sheets and corrections, was unacceptable."

Aldus PageMaker was the solution. What users could do with the personal computer and the laser printer and desktop publishing software gave the control of the publishing process to everyone. The challenge was to make the software easy to use yet retain quality typography and graphics. Brainerd was clearly pushing the edge of his own envelope. "I had good experience at the management and business side of the operation, but I was definitely not a software engineer," he admits. "I'd written software, but I was not a skilled developer of software, so I sought out people who could do that and had different experience levels to match the different pieces of the equation that we needed to work on." As it turned out, Eastman Kodak Company purchased the company for which Brainerd had been working and closed down its Redmond, Washington, facility. "There was an engineering staff there — 40 people. I basically had my pick of the very best engineers and I made offers to three or four of them.

Brainerd put together a business plan, including the concept behind the product and talked to potential customers to learn their needs. He also began to work with companies such as Adobe and Apple which were required to make all the pieces come together. But more than anything else, each morning he was on the phone trying to raise venture money. "I put up $100,000 of my own money, which lasted for six months. During that time, I went out and talked to 50 venture companies to raise additional money to bring the product to market."

Most venture capitalists did not understand software in those days, nor did they see any value in it. Brainerd was refused repeatedly and at one point Aldus was literally out of money. "I kept $5,000 in my bank account to give me time to find a new job and to pay for rent and groceries, if I had to start all over," Brainerd notes. Everything else he owned went into the seed capital.

Brainerd himself was uncertain whether he would get the money in time to make his product a reality. "There was always doubt," Brainerd acknowledges, "but once I start on something I just really focus on it and keep plugging along. I am by nature a very optimistic individual and I don't accept defeat very easily. I was brought up in a family that taught me if you work hard and are smart and continue to focus your energy, then you can make things happen."

Venture capitalists are a skeptical breed. It is their business to be so. Many never returned his call. Most people get fairly frustrated when that happens. "If I'm hitting my head against a brick wall I won't keep hitting my head against it," Brainerd advises with classical Oriental wisdom. "I'll think of a different way to approach the problem. I just kept focusing on the positive. I'd ask those who actually called back and said no who I should talk to, who would be interested in a software company. I'd get some names and out of that I'd get a lot of energy and come back the next day and make those additional calls and keep the ball rolling. I had confidence that we could make this happen, not having any glimpse of what it was going to become in just a few short years." Ultimately, Brainerd raised $860,000.

All grand ventures begin with enormous energy and metabolism as everybody jumps on board with enthusiasm. But as money becomes scarce and objectives are postponed, the troops can become restless. Brainerd's newly hired engineers were making half the salary they had before and the product was still in development. "They stayed because I understood the customers' needs and because I had done the work that this product was to do," Brainerd asserts. "I had a tremendous knowledge as an individual who had cut his fingers many times with X-Acto knives and single-edged razor blades doing paste-ups."

Brainerd and his engineers maintained their spirits through the positive feedback from potential customers. They constantly went out and explained the product. Many could see the potential, particularly those in graphic arts and those who publish newsletters such as bankers that provide interest rate sheets that varied weekly or even daily. "Those were the people that really drove this," Brainerd says. "They gave us tremendous energy and confirmed that we were in fact on to something." They were also the ones who helped forge the alliances with Apple and Adobe.

Following an unscheduled explanation at the sales office of Apple Computer in Beaverton, Oregon, an Apple employee showed up equally unannounced in Seattle and gave Brainerd a Macintosh to use in his demonstrations. "He just pulled out a Mac from his trunk, brought it in and gave it

> "All of us were in it with the attitude that no matter what happened, even if we failed, we would have learned more from doing it than from going to work for some other large corporation..."

to us. He said, 'I listened to you guys the other day and I don't really have any idea what you're doing but it sure sounds interesting and I want to give you one of these machines and I'll come back in a few weeks and see how you're doing with it.' It was that type of belief that we had something that kept us going."

The statistics of success for start-up businesses are not attractive. But, Brainerd and his band of merry men had come to believe in their product and their chances for success without equivocation. "No one said it was going to be easy and we didn't expect it to be easy," Brainerd remarks in retrospect. "All of us were in it with the attitude that no matter what happened, even if we failed, we would have learned more from doing it than from going to work for some other large corporation that none of us really wanted to do. That attitude sustained us in terms of our energy and philosophic belief. Yes, failure was certainly possible, it was always lingering in the background, but we knew if we could sustain ourselves financially we would in fact succeed."

> "I was so focused that I didn't live a balanced life. I was working 14 or more hours a day for 10 years in the process of developing the company and then running it and growing it."

Brainerd served as president of Aldus for 10 years until it merged with Adobe Systems in 1994, giving Brainerd $178 million to match substantively his "Entrepreneur of the Year" award in the Northwest, and his 1994 European Gutenberg Prize for contributions to the advancement of the art and craft of the printing industry.

Aldus PageMaker dramatically changed the lives of its users. It also dramatically changed the life of its designer. The focus that brought desktop publishing into being prevented Brainerd from a clear focus on life. "I was so focused that I didn't live a balanced life. I was working 14 or more hours a day for 10 years in the process of developing the company and then running it and growing it."

The demands never lessened. If anything they became greater as Aldus acquired more people and eventually went public. Like many small ventures that mushroom upward, Brainerd was spending less time doing the things that were enjoyable. As the business grew to over 1,000 employees and well over $200 million in sales, he found himself spending more time on financial, legal, and personnel issues and less time with the customers, who were the reason he started in the first place. "There was definitely more time spent inside the business than what any rational individual would want to do in terms of having a balanced life and having a family. I don't have children as a result. The ability to be in a normal family life was not there. It was definitely time for me to look, to move on to a third career."

The foundation was based on Brainerd's upbringing in southern Oregon. The family had a cabin in the Cascade Mountains on Forest Service land, and they would go there every weekend during the summer to hike and camp. "There's something about the outdoors for me that cleans my soul and my heart. It's an exceedingly core part of my being," Brainerd explains. "I've seen a tremendous impact on Pacific Northwest forests in my life because of the growth in population. And when I looked inside myself and identified some core values that were really important to me as an individual, the environment was clearly right on the top of my list." Brainerd spent months talking to nearly 100 journalists, academics, activists, and politicians throughout the region, asking them "If you were in my shoes, if you had my checkbook, and you could only write three checks, what would they be to." Brainerd synthesized their recommendations and added his own, formulated the foundation, and recruited staff.

The mission of his foundation is to encourage collaboration and communication among a broad base of citizens to develop strategic solutions to long-standing complex environmental issues. "If we're going to be successful in protecting the Northwest for future generations, we have to build support at the local community level," Brainerd argues. The goal of the foundation is to identify leaders from housewives to cabinetmakers, who care deeply about their communities and the forests or streams or fish runs within them and provide them with resources."

Through hundreds of ten to twenty thousand dollar grants, the foundation is cleaning up the wilderness. The recipients do not consider themselves activists. They see themselves as concerned citizens. One, a woman was arguing with a local paper mill. Built back in the forties, the mill emitted dioxins into the local waters right next to people's homes. She was concerned about the health implications to her community and started researching the dioxin dilemma. The foundation provided funding through which she organized a small citizens' committee. Two years later the mill announced it was closing down its operation. The foundation now plans to continue the funding to make sure the closure and cleanup are done in a responsible way.

Brainerd's other organization, Social Venture Partners, uses the venture capital model that funded Aldus to offer young entrepreneurs a way to help their communities without serving on a board and writing a check for their favorite charity. "They really want to give; not only dollars but other resources in the same way a good venture capitalist would," Brainerd states. They provide help in creating marketing or direct mail campaigns. They donate computers and give advice. "The venture capital model has a lot of relevance to the younger generation of people that have made money but don't know what to do with it and how to be most effective."

Brainerd sees this part of his life as a time balancing the equation of his earlier obsession. "Today's young high tech entrepreneurs believe in what they can accomplish as individuals or as a team. I try to encourage them to balance three parts of their lives: personal, career, and service to community." Brainerd recognizes that at any one time the three will not be equal, but spread over a lifetime they can be. And, as Brainerd adds, "They don't always need to give money because time and energy are just as valuable. So I try to encourage them to find their passion and apply some of their youthful energy to doing meaningful work on that passion in their communities. There's so much to be gained from that, particularly learning about oneself in the process, which is valuable in all their other demands."

Most certainly the result of what he learned about himself, Brainerd married Debbi in 1997. Together he and his wife are working on a joint project to build a children's environmental learning center on Bainbridge Island, in Washington state.

There are others who have been extraordinarily successful in technology who do not seem to have the same sense of social responsibility. Brainerd is kind on his compatriots. "I wish it would be different, but I also understand that those people have to make their own decisions about where they are in their lives." The question gets a lot of focus in Brainerd's Seattle, with people like Paul Allen and Bill Gates as neighbors. "Bill has been pretty clear that his job right now is to run Microsoft, and I can relate to that. My job was to run Aldus," Brainerd says in defense of both Gates and himself. There are a lot of things Gates does within the context of his company that are not deemed to be adequate but are certainly focused on giving back. Gates and his wife Melinda have spearheaded a number of projects, including a drive to build new libraries. Gates has said he plans on giving away 90 percent of what he has made. It is a question of time. But people are very impatient about the young generation of millionaires still in their 30s or 40s. Impatient and jealous.

> "I came from a very modest upbringing and I feel very fortunate to have the money I have. I want to give that back and do it in ways that don't necessarily bring focus back on me."

But if you look at the history of philanthropy, it is actually better now than in the past. Bill Hewlett and Dave Packard, for example, did not establish their company foundation until they were in their fifties. Their personal foundations began a bit later. "It happens late in life, once people have focused on their careers and their families, that they begin to think about service back," says Brainerd. "What I'm trying to do is advance that ten to fifteen years, because I think there's a great deal of satisfaction that can be derived addressing these issues while you are young."

Some people, of course, are envious of those that have made money and view philanthropy as just ego gratification for those that can afford it.

Brainerd tries to dispel the notion. "I don't see it that way at all. I came from a very modest upbringing and I feel very fortunate to have the money I have. I want to give that back and do it in ways that don't necessarily bring focus back on me. The act of giving and getting the satisfaction from just doing that, anonymously, is the best satisfaction of all."

The man who does not consider himself exceptional succeeded exceptionally. Through it all, he hired people that could do the job better than he could. He also enriched his own expertise by taking two weeks every year to find managerial and technical educational programs that were important for the business. He took off another week each year to hike in the wilderness.

Brainerd dreams about what is possible, about what other people would say cannot be done. Ironically, he was brought up in a family where dreams were always questioned. "There has to be realism, a practical side," Brainerd admonishes, "but often there are creative ways of achieving a result that can prevent an immediate, 'No, you can't do that.' That's probably the most valuable thing that I took away from my upbringing and living in a small town."

Growing up when he did, Brainerd never dreamed of being the guru of a new dimension in computer software, but he always had an interest in technology. He also always had a skill of building bridges between two different worlds. "I've done that throughout my career in every job that I've had. I build bridges between two different cultures, people that otherwise wouldn't talk to one another or wouldn't know how to talk to one another, and I could talk both languages and bring those two worlds together and create a result."

In the case of desktop publishing, he built bridges between creative people who use the product and the technology folks who must create it. In the case of his beloved Northwest, he is building bridges from the technology people who made money on the product to just plain folks who must live with it. "It is an incredible experience. I get tremendous satisfaction testing myself against continuous challenges where I am ill-prepared and must build the bridge to become prepared enough to accomplish the task."

We should all have the courage to cross that bridge when we come to it.

Tom Hornbein

*Member of the First American
Ascent of Mount Everest in 1963*

There are accomplishments that go beyond what most of us will ever achieve or dream that go almost unnoted in the larger world of our public awareness. Tom Hornbein, who in May 1963 was a member of the first American expedition to Mount Everest, who with Willi Unsoeld made the first ascent of Everest's West Ridge and the first traverse of a major Himalayan peak, likes it that way just fine. "The ascent that Willi and I made of Everest and the traverse has come to enjoy a historical appreciation that was never part of the reason why we were there," Hornbein begins, "so I have difficulty viewing our climb as so terribly different than what many others have done in many other locations, except that it happened to be on the highest hunk of real estate on earth."

Hornbein began dreaming of Everest when he was very young. His parents sent him to a camp in Colorado when he was 13. Soon he was consuming mountaineering literature, checking out every book on mountaineering he could find in the local libraries in St. Louis, where he grew up. At that time Everest had not been climbed, but there were accounts of those who made attempts in the 1920s and '30s. "There was an American writer, James Ramsey Ullman, who influenced me a lot," Hornbein recalls. "To him, climbers were a breed apart and he looked on them as superhuman beings. This came through in his writing."

Through books, Hornbein came to know the gripping adventures of those who tried to climb Everest in the '20s and '30s. Did George Mallory and Andrew Irvine reach the summit before they disappeared in 1924? Mallory's body was found some 2,000 feet from the top 75 years later, but provided no solution to that mystery. This is the stuff of the dreams that a young Tom Hornbein grew up on.

"The big question then was not just whether it was possible to climb to the top but whether humans could even survive at that altitude," Hornbein explains. "And it wasn't clear that it was, even climbing with supplemental oxygen, which they did use in those days although it was bulky and heavy and not very reliable. But that was my imprinting and so those dreams of climbing Everest were wonderful childhood dreams, fantasies of being up there on windswept ridges. In 1953, of course, Everest was climbed by Edmund Hillary and Tenzing Norgay and a little piece of something was suddenly taken away. Even though there was great appreciation of that incredible accomplishment, it put a pin into my balloon."

After high school, Hornbein entered college and then medical school. With his challenges focused closer to home, Hornbein's interest in Everest diminished, until an invitation came to go on the 1963 expedition. "I just kept thinking about it," Hornbein sparkles. "The highest point on earth. And I talked with Willi and Dick Emerson with whom I had shared a marvelous Himalayan adventure before and we thought, it doesn't matter if it's a big expedition, if we're all there together we will have a great time."

All three accepted. When the expedition leader, Norman Dyhrenfurth, came to San Diego where Hornbein was working as a Navy doctor, he spoke of doing something that had not been done before. "He called it a triple slam," Hornbein says. Dyhrenfurth proposed that the team climb Everest and its two neighbors, Lhotse and Nuptse, the last of which, at 25,850 feet, had not been climbed before. But sensing the attraction of Everest, Dyhrenfurth also suggested another possibility: to climb up Everest by the known South Col route and then descend the unknown West Ridge. "That struck us as a bit suicidal," Hornbein laughs. "Plunging down an unknown side of the mountain as your oxygen is getting low seemed awfully danger-ous. But the idea of going up a new route and traversing down the known route quickly followed."

Now Hornbein returned to his childhood dreams with serious intent. Using material prepared by the Swiss Foundation for Alpine Research one year after Everest was first climbed, he studied aerial photos of Everest taken by the Indian Air Force. "I looked at them and tried to figure out ways to go," Hornbein reminisces. I spotted a little snow gully that wasn't quite on the West Ridge but was over in China, which was then forbidden territory. It appeared to penetrate up through the rocks for quite a long way and then suddenly there was a blank and you couldn't tell what happens next, and then a snow-field. But it looked possible. I spent hours in fantasy, dreaming about that lit-tle area of blankness that I imagined was a horrendous rock step where it would be too difficult to carry an oxygen cylinder and still be able to climb."

Hornbein was captivated by the idea of attempting to climb Everest by an unclimbed route. Exploring the unknown transcended the desire to get to the top of the mountain. "There were several of us who were clued in to that experience as opposed to maximizing our chances of reaching the highest point on the surface of the earth," Hornbein notes. "And so we asked our-selves: if we knew there was absolutely no chance of getting to the top would we want to attempt the West Ridge. Dick Emerson said yes. Others, Willi and I among them, said no, we needed some hope, however remote it might be. In the end, the possibility of being successful, even though the odds might be very low, became a critical part of the chemistry."

Emerson, a sociologist, had the climbers keep a diary, in which he asked them to record on a scale from plus five to minus five their motivation and level of uncertainty about success on the West Ridge and South Col routes. His hypothesis was that motivation is maximized by uncertainty, that if you're certain of success or certain of failure, motivation is diminished and that the information exchanged among individuals is of the sort to enhance uncertainty.

"If we were at a spot where the certainty of success was high," Hornbein illustrates, "the information exchanged was pessimistic in order to keep uncertainty maximum. If it's a really clear blue sky and it looks like a walk up the gully, then we would express hesitations like 'Yeah, the gully looks great up to maybe 27,000 feet, but, man, we can't see beyond that. There might be a huge wall up there.' Whereas on the West Ridge where plenty of environmental input was pessimistic, we would frame comments that were more optimistic. You keep yourself right in that mid-zone, zero, between minus five and plus five, maximum doubt. Uncertainty is really an essential element of life, whether it's on a mountain or as an industrial entrepreneur."

The world of climbing mountains is a microcosm of the world at large. It has the same spectrum of humanity, although maybe not in the same mix as you see in daily life. There are people who are driven by the quest for fame and there are others for whom personal search and a great adventure with friends is the compelling force. Hornbein is in the latter camp. "It would be dishonest to say I don't have an ego and my wife would tell you I'm a liar, but there were people on our trip for whom the need to summit was transcendent. But for those of us on the West Ridge, that was clearly much less the case because we were willing to sacrifice the summit just to have the opportunity to do something that hadn't been done before and that we didn't know we could do."

One could argue that if Hornbein pulled off the more dangerous, difficult West Ridge ascent, he would acquire even greater fame, but outside the mountaineering community, fame accrues to the first to get to the top. No one among the West Ridge expedition would be the first American to reach the summit of Everest; James Whittaker earned that distinction earlier in May 1963. "We were made differently and I'm sure ego was among the motivational factors, but less so than other things."

In life, good luck and bad luck are very real. Call it whatever you want, but if suddenly out of a blue sky you are smitten with terminal cancer, you usually don't blame yourself. The same is true if you are standing on a mountainside and an avalanche takes you away. Luck is important. The mortality rate on Everest is somewhere about three percent. Hornbein tucks luck into Emerson's motivational theory of uncertainty. "When we got back to Katmandu after the expedition, there were reporters. The king of Nepal had an event one evening in our honor. I can remember talking to a Nepalese dignitary about bivouacking at 28,000 feet on the way down, spending the night out in the open. No one had ever done that before. I said we were lucky and he said, 'Luck is what you make it.' It sounds a little mystical, but I've come to believe that there is a connection between luck and what goes on in your head. That if you are in a survival situation and you are doing what you need to do to survive, sometimes it seems as if that interacts with other events over which you have absolutely no control to enable a good outcome rather than a bad outcome. Now, there is no guarantee that it is going to be the case. Anyone, no matter what their karma may be, can get blasted."

Nearly 50 years after Ed Hillary and Tenzing Norgay, Everest has become a sort of alpine safari for the rich and adventurous. One can fork out $65,000 and be taken up the mountain; in 1993 alone 129 people made it to the top. They've got to be physically very capable to get there because nobody is carrying them up but, as Hornbein asserts, "even so, these people are handicapped because they're not capable of being self-reliant and independent." But that is what guiding is all about, to enable people who have lesser skill to have experiences that they wouldn't otherwise have. "They're different in that much of the uncertainty is being managed for them. Though I don't have any reason to think that the urges that bring them there are any different than they were for us," Hornbein admits.

> "The ability to accept risk is important to creativity, whether you are climbing a mountain, creating a piece of music, or seeking a cure for cancer."

So what does it take to summit Everest and move it from fantasy to fulfillment? It begins with a certain endowed physical capacity complemented by fitness and training. It is similar to what Hornbein expects of aspiring physicians as they enter his domain at the University of Washington School of Medicine, where he is a professor of anesthesiology, physiology and biophysics. "They have to be committed to becoming the best they can possibly be," Hornbein says.

"I have difficulty tolerating anyone who floats through because anesthesiology is a specialty where if you screw up you can kill somebody. It's not just a hobby. Like climbing, it's dead serious stuff." So you tune the machine to be as strong and reliable as you can make it and that is truer today than when Hornbein climbed. "Climbing was not a profession, and the idea of training to be fit never occurred to us. We climbed to be fit. If Willi and I hadn't had 180 miles to walk we probably wouldn't have been able to get out of base camp. But by the time we got to the base of the mountain we were in a lot better shape.'

It also takes great technical climbing skill. But Hornbein believes vision and humility are at least as precious. Climbing Everest is more than just an athletic event, and he points to the world's most famous mountaineer,

Reinhold Messner, as the exemplar of both. Messner was the first to climb Everest alone without oxygen. "That was a very visionary undertaking because at the time he was up there he was completely alone on the north side of the mountain. It was not like it is now, covered with guided tours."

Messner is not a superman physically. He is fit, he has his machine tuned to be the best it can be. And he probably has a big ego. But, as Hornbein points out passionately, "He's got humility and perspective on what really matters. He knows that to push too hard simply for fame and fortune is not conducive to a long life. The sense to know when to turn around is something that he possesses that many mountaineers do not have and some of them are posthumous parts of mountaineering history now."

While many of us will make real contributions to the world we live in, Hornbein believes that major changes, breakthroughs, are rare events often brought about because someone sees things in a way that's different from what is usual. Often such new approaches are viewed not solely with skepticism but with outright hostility. "Back in the days of Copernicus," Hornbein reports half jokingly, "they burned you at the stake for pursuing new ways of thinking. But it's these major paradigm shifts that carry us into new, unimagined realms."

> "Part of life is not knowing where you go next. For me, at least, it's better that way."

Messner, Hornbein opines, was responsible for one of the more recent paradigm shifts in mountaineering, namely, the change from expedition style to alpine style climbing in the Himalayas; that is, from a pyramid of supplies and personnel that finally peaks with a couple of people at the top to just putting your tent and gear on your back and just going for it, a bold and different approach to the Himalayas. Mountaineers often view the climb Hornbein made as a precursor to Messner's, but Hornbein doesn't see it that way. "It's true, by the time we got to the end of our attempt on the West Ridge we were down to a very small number of people but nevertheless it was still in the expedition style. Our last camp was carried by five Sherpas plus the two of us. It was not just two people moving up together. It was foreshadowing only in that it showed that even on a big mountain a few individuals could do something that really stretched the limit." Hornbein may sidestep his West Ridge climb as a paradigm shift, but those knowledgeable about the history of Everest won't let him off so easily. Based upon the West Ridge climb alone, he was recently ranked by Everestnews.com as among the greatest American climbers of the last century.

Hornbein's dreaming had a practical edge to it, manifest in what is now known as the "Hornbein Mask." It all began when he was on Masherbrum in the Karakoram in 1960. The team had taken oxygen equipment like that used by the Swiss on Everest in 1956, but when they finally got to an altitude where they wanted to use it, the mask was so difficult to breathe through that they ended up climbing the mountain without using supplemental oxygen. That experience provoked Hornbein to think how he might improve the design for Everest. "I came up with an idea and milled out a prototype from Plexiglas," Hornbein demonstrates. "A simple design with only one valve to prevent your breath from going back into the oxygen reservoir so the moisture wouldn't freeze and turn the rubber bladder into a block of ice."

Later Hornbein was giving a talk about Masherbrum to medical school faculty and a patient was in the audience. Hornbein later visited him in his room. The patient's name was Fred Maytag II, then CEO of Maytag Company and grandson of the founder of the famous appliance manufacturer. He was so impressed with Hornbein's ideas on the mask he had his research and development folks transform the idea into a mold to produce a mask that was made of a single piece of rubber. "It was terrific. If moisture from breathing froze on the mask, you could just distort the rubber and break the ice off. It was a very simple thing and I put on the side of it 'Maytag Mask.' People call it the Hornbein Mask but to me it's still the Maytag Mask." Still Hornbein is reluctant to regard this creation as a paradigm shift. "If it is one, it's a real small one."

Following his historic Everest ascent, Hornbein set his Everest experience aside to focus on his medical career. Not until his mid-50s did he accept that "everything I had done in life, in medicine, with my family, and in the way I had learned from and affected other people was related to my mountaineering," and that his Everest experience could be a metaphor for the rest of life.

Everest enjoys special metaphorical stature for a couple of reasons. The first is simply that it's the highest point on the planet. Second, Everest's height appears to be very close to the limit of what an acclimatized human can endure. Filmmaker David Breashears, who has summited Everest five times and shot a recent IMAX film about the mountain, reports that the limited oxygen can force the most experienced climber to a pace of only a few feet every minute. Climbing mountains, especially the big ones, is a risky business, Hornbein says, but then risk is an inherent part of our lives. "Anesthesiology is analogous to mountaineering," he says. "Hours of sheer boredom punctuated by moments of stark terror. Crisis management links them together. In a crisis, the individual who can stay cool and continue to think and not get swept away by fear or other emotions is more capable of dealing with the events that are unfolding. That requires an enormous sense of self.

"I came to realize that risk is an essential constituent. The ability to accept risk is important to creativity, whether you are climbing a mountain, creating a piece of music, or seeking a cure for cancer. The ability to be comfortable with risk and maybe even to enjoy it to some degree is important. I learned that in the mountains, not Everest per se, though it certainly is the entity I use to paint the message for people."

Hornbein, now in his 70s, is retired as a medical school department chairman, but he will probably never retire as a man of mountains. He continues to climb, to write, and to lecture about mountaineering, human adaptation to high altitude, and, yes, the value of risk.

So where does someone who has been to the top of the world and ascended to the top of a prestigious medical school go next? Hornbein doesn't have the slightest idea and he loves it that way. "Part of life is not knowing where you go next. For me, at least, it's better that way," Hornbein says. "I wasn't someone who was born wanting to be a doc and when I stopped being a chair at the medical school I didn't have any idea where I was going to go next. I still don't.

"I know where I am right now and things will happen as they always have to define the right direction. I'm tuned in and ready to enjoy and be challenged by what comes along. I have needs deep in my soul that I have more or less always indulged. They include time to dream, the challenge of the unknown, and the richness of relationships with those whose lives I share. I have been gifted a marvelous life, though maybe to some degree that, too, is what you make it."

Mountains have always been metaphors for conquering something enormous, crossing something unknown. Maybe it's time we all found and climbed our own personal Everest.

Don Lanphere
Award-Winning Jazz Tenor Saxophonist

The fall 1994 cover of *Jazz Now* magazine bears the ponytail, double-breasted sport coat, magic fingers, puffed cheeks, and aging face of legendary tenor saxophonist Don Lanphere. In a career spanning more than 50 years, dozens of recordings, and nearly every bump on the road of hard knocks, the 72-year-old Lanphere is better than ever.

Lanphere was born in Wenatchee, a small town in the heart of Washington state's apple country. It was where his father had gone to school and courted his mother. The family moved there in 1921 from Belmont Shores, California, where Lanphere's father operated Belmont Radio store, an enterprise he continued in the Northwest. Needless to say, Lanphere grew up on a steady diet of music both on radio and on 78 RPM records with Coleman Hawkins on tenor sax, Louis Armstrong on horn, and Duke Ellington conducting. "There was always music playing around the house," Lanphere says with a wry smile.

Unknown to Lanphere at the time, his father had been a saxophone player in California, playing at dances. At seven, Lanphere was rummaging around in the basement and found his father's sax. "I'd come home after school and push the keys with no aspirations to be a musician. My dad caught me one day and asked if I would like to hear it. He played a bit for me and I liked it." Lanphere's father purchased a smaller alto sax for his son and started him on lessons. "For the first couple years, I had my eye on the clock more than on the music. I was just interested in getting my hour in and getting out of there," Lanphere admits.

But it wasn't long before Lanphere was playing better than anyone else in town. One summer while in junior high, Lanphere went to California to spend the vacation with his grandfather who took the boy and his mother to Catalina Island, a resort destination off the coast of southern California that boasted a casino and ballroom. Lanphere had his sax with him and practiced in the cabin. "There was a knock on the door and my mom opened it to two men and one said, 'Who's playing in here?' She pointed to me." The two were musicians in the Chicago-based Dick Jurgens Orchestra playing at the casino. They invited Lanphere to play during intermission that night. "It was 11 p.m. and I was in front of several thousand people in this huge ballroom with a solo." Lanphere had just won a school contest back in Washington playing Rimsky-Korsakov's "Flight of the Bumblebee." He told his accompanist, "'I'd like to play 'Stardust' and 'Flight of the Bumblebee.'"

"'Well,' the piano player said, 'I'll play Stardust, but I'm not playing 'Flight of the Bumblebee.' But he did!" Lanphere howls.

The following summer, Lanphere returned to his grandparents and remained there during the school year to avoid contracting polio that was in near epidemic proportions in Wenatchee. Lanphere and his grandfather spent a lot of time at the newly built Palladium ballroom in Los Angeles, attending concerts put on by the likes of Count Basie and Woody Herman. "It was right then that I made a definite decision," Lanphere reports, leaning forward and pointing his finger at the moment. "When I actually heard these great bands playing, I knew this is what I wanted. I told my granddad I was going to play with Woody Herman and Artie Shaw and Claude Thornhill and Charlie Barnet and all these great bands. And, over the years, I played with every one of them."

> "When the world looks at me they may say I am just a jazz musician, but I'm hoping my life might shine a bit so that people can see and feel something different."

Lanphere graduated from Wenatchee High School at 16 and headed to Northwestern University near Chicago, enrolling just after his 17th birthday. Like a hip peg in a square hole, Lanphere did not fit easily into college. No sooner had he arrived on campus then he marched into the dean's office and announced he did not want to take music history or music literature and presented an outline of his very own curriculum in harmony, counterpoint, composition, and clarinet. He countered their reticence by offering to pay full tuition and not even seek a degree. He just wanted to become a musician. "Given those circumstances, they didn't see why they couldn't do that and that was the start of special student programs at Northwestern."

By this time, Lanphere had formulated a style, copying the technique off Coleman Hawkins records. "With him as my inspiration, I went off to Chicago thinking I was the world's greatest saxophone player. I was in Wenatchee, but I wasn't in Chicago," Lanphere allows. In his first music sessions on campus, his classmates soundly dashed his pride and called his sound old-fashioned, and for good reason. Music was changing through the new sounds of young artists like the Count Basie's sax master Lester Young, Dexter Gordon of the Lionel Hampton Orchestra, and the free living Charlie Parker, king of the Savoy Ballroom. "Well, they took me into that bebop style and, immediately, I found my soul." Unfortunately,

Lanphere also found marijuana, Chicago Green. "Within a month, I was carrying good light green grass with me," Lanphere regrets.

In the late 1940s Lanphere was playing in the Johnny Bothwell Sextet. On a whim, Bothwell decided to take his act to New York. The event would change Lanphere's life. The next morning, Lanphere dropped out of school, packed, and was on his way. The band opened at the Baby Grand Club, just one block up the street from the Apollo Theater. The first night, Bothwell brought his date, Chan Richardson. "She came with my leader and left with me," Lanphere chuckles while shaking his head. "Twenty years old, and she took me home."

Needless to say, Bothwell was livid. But to keep his headliners intact, the owner of the Baby Grand forced him to keep Lanphere on for two weeks before he fired him. That proved to be enough time for Lanphere's new girl to launch his career. She coaxed her friend, Dial Records head Ross Russell, to come to the club and hear him play. As he left he gave Lanphere a note instructing him to show up at an address Friday afternoon and bring his horn.

It was November 1948 and Lanphere was about to step into the epicenter of the jazz world. "I walked in on a recording studio with Max Roach on drums and Fats Navarro on trumpet, all these idols of mine whose records I had but who I had never seen or met. Here I am in the studio with them!" The session started quickly with a tune called "Move." Navarro, an extremely talented and influential trumpeter, played melody. Despite never hearing the piece before — much less playing it — Lanphere was instructed to jump in. "The idea was to get this white kid out of the studio as rapidly as possible," Lanphere laughs. "Dinger, ringer ring, fastest tempo you could possibly imagine. I survived the trial by fire and they started taking me around to various clubs." The session produced the first recording of "Move" to be released; it was later recorded by Miles Davis and several others. "But that was the first," Lanphere beams.

From left,
Don Lanphere,
Sonny Rich and
Charlie Parker

The bebop scene in New York of the early 50s was primarily black, but there was an army of young white hopefuls and wannabes surrounding them at all times: tenor saxophonist Stan Getz, baritone sax man Gerry Mulligan, John "Zoot" Sims on the tenor sax, and Don Lanphere. They all copied Charlie Parker, transcribing recordings of the legend known simply as "Bird," studying them and playing along as the record spun. They also copied his addiction. Lanphere expanded his flirtatious interest in marijuana to heroin and found himself in a love affair with drugs and alcohol that would last 26 years. A full-blown junkie, he would finish a gig and take the subway uptown to Harlem to cop. The flat that Lanphere and Richardson took on as their own was on West 52nd Street, home base for jazz clubs and fast company. Lanphere became a card-carrying member of the community, doing drugs, listening to Dizzy Gillespie, and sharing music and friendship with none other than Charlie Parker.

Don's personally signed photo from legendary saxophonist, Charlie "Bird" Parker

The kid from the "apple capital of the world" was on a roll in the Big Apple. His early classical training merged with his passion to acquire a modern sound. Every day he listened to and studied jazz recordings. Every night he played. He learned the value of hard work from his friend Charlie Parker. Paul Desmond, formerly the sax man for Dave Brubeck's band, interviewed Parker on a college radio station in Boston and asked whether Parker's music was natural or the result of training. The reply is legendary. Parker was not musically proficient when he left school in Kansas City to go after the golden ring. As a matter of fact, in the early days the man who would eventually be called the greatest saxophonist of all time was by all accounts not a very good player at all. In the spring of 1936, the teenage Parker sat in on a jam session conducted by Jo Jones and played so poorly Jones threw his cymbal at Parker's feet and ushered him off the stage to laughter. Parker was humiliated and vowed that would never happen again. In a quote used today by young jazz musicians, "Parker reported he practiced 12 to 15 hours a day. Remembering Northwestern, so did I."

Most of the jazz musicians of that era are gone now. Many died in run-down hotels, destroyed by their addictions. Charlie Parker is a prime example. Toward the end of his life, Bird slipped into a deep depression and became increasingly erratic in his behavior. Although he looked much older, he was only 34 when he died in 1955, claimed by years of drug and alcohol abuse. Fats Navarro fared even worse, succumbing to tuberculosis and drugs in 1950, two months shy of his 27th birthday.

Lanphere is one of the survivors. He remains healthy, artistically successful, and prosperous. But in between success there was a long break. After a second two-year stint with Woody Herman, from 1949-51 and 1959-61 Lanphere disappeared from the jazz scene and returned to Wenatchee to run his father's shop. He put away his horn, stoked his pot and wafted into anonymity.

He gives all the credit to an unlikely religious experience in ultimately launching his second career. In 1969, reasonably loaded on grass, Lanphere returned from a trip to Seattle to find a psychedelic van parked in front of the store, its longhaired occupants prepping for a gig at the Bright Moon Tavern. Lanphere never made it to hear them play but he encountered one of the group — he used the name Flash — at Denny's. The two talked over coffee and then "Flash asked me to hold hands," Lanphere explains, still in shock today. "I thought this might be trouble but he started praying and I found myself repeating what he asked me to, Lord Jesus, come into my heart." Lanphere got up from the booth to leave and fell right to the floor. "When I got home, I told my wife Midge that a guy just told me I got saved. Midge asked, 'From what?'" On November 5, 1969, they both flushed their reds and yellows and grass down the toilet.

From a Carnegie Hall concert, Don Lamphere, Don Radar (on trumpet in background) and Woody Herman

Lanphere took over managing his father's store. He never returned to his former vice. Neither did he return to his old haunts in New York. He did unpack his saxophone and when he was moved to play he once again played alongside records. Lanphere's dad died in 1976. His mother died in 1985. With ties to his birthplace gone, Lanphere was resolved to renew his career. Following his wife's advice that "if you don't do it now you are never going to do it," Lanphere sold the family business and moved to Seattle for one last grasp at success. "Fear can happen in a lot of circumstances," Lanphere remarks stoically. "Like my first recording session or playing Carnegie Hall with Woody Herman's band and changes that you go through in your career. But as soon as the music starts, the passion takes over the fear." Lanphere started out with a few local gigs in Seattle, then got booked into the West End Café in Manhattan. In 1982 his career took off again. Since then he has recorded 12 albums, beginning with the appropriately-titled *From Out of Nowhere*.

Besides his recording and performing, Lanphere privately tutors about 30 students. They keep him on his toes, so he is ready when the opportunity arises to go to New York or Europe and play. "These young ones coming up are miles ahead of where I was when I was that age," Lanphere notes with delight. "They come in with their guns loaded, going to shoot the old man down today. And so I've got to stay on my toes not only to be able to play everything they play, but to think up new things for them to do to take them to another level. That gives me an advantage."

Improvisation is an important part of jazz. Musicians let their imagination, their emotions and their ear tell their fingers what to do. Lanphere's fingers have been wandering the world of music for half a century, going wherever his imagination takes them. Unlike the reckless years, his body is more in tune with his soul. Lanphere swims daily to keep in shape and his fingers limber. "I'm starting to get arthritis in my fingers. They can really hurt," Lanphere complains as he plays imaginary notes to demonstrate. "They were hurting so bad I went to a finger doctor and he was talking about restringing them, putting new things in there to make them work. So when he asked me if it hurt when I play, I said 'No!' Passion over pain works in athletes. They go out there with fractured ribs and as soon as they get into the physical part of the game, the passion for it takes over the pain. This is true for me."

Some athletes wear Super Bowl rings or have memorabilia that suggest conquests and victories. Lanphere has memories. "I treasure my photograph from Charlie Parker that he signed 'To Don— a friendship unending. Sincerely, Charlie Parker.' Few folks ever got a picture signed by him," Lanphere notes with pride. Probably few folks ever lost a girlfriend to him either. Ironically, Chan Richardson left Lanphere not too long after 52nd Street to become Mrs. Charlie Parker.

Lanphere does have some plaques, like several Record of the Year awards. One wall, like an athlete. The other walls are covered with pictures of people who were a part of the journey, like Lester Young, Miles Davis, and pianist Jimmy Rowles, "musicians I want my students to see and ask questions about and come to know," Lanphere says of the people in his life. "People are always more interested in what you do with your hands, like my sax, than who you are. Everybody always talks about Jesus when he calmed the sea. Don't look at Jesus' hands to watch what he did, look at his face to see who he is. When the world looks at me they may say I am just a jazz musician, but I'm hoping my life might shine a bit so that people can see and feel something different."

The wonderful jazz artists of the bebop era all learned by listening. Let's hope the rest of us can.

Roger McGuinn
*Writer/Singer Who Founded America's
First Rock Supergroup, The Byrds*

The History of Rock-n-Roll and *The Best of the Ed
Sullivan Show, Volume 2* videos include him among
their legends. *The Sixties Superstars* video and
Hullabaloo, Volume 2 portray him as an icon.
Historians and musicologists at the Rock and Roll
Hall of Fame identify him among the three greatest rock and roll performers of all time. "I have no
idea why. I don't pay them," Roger McGuinn
shrugs. Now in his fifth decade of rock concerts,
seated in the fully equipped van that takes him on
the road from gig to gig, he simply says, "That's an
area that I don't deal with. It's not my job to worry
about acclaim. I just go on and do what I do."

In 1964, McGuinn was co-founder of
America's first super group, The Byrds. Although
only in his early 20s at the time, McGuinn already
had an impressive musical résumé. He was an
accompanist for the Limeliters, the Chad Mitchell
Trio, and Bobby Darin, recorded with Hoyt Axton
and the folk duo Tom and Jerry (who would later
be known as Simon and Garfunkel), and was musical director for Judy Collins.

One day, he was performing solo at the
Troubadour folk club in Los Angeles. Singer/gui-
tarist Gene Clark, who had just left the New

Photo credit: Daniela

Christy Minstrels, was in the audience and liked the blend of folk and rock
that McGuinn was playing. After the show they talked about writing some
music together. The two formed a band initially called Jet Set along with
David Crosby, a talented local singer/guitarist, and released a single as the
Beefeaters which was ignored. But not long after, bassist Chris Hillman and
drummer Michael Clarke joined the group and a legend was born.

"My talent is experimentation," McGuinn notes. "I don't see things written in granite so they can't be moved. I wasn't afraid to put a rock beat to folk
or do country when country wasn't cool. I came up with a new genre by taking things off the shelf and combining them in ways they hadn't been used
before. It's an attitude thing. If you're open to experimentation, it'll happen."

McGuinn was putting a beat to folk songs early in his career but it wasn't
going over very well. "Audiences thought it was an abomination. You know,
'This is terrible. Get this guy out of here.'" One night McGuinn was on with

Roger Miller and, after he had performed, he came backstage angry at the audience because they didn't like his music. "Roger said, 'I like what you're doing up there but you'd probably do better if you didn't get mad at the audience because they can see that. It makes them not like you even more.' I started being nicer and it worked."

Audience reaction is very important, more so than audiences realize. There are very few artists who are capable of being totally independent of the audiences' reaction. "I am not able to do that at all," McGuinn acknowledges. "I am very dependent of the reaction. When they're into it, when they're with me, it can really soar, and when they're not, it's like a magician whose tricks don't work. Everything falls apart. You can't tell by looking at them. You can only tell by how they behave after you do a couple of songs. Sometimes they're a hard sell."

It is risky to move the genre and McGuinn has suffered in sales over the years because he took chances artistically. But it pays off in the long run. He is still performing. A lot of groups and musicians are hanging in there longer than one would ever assume. In most cases, money is driving them. Not McGuinn or his long-time associates. "I was privileged to work with Stevie Nicks just before she got back with Fleetwood Mac," he recalls nostalgically. "We did a concert together that was pivotal in her career. She hadn't performed for a while and she got up in front of this audience — about 4,000 outdoors in Arizona — and they went crazy for her. When she got off stage I was standing in the wings and as she came by she went, 'Wow, I haven't done that in awhile. I forgot how much I liked that.' Right after, she got back with Fleetwood. It isn't money that keeps us going. We love what we do and we love the art."

> "It's an attitude thing. If you're open to experimentation, it'll happen."

Soon after Hillman and Clarke joined the band, the five musicians debated a new name over Thanksgiving dinner in Los Angeles when someone suggested "The Birds." But the word was a slang term used in England for women and the band didn't want to be called "The Girls," so McGuinn changed the spelling. They all loved "The Byrds" because it had the "b" sound of the Beatles who had recently exploded onto the worldwide music scene.

Inspired by the Beatles, the group went to see the Beatles movie, *A Hard Day's Night*, and studied the instruments they were using. Immediately they traded in their old instruments. With a $5,000 loan from a friend they purchased what they needed, right down to the black suits with velvet collars just like the Beatles wore. The transition was less than smooth at times. Hillman was a mandolinist and prior to the Byrds had never played electric bass. Clarke actually used cardboard boxes in lieu of drums during the band's first rehearsals. But the quintet was determined to craft their sound and persevered.

"Cream rises to the top, so you're going to get some recognition if you're really good," McGuinn reports. "You get to Carnegie Hall because you practice. You don't get there because you are a celebrity. There is a lot of manipulation in the industry and you know that. But you accept it, do your thing, and don't worry about it."

No need. Released in 1965, The Byrds' first single was a cover of Bob Dylan's "Mr. Tambourine Man," a song destined to become one of the definitive tracks of the 1960s. Later that year, Pete Seeger's "Turn! Turn! Turn!" became the band's second number one song. Both songs are driven by McGuinn's jangly 12-string Rickenbacker, which over the years became his trademark. An original song, "Eight Miles High," cracked the top 20 in 1966 despite being banned by many radio stations for alleged drug references. The song is credited with creating the psychedelic style in rock and roll.

But like most bands, with success came tension. Gene Clark left the band soon after "Eight Miles High," ironically because of fear of flying. Creative differences forced David Crosby out in 1967; he went on to huge success with Crosby, Stills and Nash. By decade's end, McGuinn was the only original band member left. The Byrds would never again attain the commercial success they enjoyed in its early days. After a disappointing 1973 reunion album, the band was effectively finished. Rock would never be the same.

Actually, neither would McGuinn's name. Born James Joseph McGuinn III, he changed his name in 1967 because a guru told him a new name would vibrate better with the universe. The maharishi also sent him the letter "R" and asked him to send back 10 names starting with that letter. Because McGuinn was into science fiction, he sent, among others, "Rocket," "Ramjet," and "Roger," because space guys used it for radio messages to mean things were OK. The guru picked Roger. As for vibrating with the universe, McGuinn didn't notice any changes and would have changed his name back to Jim, which he preferred, but it would have been confusing.

McGuinn's life was confusing enough. There wasn't a point when he decided to be a rock musician; like so many other things, it just happened. "I didn't know what I was going to do with my life," McGuinn admits. "I took up guitar at 13 because I liked Elvis Presley's 'Heartbreak Hotel.' I never thought about doing that for a living. But when I graduated from high school I got a job playing and that was it. I was on the road. My folks didn't play music but they were very sympathetic. They didn't have a my-son-has-to-be-a-doctor kind of attitude."

McGuinn found himself working with a number of groups playing different styles of music but ultimately turned to folk music and stayed with that until The Byrds. For most of the last 25 years he has worked alone. "I like it better alone because you don't have to wait for the drummer to get out of the shower and you don't have to carry around all that gear," McGuinn jokes. "As an artist, I enjoy the repertoire I have as a solo performer. I have more control. I get up there and I do anything I want."

You cannot walk out on to any stage without a certain amount of ego and McGuinn is no exception to the rule. "I'm a ham and I have to be out there," he says point blank. But the songwriter-singer is also deeper than that. "It's like the engine under the hood. You don't want it to get out of control. It's running things. It's working for you. You have to keep it in its place. A lot of things keep my ego in check." His wife Camilla is one. She does not like to call herself a manager, but she does a lot of things that manage. She is road manager and accountant manager and audio engineer. McGuinn decided not to have a personal manager after The Byrds broke up. "I came to the conclusion it was a form of white collar crime, but Camilla's great," McGuinn smiles. "There's a risk in performing of an inflated sense of self worth. I've had that at times. Camilla will bust me for it and put it in nice terms. 'Roger, I think you have an inflated sense of self-importance right now.' I'm like, 'Thanks.' She says it sweetly though. Nice but firm. She doesn't tell me what to do and I don't tell her what to do. We're a team."

They are also no longer in the limelight. The ham is no longer on Ed Sullivan. The ego is checked at the door. McGuinn likes it that way. "I still get recognition," McGuinn insists. "It's all very kind. 'Gee, I like your music.' Nobody tries to tear your clothes off like they did back with The Byrds. I'm very happy with that. Plus I can go places where I couldn't go if I was more popular."

Places like the supermarket. Tucked in a Safeway parking lot in his blue van, McGuinn is the same man in the produce aisle as he is on stage. "I'm not that concerned about success. It's not my primary objective. I am already a success in the way I feel about it," McGuinn asserts. "I make a good living. I'm happy with what I do."

No longer a household name like his 1960s super group, McGuinn is content with his limited notoriety. "I know what it entails to be a celebrity and it's no fun. You're on call 24 hours a day. You have to do interviews like this all day long and then a show and then the next day do it again. You can't live your life because you've given up your life for an image that's plastic. Now, I didn't recognize it when I was in it. It's like you're in the eye of the hurricane. You're wrapped up in it and you can't get out of it. I don't mean to go sour grapes but success is not any fun. It's really a lot tougher than it looks."

But once you have been there, it is all the more tempting to look at those who have mega-platinum hits and ask, "How come I'm not doing that?"

"You do that," McGuinn confesses, "and then you remind yourself that's not really that important." The twinge of jealousy is always subdued by the notion that serendipity plays such a big role in all of this. The career launching success of "Mr. Tambourine Man" is a clear-cut example. It was a matter of happenstance. The Byrds were writing songs that didn't feel right. But they had a one-single deal with Columbia Records, so they needed something hot. Their manager heard of a Dylan song that was rejected so the song was up for grabs and he got a copy of it sent to Los Angeles. "We learned it and recorded it. Dylan even liked it," McGuinn recalls with more delight than usual. "He came to our rehearsal and he liked what we were doing and at one point he said, 'What was that?' and I said, 'That's one of your songs.' He didn't recognize it."

McGuinn is grateful for both the past and the present. He often sees musicians at local hotels that play really well and he wonders why they are playing at a Holiday Inn and he played at the Hollywood Bowl. To answer the question, McGuinn once took to the sidewalk, opened up his guitar case and started playing. "I just wanted to see if I could make money by my raw talent or if the early success was a fluke. Unfortunately, people recognized me and started yelling out Byrds' songs. So I got back in the limo and drove away. The guy with the six bucks in the guitar case owns a limo. It was pretty funny."

"Cream rises to the top, so you're going to get some recognition if you're really good."

Talent is a small part of success in rock music. It is really emotion and soul, not only musicality. There is a certain element of technical virtuosity that is necessary to do rock well, but it's not as critical as it is in classical or in jazz. You have to be able to sing in tune but you can be absolutely extraordinary, technically, but if the audience doesn't connect on an emotional level with the music they are not going to respond. "I have always missed the boat on the massive feel thing," McGuinn accepts. "I've never been able to nail it down, except with The Byrds. On my own, I've never been able to find that secret button that makes it go like that."

Part of the problem may be the genre. Folk music is indefinable. There are traditionalists who say it has to be at least a hundred years old and written by someone anonymous. Others say everything the Beatles did was folk because folk music is music that folks sing. McGuinn is "more in that camp of thinking. We're storytellers. There isn't an overriding story. It's just a narrative of small stories and little mind trips that make it interesting. It's like a mosaic that adds up to life is good or life is interesting."

There have been only a few who have become legends out of the folk genre: Bob Dylan, Woody Guthrie, Arlo Guthrie, Pete Seeger, arguably Paul Simon. It's been made more difficult because music today is more visual with rock videos and lasers at concerts. Folk is a medium that lacks a lot of visual assistance. "I'm just a guy sitting on stage with some lights," McGuinn declares. "Audiences are spoiled. In the old days, classical guitarist Andres Segovia would just sit there with a chair and it was wonderful. I could carry a laser show with me, maybe some sort of audio-visual presentation behind me, but it'd be ludicrous. I don't worry about it."

McGuinn continues to perform from the repertoire of his roots, concentrating on folk, dusting off something old that becomes something new again. "It's like when you go out to the garage and find something that you haven't played with in a long time and it's fun to see it again. I'm just having fun making people happy with music," McGuinn states and then pauses. "Some of the music makes them cry because of what they're thinking when they're hearing it. That's great, too. It reminds them of things they did and it's really nice to have that. I don't have a big message. I'm not trying to evangelize the world or do any kind of political agenda."

There are no limousines and no black velvet suits. Four of the five guys are gone and so are the paparazzi and the screaming fans. "You wonder some times. It's like bad weather," a tired McGuinn explains. "You have your little storms of that kind of thing, but hang in there and it goes away. You just let it go. You can't ruminate about it or beat yourself up over it. It's not worth it. You just waste a lot of time and energy. I feel good about what I do now. I am doing quality work and I enjoy it and other people do too."

Forty years ago McGuinn asked Bobby Darin what he needed to do to make it in show business. He told McGuinn, "Well, get up on stage as much as you can because it doesn't matter how good you are in your living room or in front of a mirror. You have to test it under fire because that adrenaline happens only when you have an audience and you don't have an audience unless you practice, give it total commitment, and hang in there and keep doing it because you love it."

It is easier said than done, of course. Now ready to return home to practice, McGuinn exposes the embers of a dream. "I would love to get a 5,000-seat auditorium kind of audience. Like Joan Baez or Judy Collins. I'd like to get into that group. *The History of Rock and Roll* spot on PBS kind of gave me a boost in that direction. You know, Andres Segovia was scheduled to play Carnegie Hall the month he died. I want to do it like Segovia, 'till I die. That's all there is to it. It's very simple and straightforward. I am very happy."

Hey! Mr. Tambourine Man. Play that song for all of us; for without it, there ain't no place we're going to.

Chapter 9

It's Leading People Without Leading Them By the Nose

Red Auerbach

Former Coach of Nine-Time
NBA Champion Boston Celtics

Arnold "Red" Auerbach once said, "The Boston Celtics are not a basketball team. They are a way of life." One of basketball's truly great figures, Auerbach was part of the NBA before it was even called the NBA. He has been with the Celtics organization since 1950. Auerbach is as much a part of the tradition as the parquet floor the team played on.

Photo credit: Dick Raphael

As he does every day at 9 a.m., Auerbach sits at his desk opening a pile of mail. He is dressed casually: golf slacks, sport shirt, and a baseball cap. Every wall of his office is covered with photographs of his famous teams and players. The room's kelly green wainscot wraps around Auerbach like a Christmas ribbon. The carpet bears the Celtics' familiar leprechaun logo. The wall just behind his head is adorned with a larger than life painting of his trademark cigar.

"It starts with the talent you're born with," declares the team's vice chairman of the board. "Everybody has a potential limit. Say my potential limit is to long jump 15 feet. With training, hard work, perseverance — what I call paying the price — I get as far as 14 feet. You have the same potential limit but you say, 'Thirteen feet's good enough for me,' so that's all you do. I become great and you don't. You take three guys that are born with the same talent and one will become great and the other two will not simply because they were not willing to pay the price."

Auerbach paid that price. After one year of community college in New York, the Brooklyn-born Auerbach attended George Washington University in Washington, D.C. He played three years of college basketball at GWU and was the team's leading scorer and defensive specialist. "There was no pro ball then, see," Auerbach punctuates. "So my ambition was to be a physical education teacher and high school coach, which I was." Auerbach obtained his BS in education in 1940 and a master's in education the following year. "But as opportunities came along, I took the gamble," Auerbach states with pride. "I gave up the security to go into this pro basketball thing and I was lucky."

In 1946, a time when professional sports in general — and basketball in particular — were considered a novelty with only regional appeal, Auerbach became head coach of the Washington Capitols, one of 11 teams in the new Basketball Association of America. Auerbach coached the Capitols for three seasons, winning his division twice. In 1949, after the BAA merged with the National Basketball League to form the NBA, Auerbach took the coaching job with the Moline, Illinois-based Tri-Cities Blackhawks. "I tried to put a competitive team on the floor that was pleasant to watch," Auerbach says of his initial efforts. "See, some coaches were scared of their job and would play slow-up basketball. They wanted to keep the game close so they could say, 'We only lost by four and with one little break would've had it.' So they played scared, holding the ball. All they were doing was looking for excuses to lose.

"I didn't believe in that, still don't. You play the game and let the chips fall. If I'm going to lose my job, I'm going to lose the job, but not because of being scared of losing the job. I didn't lack the guts. I'm going to do what I think is the thing to do."

> "You take three guys that are born with the same talent and one will become great and the other two will not simply because they were not willing to pay the price."

The struggling Boston Celtics thought the thing to do was gamble on Auerbach, hiring him for the 1950-51 season after the young coach took the Capitols to the NBA Finals two seasons before. Auerbach quickly built solid teams in Boston, finishing either second or third in the Eastern Division for six straight years. Then in 1956, the Celtics traded Ed Macauley and Cliff Hagan to the St. Louis Hawks for their first-round draft pick that year, a promising 6'-10" center from the University of San Francisco named Bill Russell. Boston then used its second-round pick to select another future star, K.C. Jones. The result: the Celtics were no longer a merely good team, but instead the most dominant franchise in pro-basketball history, perhaps the most dominant professional sports team ever. Over the next 10 seasons, Auerbach coached the Celtics to nine NBA titles, including eight in a row from 1959 through 1966. Auerbach retired from coaching after the 1966 NBA Finals to take a job in the Celtics front office, where he remains to this day.

Auerbach doesn't dwell on the numbers, although his numbers are amazing. In 20 seasons as a head coach, Auerbach compiled an astounding 938-479 record for a .662 winning percentage. As of the 1999-2000 season, only Lenny Wilkens and Bill Fitch, who both coached longer than Auerbach, won more games. His playoff record is equally impressive at 99-69 (.589). Auerbach attributes the record to some simple facts of life. First, you need an eye for good people. "You try to visualize how a guy is going to mature mentally and physically," Auerbach explains, "what his attitude is, what type of system would best suit his skills." But, as he is always prone to do, he adds, "and you need an element of luck because you don't know if the guy is a drunkard on the side. I drafted a guy one time, hell of a player. He won't fly. He won't get on an airplane so he never had a career in basketball. Can you believe that?"

But luck goes both ways and Auerbach accepts the fickleness of sport with his usual demeanor. "In the seventh game of a playoff, the score was tied, and one of my players shot the ball at the buzzer. It hit the rim, hit the backboard, hit the rim, hit the rim again, and slopped in. Made me a great coach. We won the title. What can I tell you? It's like that." Auerbach chuckles.

Auerbach chose skilled people for his roster. My favorite was Bob Cousy, who 40 years ago would pass or dribble the ball behind his back to beat an opponent that was over-playing him. He was beautiful to watch and the only player in that era to display such wizardry. Today, children in elementary school dribble behind their backs or between their legs when they're walking down the street. At one time it was a phenomenon; today it's commonplace.

Many use this fact to suggest that athletes today are bigger, faster, stronger and smarter. "Just not so," Auerbach retorts. Auerbach figures he could put together a team from his era that is better than any of today's dream teams. "I'd have Bill Russell, Wilt Chamberlain and Kareem Abdul-Jabbar, three big centers better than what they got now. Elgin Baylor, Bob Pettit, Julius Erving, and Dolph Schayes at forward. In the backcourt Oscar Robertson, Jerry West, Bob Cousy, John Havlicek. No dream team's going to beat that. The frontcourt is better. The backcourt is just as big and we've got a big edge at center. We can score. And our rebounding? No way they're going to get more than one shot. The difference is today there are more of them. They're not better, just more. That's the only difference."

The second Auerbach axiom is to play smart. "I was a thinker," Auerbach notes, tapping his index finger on the side of his baseball cap. In fact, there was a certain time in a game when Auerbach was actually preparing for the next one. Whenever the Celtics got an insurmountable lead, Auerbach gave his starters a rest so they would be fresh for the next game. "That's what started me lighting up the cigar," Auerbach says about his trademark behavior. "It was a way of relaxing and thinking. Besides, other guys were smoking cigarettes on the bench, so I lit up a cigar. At the right moment, I knew it was time and all of a sudden, poof."

Auerbach re-lights the cigar he has been savoring all morning. For a split second he becomes an exact likeness of the painting behind him. "Now, today," Auerbach adds drawing in another puff, "you can't do that because you're affecting the averages of these players. They want to be in there in the garbage time, get easy baskets, put up the points for their contract negotiations," he points out, exhaling.

Identifying talent and crafting game plans are the bread and butter duties for any coach. What may have been the real difference between Auerbach and the others was the man behind the cigar. "I had a certain philosophy that I lived by," Auerbach states. "Everybody would ask me, 'How did you handle those personalities, those egos?' I would always tell them that you don't handle them. You handle animals. You deal with people." Auerbach draws in a full breath from his cigar and slowly blows out a silent stream of smoke savoring his idea as much as his tobacco.

As a part of the way Auerbach dealt with his people, he never fined his players. He found other ways to discipline. "You don't gain anything by fining," Auerbach argues. "People say fine him and if he does it again, suspend him. Why? You only hurt yourself."

After Auerbach retired as coach to assume full-time duties as general manager, one of the players missed a flight. Bill Russell, who succeeded Auerbach as coach, asked him how much to fine the player. "Nothing!" was Auerbach's reply. "I told him that you never got fined when you played for me and he says, 'But we've got rules.' Yeah, but it doesn't say what you've got to do to the guy. It happened. So what? Now he owes you one, see?" Auerbach had rules but he never identified the punishments. "If my job depends on winning and I have a rule that says if you're late for curfew you're suspended, I don't hurt the kid as much as I hurt myself. You should have your rules but the punishment should be different with every case. If a guy keeps breaking your rules, you get rid of him."

As a part of the way Auerbach dealt with his people, he talked to every one of them, one on one. If anybody ever says that you should treat everybody alike, Auerbach will set you straight. "They're wrong. You don't. You don't have two sets of standards but personalities are different." Moreover, Auerbach appreciated the fact these were college graduates in their late 20s or early 30s. "They're not kids, so why do I have to show them I'm boss every day and show them all this ridiculous discipline? They know I'm in charge. So you don't have to be demonstrative to show them you're the boss. But you do have to understand them."

Even though they may be good, NBA coaches rarely stay in the same place for more than four seasons. "They get these players as young guys and after four years the training camp is the same, the pre-game talks are the same, the practices are the same two-and-a-half hours even though the plays haven't changed. The kids get bored and as a result their production goes down and they're not as good as they should be. Next thing you know, the coach leaves. I won't name any guys, but I could name you 10 guys like that in the NBA; after four years they're gone because they don't change with the players."

Auerbach was an exception, coaching in Boston for 16 years. He did it by being in constant evolution. He never ran his practices by the clock. Instead, he ran practice only for as long as it took to accomplish his agenda. "By the time several years had gone by with these guys, I could run a practice in 40 minutes," Auerbach asserts. "Today, they go two-and-a-half hours, come hell or high water, because they don't think their players know the stuff. I respected them as men and treated them as men. That's the main thing."

Auerbach made a habit of studying his players. He came to understand how they thought and appreciated their personalities. "Cousy was emotional and he gave me everything he had," Auerbach says of his former captain. "If he made a mistake, he made a mistake. I didn't have to yell at him. Same with K.C. Jones, he's another sensitive guy. But other guys like Tom Heinsohn and Jim Loscutoff, you had to get on their tail. I used to get on Russell a lot."

One evening, Boston was buried in a blizzard but the Celtics played their scheduled game. Player-coach Russell was a no-show. There were no assistants to help; Auerbach did not believe in assistant coaches ("It's just 10 guys," he notes). So Auerbach came out of the stands and coached the team. With seconds remaining and the Celtics ahead, Russell arrived wearing a derby and cape and smiled at the score. In the locker room afterwards, Auerbach took hold of him and yelled, " 'You big, no good, SOB, where the hell were you?' He said he got caught in the blizzard and I shouted, 'Havlicek walked four miles! Next time you leave your goddamn Lamborghini with the six carburetors because when you're not here, it's two people missing. It's Russell the coach and Russell the player.' I just laid into him. I didn't want to let it drop; I wanted him to owe me one big time. I wanted a big performance, which we got, and we won the next game."

Auerbach was not just a psychological warrior with his stars. He paid significant attention to his bench. "I tried to keep them happy because I know how it feels when you're not playing, when you're sitting there," Auerbach remarks. "I would practice them a lot and tell them your chance will come but you've got to have the balls to hang in there." Sam and K.C. Jones, subs then, listened, paid the price of perseverance, and took over for Cousy and Bill Sharman when they retired.

A lot of players retired as Celtics. During Auerbach's tenure, more began and ended their careers with Boston than did players from the rest of the NBA teams combined. His players respected him because he knew the game. They appreciated him because they knew his word was his bond and he would treat them fairly, one on one. "Players today are looking for commercials and how to maneuver their stats to get more money," Auerbach snaps. "While they're playing, the cash register is in their mind. 'If I average 12 points a game, my agent can get me $2 million, but if I can average 17, I could

"Everybody would ask me, 'How did you handle those personalities, those egos?' I would always tell them that you don't handle them. You handle animals. You deal with people."

get $3 million.' So they're out there counting." He didn't have that problem. Auerbach was salary czar as well as coach, and salary was solely dependent on a player's contribution to winning, not his statistics. "I wasn't interested in whether a guy had six rebounds and 15 points per game. You can get 15, play lousy defense, give up 18, and we get beat. It was all about contribution towards winning and they bought it."

Auerbach remains in contact with his former players. He possesses a genuine affection for every one of them. "I've affected them and they've affected me," Auerbach expresses tenderly. "We had a true family feeling which it's impossible to have today." For sure, his players stay connected out of admiration for their former coach. But it is also because a lot of fun occurred along the way. "There's no fun off the court today," Auerbach points out. "We used to go to movies together." Can you picture Dennis Rodman and Phil Jackson at the Bijou? Auerbach starts to chuckle.

Photo credit: Dick Raphael

"My first year, we're going on trains with sleepers and I've got to figure out who goes in the upper berth, who goes in the lower berth. I said, 'Fellas, I measured the berths and the upper berth is four inches bigger, so in all fairness I want the five biggest guys to have the upper berth.' They go, 'OK.' All of a sudden about March, one guy comes over and says, 'Coach, I measured the berths, they're the same size.' I said, 'I'm humbled.'"

Auerbach actually is a humble icon of the game. There is no glitz, no glamour, no glory. Just story after story about how much he loved the game and his players. One of his favorite tales is when he had the chance to beat his own record of 17 straight wins. "We were playing Detroit, one of the worst teams in the league, for the 18th win," Auerbach recalls and leans back in his chair. "It was on New Years' Day so I told the guys I'd supply the beer and pretzels and we'd stay in and play cards, get to bed early New Year's Eve. We were asleep about 12:30. Next day they clobbered us, beat us by 30. The easiest team for us to play to break the record. It taught me a lesson. After that, I took it one game at a time and to hell with all the records."

Auerbach finishes his mail and turns his attention to the memorabilia that surround him. When Auerbach was a high school teacher and coach, he wrote an article about training based on an obstacle course he built. It is framed on his wall. "Very simple. I'm not a very complicated person, not a computer guy or any of that stuff. That was one of the big thrills of my life, to have that published." Near his desk is his book about basketball, one copy for each language in which it was printed. "I wrote every bit of that myself, in longhand because I couldn't type anything. Here it is in Japanese, Burmese, Russian, Polish, Italian, and English. That book will teach you everything you need to know. The game hasn't changed. The fundamentals are the same."

More philosophical than before, Auerbach notes, "You get certain thrills in life which stay with you." He points to the photo of legendary college coach Hank Iba. "I was playing college ball and we played Oklahoma A&M where Iba was coaching, and after the game he came to the locker room just to see me and congratulate me on a great game. People sometimes say Red wasn't a player. He was one goddamn player," Auerbach says matter-of-factly with a nod and a wink. "Of course you get better as you get older. I don't know whether I could have made the pros. It would have been close." Auerbach points to another picture of himself with Iba and University of Kentucky coaching legend Adolph Rupp, and another with UCLA's John Wooden. "Next thing you know, they're friends of yours. Ain't that just the greatest?"

If only they all thought the way you do, Red.

Daniel J. Edelman
Founder and Chairman of
Edelman Public Relations Worldwide

Daniel J. Edelman is the founder and chairman of Daniel J. Edelman, Inc., the largest privately held independent public relations firm in the world and the sixth largest overall. There are two operating companies, Edelman Public Relations Worldwide and PR 21. A staff of 1,800 works out of 42 offices in North America, Latin America, Europe and Asia. In 1999, Edelman generated $193 million in revenue. Forty-eight years after establishing the agency, he still stays close to his roots.

"I have always thought of myself as a journalist." In his trademark gentle, deliberate voice, Edelman reflects on those early beginnings with obvious delight. "I started writing on a typewriter when I was five years old. I had mumps and I wrote notes to my mother. I was put in the maid's room in the corner near the kitchen so I wouldn't infect the other kids. I would type up notes as to what I wanted for lunch and slip them under the door. I began to write when I was about 11. A friend of mine and I did a newspaper for the neighborhood. We had a kind of a gelatin material to make copies and distributed them to all our friends and families. We had maybe a hundred in circulation. A freebie, no ads, no price, just fun."

As a high school student, Edelman served as sports editor of the *DeWitt Clinton News* in the Bronx. Gifted with many talents and a sharp mind, he recalls an early turning point in life when he was forced to decide whether to report the news or make it. "The sports editor just before me at the *News* was Jack Rosenblatt, who later became Jack Raymond, a front page writer for the *New York Times*, who covered Yugoslavia and later wrote a book about the Defense Department. Jack took a liking to me and sponsored me to run for high school president. I lost by a rather narrow margin and we couldn't figure out why, so we did a little investigation and found a lot of my ballots in the toilet, a typical Tammany Hall operation. I thought a lot about that incident. Maybe I would have won and maybe I wouldn't, but it was kind of reflective of this struggle going on within me: do I really want to be a reporter or do I really want to be a doer?"

The dilemma lingered through Columbia College as he wrote for *The Spectator*, became president of his fraternity, served on the student board, and was graduated Phi Beta Kappa and ranked among the top 15 people in his class. But options were limited. World War II was pressing forward, but with two older brothers already in the service his father asked him not to volunteer. Edelman knew there wouldn't be much time, so he seized the moment to enroll in the Columbia Graduate School of Journalism. He then took a job in Poughkeepsie, New York, as a news writer on a local paper owned by the family of one his classmates in journalism school.

Quickly, Edelman became sports editor of the *Sunday Courier* and also did some daily writing for the *Eagle*, which later became the *New Yorker*, the daily paper. He also explored other elements of his beloved journalism. "I'd never been a photographer before, but that was part of being the sports editor. I took a lot of pictures with my Speed Graphic. One day, I went up to Hyde Park and took a picture of President and Mrs. Roosevelt emerging from church with their guest, Queen Juliana of The Netherlands. A little girl gave the Queen a bouquet. I happened to be going to Manhattan to see my folks so I dropped off one of the pictures at the *New York Daily News*. It was on the front page the next day with the caption, 'A Queen Bows.' It ran on the AP and appeared all over the country. It was a beautiful picture. I still have it."

Edelman was drafted into the Army in December 1942, a year after Pearl Harbor. He was immediately assigned to public relations and then the Army Specialized Training Program. "They thought that they'd invade Spain or France, so they had thousands of us studying those languages at different universities. I was studying Spanish at Ohio State. Later, I was assigned to psychological warfare in the Fifth Mobile Radio Broadcasting company. We trained in Bloomsbury, a suburb of London. On the boat going over, there were 3,000 guys, and I did a daily newspaper. I listened to the radio all day and wrote the paper in the afternoon."

Edelman's military journey further honed his writing skills. Not long after the Allies established a foothold in France after D-Day, he was summoned to the Continent to assist a Columbia classmate who was editor of the nightly analysis of German propaganda. When his friend was transferred, Edelman took over. "I was flown to Paris and wrote the analysis for months in Verdun. It was fascinating, assessing the German claims that their V-bombs were destroying London and communicating what Goebbels was saying in his 'Das Reich' editorials. My report went to general officers all across the front, from General Omar Bradley on down, and to our propaganda people to help them offset the Nazi claims in our radio broadcasts that reached the German troops and the whole war region. When the war ended, I did a survey of German reactions to the peace. I covered Nuremberg and wrote reports on the Nuremberg trial. There's a relationship between psychological warfare and propaganda and journalism. In a way I've always felt that psychological warfare oriented me to public relations. People sometimes kid me when I say that."

Edelman returned to the United States a master craftsman of his trade. He is unequivocal in characterizing the value of his training. "I just addressed our 20 interns who are winding up a summer stay in our office. I told them that the most important attribute to success is to have a skill that's better than anyone else's and to keep pursuing and to build your own special knowledge and strength. It gives you an edge. I told them that in public relations these days they have to get strong in medicine, technology, finance, consumer behavior, or tourism. I told them they will have their best chance of success by building a niche capability."

Edelman believes that the success of his company is framed in the extent to which his employees understand that message. "It's true of business in general. Companies are built by having a unique offering. They may be diversified later but great companies are built first and foremost by individuals who are great at their specialty. It's key," he states emphatically.

> "I really like working. It was unusual for me to take two weeks off ... The first week was fine but by the second week I was back working."

But adaptation is the antidote to the disasters of a rapidly changing corporate environment. "You have to stay with it no matter what happens because in this business things change quickly and you can fall off the top at any moment. There isn't a year that passes that we don't have to close an office or change managers. Three or four of the managers from last year are not here. We close offices. We open new ones. We have to be very quick. You've got to attend to business. You have to continue to learn.

"College is just the beginning of education. You must continue to study. You've got to continue to read, go to the opera, the theater, movies, listen to jazz. In order to be current in our business and to be productive and creative, you have to have a sense of what's going on in society and our culture. Sharpen your talents; learn and master new ones."

The passion to master his specialty, to write, continues to occupy Edelman on a daily basis. "What I have is the ability to write and edit, and I still enjoy it. We have an internal newsletter called 'Edelman Talk.' It comes out every Friday. I'm still the editor. I don't write it. The news comes from our status reports from all the managers, and one of our guys writes it, but I'm editing the thing as if it were years ago and I enjoy doing that. I am also very involved in the editing of our corporate brochures."

Given an opening, Edelman is relentless in preaching the gospel of mastery. "When you take a look at the pyramid of people trying to get ahead, the skills of the people at the bottom are not significantly differentiated. But as you approach the top of the triangle, you are staring at people with super skill. Michael Jordan is the perfect example. He developed his skill beyond belief. He achieved perfection with his incredible and unparalleled basketball talent. It's the same for somebody who's a great ballerina or a sculptor or a painter or a writer."

Taking one's skill to such levels requires sacrifice and self-control. "You have to be committed but not fanatical. You have to be directed, have to pursue success with zeal. But fanatics may or may not be good leaders. There are people here who are neurotic and work too many hours and devote their whole lives to the business. Up to a point they're terrific; they really get a lot done. Afterward when they move up and become supervisors, they expect everybody else to act the same way. Fanatics often expect everybody else to be like them. They're not very good supervisors. There's a limit to their growth because they're not balanced leaders."

Edelman is the first to admit he has not always been true to his own advice. At a time in his life when most men with half of his success retire to the country club, he continues to look for new skills to master. "I honestly don't know where I'll go from here. I really like working. It was unusual

Edelman, far right, and his wife, with Henry Kissinger and Illinois Senator Chuck Percy

for me to take two weeks off, which I tried this summer. The first week was fine but by the second week I was back working. I played tennis in the morning and then read the *New York Times* and the *Wall Street Journal* and worked every afternoon, dictating and so forth. I enjoy working. I like the stimulation."

Fiercely proud of the success of his family-owned business, Edelman realizes that avoiding a merger will be one of his biggest challenges. "We have maintained independence, which is very unusual among the leading firms in PR. Most of them have sold out to ad agencies. So we're the largest independent firm in the world and the only independent in the top 10. We believe public relations is a separate discipline and shouldn't be subsumed under advertising. It changes, in some ways, the recognition of public relations as a fundamental, basic, professional service."

But writing isn't the only skill Edelman has developed. After nearly a half century of work with Fortune 500 companies, Edelman has mastered the art of communication in general. "We spend a lot more time with government relations or crisis problems. We represent AT&T in the continuing battle with the Baby Bells to get into local service. We handled the Odwalla apple juice recall using the Internet. We deal with mergers and acquisitions constantly, stopping them, winning them. It's the most interesting and professionally challenging thing I could imagine because you have to work with the chairman and CEO and the key people on strategies and operations. It isn't just putting out a commercial."

Whether business historians make note of landmark Edelman promotions such as the first Concorde landing in the US, the StarKist/Heinz cam-

Edelman, left, hosting a conference with General Eisenhower and Tom Turner of Chicago's Columbia University Club

paign for dolphin safe tuna, clearing the way for the Vietnam Veterans War Memorial, or facilitating the Viacom-Blockbuster merger, Edelman is much more pragmatic about his achievements. "The greatest high is the realization that over a period of time we have become very successful. You don't think about that very often and you keep waking up every day and you hear what accounts you're going to lose, and what the competition is doing. But the years have passed and no client represents that large a percentage of our total volume. We don't have to run as scared as we did earlier."

The tough days are gone indeed. But they are not forgotten and serve as corporate folklore — wonderful Yiddish stories — to remember the past and admonish the future. "The toughest day of my career was when we still had a pretty small operation, maybe we had 20 people. I came in one day and there was a note signed by seven of our staff that they had left and set up their own office across the street. And obviously they had been planning this for months because they had the office all set up. Our files were missing. I worked night and day for about three weeks and I visited every client. We didn't lose any then, but it weakened our position with several of them which we lost later. This new firm lasted two or three years, then collapsed. But seven out of 20 people? You just don't think people will do that to you."

As you walk through his Chicago corporate museum on the 63rd floor overlooking Lake Michigan, Edelman pontificates on the meaning of newspaper clippings, letters of testimony, and his industry's equivalent to the Oscars, the Silver Anvil Awards. "We always have said what we think. We emphasize the truth in communicating to the public — telling the truth and telling it immediately and saying what you're going to do about it if it's a problem. So I think that knowing that I've helped contribute to the standards of the practice of public relations, to the ethical standards, has been an ongoing and growing satisfaction for me."

Edelman and his wife, Ruth, of 47 years are especially proud that their three children occupy key positions in the company. Richard is president and chief executive officer; Renee is executive vice president at PR 21, specializing in new media, and John is international director of human resources.

Daniel J. Edelman has a gift for words that he has sculpted into an art form and used to build a business into an archetype. "Leadership involves making decisions sometimes by yourself, about important issues that confront you. In running a business you have to get the job done and that means you have to be prepared, have your skill as developed as it can be, take risks. We've made mistakes, but we also have had successes in hiring terrific people, opening up offices or making an acquisition. It's a matter of being a decision-maker and being willing to take the good with the bad. I feel I'm ready for whatever comes next."

Bill McCartney

Founder and President of
Promise Keepers Christian Ministry

William P. McCartney turned 60 in the first summer of the new millennium. For most of those years, life was football. McCartney attended the University of Missouri, playing linebacker on the football team. After graduating with a BA in education, he continued with the game he loved as a coach. In 1982, the University of Colorado hired him to turn its long-mediocre program around. Over the next 13 years, the Golden Buffaloes under McCartney became one of college football's elite teams, culminating in a share of the 1990 national championship.

McCartney was so successful he was twice named Coach of the Year by the sportswriters of United Press International and three times by the coaches in the Big Eight Conference. His exemplary career placed him in the Colorado Sports Hall of Fame and the Orange Bowl Hall of Fame. McCartney retired from coaching on January 1, 1995, immediately following the Fiesta Bowl, to pursue a closer personal relationship with God and to lead the budding Promise Keepers ministry he founded in 1990, dedicated to "uniting men to become godly influences in their world. It's completely opposite of football," McCartney notes with deep seriousness. "The three most important words are yield, surrender, and obey. To be great in the kingdom of God, you have to see others as better than yourself and take on a posture of servanthood."

In March 1990, coach McCartney and a friend, Dave Wardell, were on a three-hour car ride to a Fellowship of Christian Athletes meeting, when they first discussed the idea of filling a stadium with Christian men. Later that year, 72 men fasted and prayed about the concept of thousands of men coming together for the purpose of Christian discipleship. In July 1991, 4,200 men gathered for the first Promise Keepers conference at the University of Colorado basketball arena. Since then, more than 3.5 million men have attended Promise Keepers stadium and arena conferences, organized by nearly 200 staff members operating under a $41 million budget, and assisted by 20,000 men and women volunteers across the country.

McCartney draws on the Bible for his personal direction, his Promise Keepers homilies, and his philosophy about leadership. In what may be

Jesus' most famous lecture, McCartney points to the Sermon on the Mount as the fundamental starting point. "Jesus said, 'Blessed are the poor in spirit, for they and they alone shall gain the kingdom of heaven.' Blessed are those who realize that in and of themselves they can do nothing, and only through the power of God they can do anything. There is corruption in your heart. It is deceitful, and the more you walk with Christ, the more you realize your total dependence upon Him." McCartney invokes the words of early 20th Century Scottish minister Oswald Chambers and concludes, "You must attend the funeral of your independence."

McCartney is visibly intense, genuine, and hard at work convincing those who listen. His style is part preacher, part coach, and the combination is reminiscent of football's greatest locker room speeches. "In order to handle those egos and to work in the company of skilled and tempered athletes, or others that have tremendous gifts, you have to have humility. It's the only way you can corral them," McCartney proposes. Always mindful of the skepticism in his audience, McCartney illuminates his discourse with images. "When they raced chariots, they would use as many as eight stallions to pull those big wagons. The implement they put on the horses to get them to run in unison was called a *humilité*. That's where the word humility gets its purest derivative. Harnessed power; that's humility." In addition to humility, there is meekness, which McCartney defines as a blend of strength, courage, and kindness. "Great coaches coach with meekness. They have tremendous empathy for their players and they are courageous in the way they make decisions. It takes strength to do both. The really great coaches have tapped into kingdom principles that will go the distance in whatever you do."

Whether uniting men of faith or men on the gridiron, McCartney is a Rocky Mountain guru in team building. And people must be taught to become a team. It is not inherent to human nature. "The greatest craving of the human spirit is for significance," McCartney proclaims. "I have never met a man that didn't need to be affirmed every day." To tackle that, McCartney has created two operating definitions for success, one is improvement and the other is "when those who know you best love you most," McCartney adds tenderly. McCartney will never coach again, but if he did, he would follow the tenets implied in his favorite couplet: "Do you love me, do you love me not? You told me once, but I forgot." As though drafted from a lecture on Maslow's hierarchy of needs, McCartney is adamant that "every guy needs to be told every day that you love him. Not necessarily in those words. Sometimes it's a pat on the back, sometimes you rustle his hair, sometimes you call him on the phone. Some guys need to be affirmed with more exhortation than others, but every guy needs to be affirmed, needs to be reinforced."

For McCartney, achievement in football and in life is as much about morale as it is about talent and work. He even has a recipe for mixing the ingredients. "It's four times as important the spirit you bring into the situation than your actual abilities. Ability just gives you a chance to be good, but if you have a whole-hearted spirit, then you have the quality that allows your abilities to surface." A good coach calls out the spirit of the team, convinces the players that the sacrifices are worth it and encourages them to raise the standard so their abilities might flourish. All of that is done by mastering the fundamentals. "You hear people say, you've got to make it fun. They misunderstand," McCartney admonishes. "Fun is when you learn to do it right. It doesn't matter whether you're a sales clerk or waiting tables or a CEO. The person who knows what they're doing is the person who's having fun. Fun is the first three letters of fundamentals. So great coaches are the ones that keep finding ways to get these guys to master the basics."

McCartney points to former Baltimore Colts and Miami Dolphins coach Don Shula as such a coach. Shula won 347 NFL games including playoffs, took six teams to the Super Bowl, including his 1972 17-0 Dolphins, the only undefeated team in NFL history. In *The Winning Edge*, the book he wrote after retiring, Shula spoke about what McCartney calls "conviction-driven leadership based on a vision of perfection." Shula had such a keen vision for what he wanted to have happen on the field that when his offensive teams would practice a play, he would ask them to run it again for only the slightest imperfection. "He knew exactly what he wanted and the same thing's true in whatever you lead. The leader has to show what it looks like and unfold it like an artist does on a canvas." And then the leader must build that spirit, that morale. This time, McCartney, points to coaching colleague Bo Schembechler of the University of Michigan, whose 194 wins, 17 bowl appearances, and 13 Big Ten Conference championships in 21 years remain unprecedented. "Tremendous motivation, determination, drive, passion, work ethic, all those things. He was a hard-driving, hard-charging guy from day one and yet the guys loved him. He was able to extract something special and the way he did it was he sold his team on the spirit of interdependence."

> "Fun is when you learn to do it right...whether you're a sales clerk or waiting tables or a CEO. The person who knows what they're doing is the person who's having fun."

In an earlier era, the spirit enabled McCartney to win football games. Today the Spirit is helping him win souls. Through stadium conferences, ongoing local small groups, educational seminars, resource materials, and local churches, Promise Keepers encourages men to live godly lives and to keep seven basic promises to God (engaging in worship and living in purity), to family (building strong marriages), to fellow men (building nurturing relationships), to humankind (displaying racial and denominational ecumenism), and to the church (providing prayer and resources). These are made manifest and culminate through the seventh commitment to lead a life of influence by being obedient to the Great Commandment (Mark 12:30-31): "Thou shalt love the Lord thy God with all thy heart and with all thy soul and with all thy mind and with all thy strength and thy neighbor as thyself" — and the Great Commission (Matthew 28:19-20): "Go and teach all nations, baptizing them in the Name of the Father, and of the Son, and of the Holy Ghost, to observe all things whatsoever I have commanded you."

"As God's Holy Spirit gains dominion in a man's heart, you see a man change," McCartney says with profound joy. "No one but God can change a man's heart. That's why we need the Lord. The moment you receive Christ in your heart, in the form of God's Holy Spirit, you start a process in life of learning to surrender to God and yield to His prompting in your life. In that stadium, they're all at different places in the process. Some have backslid, some are living lives of contradiction, some walk intimately with God. We have this incredible spectrum and we're feeding them with the truths of God's word so they might come together to stand strong for the gospel of Jesus Christ."

Christians are supposed to be set apart, supposed to look different to the world, so people will like what they see and want some of that for themselves. Martin Luther King clearly denied himself for humanity and won the accolades of the planet. But most Christians have seldom been like that. Instead of being a people set apart, truly humble, yielded, living lives of love and service, they have more often grabbed for the golden ring than marched toward the golden throne. For McCartney, the duplicity is "because basic human nature is sinful. Left to ourselves, we self-destruct. Jesus came to win back for us access to a holy life. God is the biggest love story ever seen. You've never understood the word love until you see the way God operates. If we turn towards Him, just turn, He comes running. He doesn't sit back and wonder if you really mean it, he comes. That relationship is what builds our identity and transforms our behavior."

To demonstrate a suitable model of such transformation, McCartney takes his audience outside the stadium. Mother Theresa not only captured the planet, she captured McCartney. "She lived a life of servitude," McCartney characterizes. "She was inconspicuous most of her life. She possessed meekness: strength and courage coupled with kindness. She served people who were hopelessly ravaged. It doesn't make any sense to the natural mind. But Jesus taught in the 25th chapter of Matthew that whenever you see someone who is naked and clothe them or you see somebody who is hungry and feed him, it's as if 'you did it unto me.' Mother Teresa had the right heart. She walked so intimately with the Lord and when you turn towards God he will clean your heart and keep you in front of him."

Less than a decade ago, McCartney was yearning for championships and gaining awards. The objectives and the rewards are dramatically different today. "I still have goals," McCartney states and then qualifies. "The Bible says in Proverbs, 'Where there is no vision people perish.' If you don't know where you're going, you miss opportunities along the way. But when you've been born of the spirit of God, you know who you are, you know whom you serve, you know where you're going. In that context I have goals. In other words, the Lord has plans for me. My goal is how can I please the Lord because the reputation of Jesus Christ is at stake. Jesus Christ is not at stake; He is God. But his reputation on earth is tarnished because His sons have compromised who He is and are not walking obediently and faithfully. And so I have goals."

Bill with wife Lyndi

McCartney is the first to admit he fails more at these goals than those he set as one of America's foremost coaches. "I am not doing as well as I should. My heart is selfish and I'm thinking about my comfort zone, of choking my motor down and idling." He also is the first to admit he feels totally inadequate for the task. "No one would ever have chosen me to do this and I wouldn't have chosen me. I don't qualify. My life is full of holes and contradictions. There are guys who are much more godly. But somehow the Lord, in His humor, reached into life and pulled me out and gave me this favor. I don't even know what to do with it, let alone run it."

But McCartney need not worry. He has a team. A lot of the plans for Promise Keepers come through his wife Lyndi. "Most of my life I was a taker and she was a giver," McCartney admits. "I didn't figure that out for the longest time. It was always about my dreams, my gifts, what I had longed to do." Throughout the years, his wife put her dreams on the back burner and rallied alongside her husband and championed what he was doing. Now her gifts are coming to bear within the ministry. "She's more talented than I am. She can do instinctively what I can't figure out for two weeks. It's very humbling to see how she just quietly serves me while I am Mr. Wonderful in public. She is really the one who has the character and the values."

If my memory is correct, there is a verse in the Bible somewhere, that says "Let not the wise man boast in his wisdom, let not the rich man boast in his riches, but let him who boasts, boast that he knows me, the one true God." Something to that effect, anyway. It is really McCartney's mantra. He has been the best in the game. He has garnered all the prizes. And it is not those things that make him sing. "I tell guys with great aspirations and great potential and obvious gifts, if you chase all those other things you're going to come up empty," McCartney warns. "Those things do not satisfy. There's a void within every man and every woman that only God can fill." The message is crystal clear. If you chase all the things society says are important and you build your hopes and your dreams and your future on all those things, one day you will realize that life threw you a no-hitter. It is also foreboding. When you have one hour left to live, you are not going to look back on all those things because you have too little time to sort it all out. You are going to look at where you go from here, what is in store next. McCartney is ready for that moment and pleads for those who are not. "You're either going to spend all eternity separated from God or all eternity in relationship with God. Life is a test and God offers a free answer sheet in Jesus Christ. Don't miss it."

Rhetoric worth a review. There are a lot of empty people out there with a lot of awards on their wall. They are lost and aching and do not even know what they are aching for. "That's so true," McCartney agrees knowing the extent of his own trophy case. "That's why we've got to tell everybody who will listen about Jesus. He's the answer but most people can't see it." But while he is at the center of the movement, McCartney does not want to be the center of attention. "I don't want them to see me at all," McCartney exclaims. "If they see me, they're going to see the wrong thing, because all of us fall short of what God would intend for us to be like. I am merely a vessel to pour God into others. I am one of the horses in the harness, pulling God's chariot. I draw all my esteem from who He is. See, it isn't about us, it's about who He is and receiving what He gives us."

Hugh Wolff
*Former Music Director of
the St. Paul Chamber Orchestra*

It's 8:00 in the morning on one of those rare weather perfect summer days in Minneapolis. The sky is cloudless and blue to the horizon. The temperature and humidity are low. The horseflies and mosquitoes are quiet. There is a slight hint of fall in the air as a few towering oak trees model the bright yellow leaves they will wear throughout September. From the outside of his stately brick city home, it would appear Hugh Wolff and family are asleep or enjoying the tranquility of life near Lake Harriet. Not so. Inside, young children are bustling up and down the grand staircase in response to their mother's voice and an imminent departure for school. Hugh Wolff, music director of the 33-member St. Paul Chamber Orchestra, dressed in khaki pants, blue polo shirt and wool socks, is already hard at work reviewing a musical score.

"It's a huge repertoire," declares Wolff. "It's a fantastic art form. It's a lifetime of study. To be in this business you have to love to study. You've got to love to be all alone in your room, in your head, staring at a score for four hours at a stretch, without any hope of ever performing it. If that makes you antsy, nervous, or if that is not just completely, emotionally and intellectually satisfying in and of itself, then you're in the wrong field."

Whether it is the rumpled clothing and the tousled hair that reveal the early hours he has already spent or the shear energy in his voice, it is clear Wolff is in the right place. "That's always been the case for me," Wolff chimes. "I'm happy just to sit and think about how cool this is."

Wolff examines every score to discover what the composer did musically, what the music is about, his feelings on the piece, what the composer may have been feeling, what the composer was hoping the audience would feel. From this, Wolff determines how the score is put together, what he must do to make it happen the way it was intended and what it will sound like. "It's like walking through a gallery and spending an hour in front of a picture, admiring it, trying to understand. That is motivation enough. That's what's so fabulous about the art form. It exists to perform and it exists like a novel. You read a novel but you don't perform a novel. We exist on both levels and that's quite wonderful and special but you have to be absolutely comfortable in the solitary aspect of it."

In addition to his duties in St. Paul, Wolff is also the chief conductor of the 120-member Frankfurt, Germany, Radio Orchestra. He also engages in numerous guest-conducting opportunities around the world. Such devotion to duty does come with a price. He is away from home much of the time. The way conductors work in today's society, that is inevitable. Wolff finds the separation regrettable having grown up in a household where his father and mother were separated from each other only a few times in almost 50 years of marriage. "I'm away from home a hundred nights a year and I've got three kids," bemoans Wolff. "I try to keep it under a hundred nights and sometimes, since the kids are getting a little older, we travel together."

But travel is not the only factor. Wolff keeps very odd hours. Often, like today, he is home during the day when the children are at school. And then he is gone each concert evening from 6:00 p.m. until well after they are asleep. The notion of a traditional family in which he was raised is very hard to recreate in his family. "I've been very lucky to make such a wonderful living," Wolff admits, "and it's tremendously satisfying and rewarding from all the other standard assessments. But I have this terrible juggling act with travel, my concert responsibilities, and my home life."

Without the tuxedo and grooming, Wolff appears to be anything but a concertmaster. His young face and blithe body suggest he is an aspiring musician. His discography reports otherwise. After 15 years of serious piano study and composing Wolff began and continues a career in orchestral leadership that is remarkable in its speed and effectiveness. He has never tried to plan his career. Every position he has ever held was offered to him. While he received numerous invitations to leave the chamber orchestra, he always remained content in the smaller theater of St. Paul. While he admits he has a healthy ego, he doesn't have an overwhelming sense of ambition. "I've done a lot of the things that I thought, 'If I ever do that, great.' And I can look back with a lot of pride but I'm not burning with the desire to be the sole chief conductor of the Berlin Philharmonic. I can live my life without that level of achievement."

Wolff's hours of solitude and reflection, his confident sense of self and his understanding of those with whom he works combine to make him an extraordinary achiever and master of his own destiny. What makes Wolff an effective conductor is very similar to what makes an effective CEO. "It's leading people without leading them by the nose," Wolff explains. "Every conductor works with a hundred or more exceptionally talented individuals. They have strong points of view. They have very strong desires. They have big egos, just the way we do. It's the conductor's job to get them to work together, to subsume their egos to the conductor's."

But nothing about Wolff connotes a misuse of power. On stage and in his living room he seems content and comfortable. Wolff recognizes that his orchestra must not subsume their egos entirely to his. Some sense of individual ego has to be balanced with group cooperation. The conductor must coordinate people and show them its value and how they can achieve a higher level of performance. So Wolff must exercise psychological skills with his musicians to inspire them to put aside their individual preferences for his. Wolff states that "a lot of what we do in rehearsal, and in performance, is more about people than it is about musical correctness and instrument balance."

The orchestra conductor is a fascinating oddity, the object of all the public acclaim while the talented and almost always anonymous musicians are the ones actually playing the music. Conducting is a very interesting discipline and, in many ways, the last of its kind, a throwback to another era. Conductors have absolute power. An orchestra rehearsal is run in a very odd way where there isn't much room for dissent. Wolff repeatedly draws a parallel between the concert hall and the boardroom to explain his style. "With the Chamber Orchestra we've tried to set up a different kind of structure. There are only 33 people in the orchestra. I've spoken a lot publicly and with the orchestra about how different opinions can be voiced and entertained. But ultimately, when you get down to it, the buck stops there and that's true in any leadership position."

Like any chief executive, Wolff believes leaders must have the ability to disregard impulses for popularity and feelings of alienation as they try to persuade people to perform at their highest level for them and with them. Wolff is not naive and realizes that he is asking some people to perform in a way that they'd rather not perform. Their taste, their style, their sense of the music would take them in a different direction. "They're not going to love me and my way of doing it," Wolff acknowledges. "But, hopefully they're going to respect it and want to do it my way out of some sense of responsibility and, presumably, with some admiration for who I am and the way I'm going about my business."

The leader that is driven by the need to be loved will have a very different result than the leader that can accept the notion that some people like you and some people might not like you, or your views, or your talent. Aware of the danger, Wolff warns, "It's important to have a relatively thick skin in a leadership position."

It is also important to remember who is inside the skins of the musicians, and so the way Wolff addresses one musician might be very different from the way he addresses another musician right in front of everybody. "I have a certain style with one person and a different style with another person in the hopes of achieving the kind of give and take that is positive for everyone," says Wolff. "A good conductor is very psychologically sensitive."

It takes time to develop a relationship with an orchestra and to really come to know their individual personalities. But often, due to the nature of the industry, there is no time. As a frequent guest conductor in front of an orchestra he has never met, a hundred people he has never seen in his life, Wolff must begin telling them what to do and immediately sense who they are, what they want, what they need, and what they can offer. "There's a tremendous amount of mutual vibration going on," Wolff notes, "and you have to have really, really good antennae."

Wolff believes you develop these antennae in part through experience. But in greater part, he views them as just a sixth sense that leaders must have. "Great leaders have a presence," Wolff marvels. "People talk about them when they walk into the room and the room is energized by them." Where they acquired it and how to define it remains a mystery. But like any leader, "conductors have to have that quality so when you're standing one foot above everybody else on the podium and you open your mouth people will stop what they're doing and listen."

What happens on the concert stage is a combination of a million things all operating on such a subtle level that you can't measure each one individually but you know they are there. They are combinations of personality, ability to communicate in a language that does not involve speech, ability to communicate feelings and emotions that the music is stating and the conductor is experiencing, and the ability of the people a hundred and twenty feet away to actually hear and sense all of that. It is even in the body language.

"What is it about Itzhak Perlman?" asks Wolff. "The way his face moves, the way he smiles, the way his body moves when he plays? These are very subtle, hard to define, but they all add up to what we call presence because they are genuine and they add up to something big. You know it incrementally. It's similar to the different ways people respond to baseball players Ken Griffey Jr. and Albert Belle. When Ken Griffey smiles as he swings, it's different than Albert Belle who frowns when he swings. Whether we like it or not, and certainly Albert Belle doesn't like it, the public responds to one more than the other."

Truly great performers perform for themselves and for their relationship to what they're doing, for their art form. The public has an uncanny ability to winnow out affectation, not 100 percent of the time but in general, as Wolff suggests, "they know who is doing a lot of extra stuff and it's bullshit because it doesn't come naturally to them and they will give less of a response to them than to those who are genuine."

In conducting, Leonard Bernstein may have done it best. He possessed a powerful personality. When you saw Bernstein perform, you never felt he was

> "To be in this business you have to love to study. You've got to love to be all alone in your room, in your head, staring at a score for four hours at a stretch without any hope of ever performing it."

interpreting it. He was so magnetic, he convinced you that was the way it had to be. He captured you.

Ever the baseball fan, Wolff points to Cincinnati Reds outfielder Ken Griffey Jr. as the paragon of such personality. "I don't know the guy at all, but there is this sense that he is incredibly comfortable in his skin, that he never puts on an act any of the time, and that his talent and his love for what he does are paramount; they drive him and everything else takes care of itself." It is a very important and powerful concept and it is apparent to baseball fans everywhere. Even cynics look at Griffey and agree he is for real. We are able to do so because of the antennae Wolff intimates we all possess to sense genuineness in other people, to sense when someone is phony or not.

Griffey is among the rare individuals who are obviously genuine. As for the others, Wolff laments that "many of the more complicated, less popular, but really gifted individuals have demons inside that they're grappling with while they're exercising their amazing talents. They have less of that comfortableness in their body, in their skin, in their personality. There's less of a wholeness — it's not as congruent, who they are, their personality and their talents."

At the end of the 1999-2000 season, Wolff ended his 12-year relationship with the St. Paul Chamber Orchestra, four as principal conductor and eight as music director. He led the orchestra in more than 600 concerts (more than any other conductor in the orchestra's 41-year history), guided them on tours of Europe and Japan, made 20 recordings, unveiled a variety of seldom-heard works for chamber orchestra, and twice earned awards for adventurous programming of contemporary music. Wolff says "I am saying goodbye to an orchestra that I've been very close to."

Everyone who knows Wolff doubts he will look for a position because it is in a prestigious city or it is a career-building opportunity. "I'm honestly not planning what the next step will be," Wolff concurs. "I can honestly say that I have less ambition than a lot of people in this business. I like what I do. I find it challenging. But I'm not burning to figure out what's the next level I should be at. I have three kids I wish I could spend more time with and I feel that further ambition could actually be detrimental to raising them and having another life as well."

Slouched back against the armrest of his sofa, Hugh Wolff is content with himself and comfortable with all of his musical world.

Chapter 10

You Have to Face Your Own Terror and Pain

Rebekka Armstrong

*Former Playboy Model and
Centerfold Turned AIDS Activist*

Rebekka Armstrong grew up in the middle of the Mojave Desert, a sand-racing tomboy bent on being a professional motocross racer. But at sixteen, Armstrong quit racing, dropped out of school and moved away from her dysfunctional family and into her own place. Sixteen was also the age she first admitted publicly that she wanted to pose for *Playboy*. "I don't remember where the idea came from," Armstrong giggles. Maybe not, but she does remember her grandfather's *Playboy* collection she would secretly admire. "I would look through magazines and I wanted to do that, but I never thought that I was pretty enough or that I'd ever really be able to do it." Embarrassed, she told no one until her sixteenth birthday when she told her mother. "My mom said, 'Go for it. You can do it,' and then I just put it out of my mind." Two years later, on her eighteenth birthday, she made a phone call to *Playboy*.

A close friend of her grandfather who had a connection to the magazine came to the Desert to shoot the photos she would submit and arranged an introduction. "I was shy and a little embarrassed, like anybody is anytime you take your clothes off for the first time in front of somebody," she recalls. At the *Playboy* Mansion, she met Hugh Hefner, the founder of the magazine. "I was so nervous. Here was this man I had to impress. And it's not like you have to have a particular look for *Playboy*. It's not all just big boobs and blonde hair," Armstrong reports, accentuating the comment by building enormous imaginary bosoms. "It's about what you do. After the test shots come back, if you don't carry yourself well and you act like a bitch, you're not going to make it." After making it, she spent the next eight months awakening for 4:00 a.m. sunrise shoots. Armstrong eventually joined the Playmate lineup as Miss September 1986, in a spread that cast her as the quintessential wholesome all-American blonde turned femme-fatale. The young model was so busy with shooting and a promotional schedule, she never saw the photos until they hit the street. "I had been in Jamaica where I was shooting swimwear and I got off the plane and I knew my issue was supposed to hit the stands so as I was walking through the airport, I stopped and looked through it. I just said, 'Oh my gosh,' put it down, and hurried out of the airport."

The exposure led to modeling and playing dumb blondes in softcore *Playboy* comedies on their cable channel. She was on billboards all around Los Angeles. "I really wanted to model and to act. It was a way of expressing myself," Armstrong explains. "Even when you're modeling you're acting, because you need to act out whatever it is that they want to see. And I believed that I was really good at what I did. I don't really know how far the dream went. I do know that it kept getting bigger and bigger the better I got, the more I would want and I allowed myself to dream a little higher."

But the dream turned out to be a nightmare. From her small town beginning, Armstrong had no idea of what life was like in Glamour City. "I didn't have a clue what existed out there. I just pictured fancy things that a young kid would picture, like a dress that sparkled, not knowing all of these other things existed because I didn't have a clue about them." What she discovered was that it was very hard work and that the pressure was intense and it was relentless. "Women feel pressure to look good as a rule. But in this, not only do you gotta look good, you gotta look damn perfect. You can't even accidentally have a bruise. Everything has to be perfect. The toenails, fingernails, or whatever else they state. Everything, constantly. You couldn't have an ugly day. It wasn't allowed."

To stay perfect, Armstrong experimented with drugs, the one thing her small town had taught her. The Mojave is an easy and secluded drop for planes smuggling drugs from Mexico, and Armstrong knew all about the metabolic advantages of "speed," which kept the weight off, pasted a permanent smile, and boosted the energy. "I wasn't using drugs when I first started at *Playboy*. And it wasn't Playboy that made me do the drugs, it was me," Armstrong admits. "But when the editor said to me after a test shot, 'We've got to trim the hips a bit — it's a little wide through here,' I panicked. This was something I really wanted so I had to trim down those hips. Almost everybody was into drugs. A lot of girls did coke. I did speed to stay like this," Armstrong says, holding up her baby finger. "It kept me awake. I wasn't as tired. I could get up and function. But I became addicted to it and began using it all the time. Well, I ended up losing almost 30 pounds. I ended up with no hips at all." Fearful of reprisals for her addiction, Armstrong claimed she was ill. Her editor moved her into the mansion for supervision.

Armstrong claims there were good times in her life as a Playmate but she cannot pinpoint a specific one and "things that were good then are not necessarily great now," she offers quietly and very tenderly. "Then" she was making $500 for each public appearance. That was good money for an 18-year old. "The money drives you, and you just get caught in all the other aspects of it. I just hopped on this boat and I was going down this river. I was content, happy, fulfilled, satisfied. It was good and I never had a problem getting a date." But dating became the source of her biggest problem. Equally attracted to men and women, she found herself in a string of unfulfilling relationships. While breaking up with a boyfriend, Armstrong, fearing pregnancy, decided to get a physical. The examination included a test for HIV. The test was positive. Now she is living with AIDS.

At twenty-one, Armstrong was dying. "There wasn't a second that didn't go by for the longest time that I didn't think about it," she recounts in almost a whisper. "I alienated myself. I stayed away from my family, from everybody." Because she wasn't working, her bills became delinquent and her life went from bad to worse. "I went from one extreme to the next," Armstrong nearly shouts. "I would go through the 'I don't give a shit, I'm dying attitude' so party on, do whatever the hell you want to do, to the other extreme of jogging every day and eating extra oranges." At the lowest point Armstrong gave up hope and tried to commit suicide, creating a pharmacological cocktail using nearly everything she had in her well-equipped AIDS medicine cabinet. "I'd just had it. I couldn't tell anybody because when you do, you're treated like toxic waste. So I hid it for the longest time. I was so sick I had totally forgotten that I was supposed to fly somewhere to work so I was getting this terrible reputation I was unreliable. And I didn't look that good anymore and nobody knew why. I lost my house, I lost my car, I started losing everything. But suicide didn't even work. I screwed that up too!" She awakened from a coma days later, in terrible pain from the stomach pumping and drug damage to the body.

"Before, I offered my body; I offered my looks. Now, I'm giving information to kids so that they can make their own decisions and that can possibly save their lives."

With the help of some friends and a couple of AIDS groups, Armstrong pulled herself together. She also sought out each of her former sex partners. "Don't think that I was just being the responsible woman and meeting with these people because I needed to tell them that I was infected. I wanted to find out who in the hell did this to me," Armstrong roars. "I confronted them. I was angry. And I was terrified. Terrified for me and terrified at how many people I had given it to because I was on the pill. I didn't need to use condoms. That was for gay men, and that was for people that used IV drugs." That's what we knew in 1989. Surprisingly, her former lovers cooperated. Everybody turned out negative. "There's one guy I couldn't find. He was a model for a magazine and everyone suspected he was involved in sexual favors for the editor who passed away due to complications of the AIDS virus."

Armstrong stopped her search. She has also stopped her anger. "It takes two. We both chose to have unprotected sex and it was only that one time, but one's all you need. We were both responsible." There is one other possibility. At sixteen, besides expressing her desire to be in *Playboy*, Armstrong became pregnant and had an abortion at a clinic where she received blood. "Either way, I got it through unprotected sex because I wouldn't have been having an abortion had I not had unprotected sex. So whether or not I got it from the actual sex act or from the blood it makes no difference."

In 1994, Armstrong went public about her disease. Not long after, she developed full-blown AIDS. She began a new career as a safe-sex educator and a new life, in rural New England. "I look at life as before HIV and after HIV." Before, it was a fashion runway for money. After, it is a high school auditorium, for free. With some assistance from *Playboy* magazine, Armstrong the ex-centerfold is now a crusader for safe sex. "Being a Playmate has definitely given me a voice. And I am so thankful for that. If that's what's getting them in there to listen to what I have to say, if these little 15 year old boys want to come and gawk at a *Playboy* model, fine. Then, it's up to me. Can I break that wall and get them to forget about that *Playboy* thing and listen to what it is I'm saying? And I do a damn good job at it."

Anyone at Lawrence Academy will vouch for that. It was her first gig. After Armstrong arrived in the small New England town, the school's nurse learned about Armstrong's interest in speaking to students. A young law student who lived in the house where Armstrong lived also worked at the local pizza place to pay for rent and tuition. With only one pizza parlor in town, it is where every student in the village hung out. One evening, they overheard the tenant say, "Yeah, that *Playboy* girl lives at my house." The revelation got back to school, and Armstrong has been a fixture ever since. "They are getting to know me because I'm on their level. It's not like I am the adult they're going to just have to listen," Armstrong clarifies, energized with the opportunity. "I go to their basketball games. I'm not trying to act above them. I'm trying to be right there with them so they will want to listen to what I have to say. You can have something to say but if you're giving it to them like you are so much smarter than them and so much above them, then they're going to block you out. For lack of a better word, I hope they think that I'm cool. I don't know why that's important, but it's important to me that they think that I'm cool."

Drugs similar to those she once used to kill herself are now sustaining her. Her current cocktail of Viramune, Ziagen and Zerit have boosted her T-cells to a normal percentage and the viral load is undetectable. As a result, Armstrong has become very involved in physical fitness and is currently training for an AIDS Marathon in Chicago. "I believe that the stronger I make my body the harder I make it for the virus to grab a hold of me and kick my butt," Armstrong blurts out with a smile.

Rejuvenated for the last six years, Armstrong has been talking to teens as frequently as she is feeling good enough to do so. "All I want them to do is just listen. I'm not a teacher speaking from a textbook and telling them medical this-and-that and how the virus attacks the cell. I'm telling them a story about my life," she proclaims. Sometimes there are tears, from both sides. Frequently young girls come up to her after the presentation and start crying because they have friends that are having unprotected sex and they are terrified now for them. Always, Armstrong is impassioned. "It's so important for me for many reasons. The fact that I was most likely infected at about their age. The fact that nobody was telling *me* about this virus. And now that I have gotten so involved in it, there are new reasons like the fact that women were being given drugs that had only been tested on men resulting in serious adverse reactions, even death. And motherhood issues. Women that were infected, who are dying, who need help caring for their children or placing them in homes." In a recent presentation in Atlanta, a woman thanked Armstrong for helping her get information on how to legally place her children with a foster home. She was in the final stages of the disease and barely able to walk. "It doesn't make me feel like a hero, but makes me feel like I really did something good for somebody, you know?"

The beach communities of Southern California where Armstrong lives now are about as far removed from the deserts where she grew up as you can go. About the same distance as a pinup from preacher. And Armstrong spends a lot of time looking back. "AIDS has given me a different outlook on life. It's given me a different reason to want to live. It's given me a different reason for being who I am," Armstrong reveals. "Now, I'm a better person. I have more to offer. Before I offered my body, I offered my looks. Now, I'm giving information to kids so that they can make their own decisions and that can possibly save their lives. I sure in hell feel better about what I'm doing now."

Fame means different things to different people. At one time for Armstrong it meant movie stars and models, people that were on the coffee table magazines, household names from television. It is entirely different now. "When kids meet me, for the most part, that's the first time that they've been in a room knowingly with somebody who has HIV. And that makes me feel famous because I'm the only they know and they have all these questions and I'm the only one who can answer them."

She also spends a lot of time looking forward. Ironically, the new wave of drugs, the inhibitors, the combination therapies, frightened Armstrong. "This is going to sound crazy," Armstrong begins, checking around to see if anyone else is listening, "but I have to be honest, it scared me for a second. I was like, 'Shit! If I get cured, what the hell am I going to do then? I'm not going to have this life anymore and I can't go back to the old one.' Of course, I only thought that for a second because we know that they're not a cure." But they are making life livable, and Armstrong can now also tell you about new dreams she would like to experience that have replaced the old. "I hope to travel all over the country educating others about safe sex and HIV," Armstrong says proudly. "I am due to go to the UK to speak to several schools." In the meantime, she is a certified Phlebotomist and works part time drawing blood and doing tests for sexually transmitted diseases. She is putting together a cookbook with information, tips and recipes that she believes have helped to keep her healthy. She is writing a column and an autobiography. "I would like to continue to help somebody or something somewhere."

But those are easy dreams, unguarded dreams. The bigger ones are still impossible dreams. "Oh yes, I'm going to get cured and I'm going to have babies," Armstrong says laughing and then quickly stops. "No, it's not a risk I'm willing to take. I can't guarantee I'll be around for that child to grow up and I can't guarantee that I'll be able to raise that child. And I think that's kind of an unfair thing for someone to do. Some women do make that choice. But I just can't."

Armstrong sobs quietly and wipes her eyes and nose with a tissue. I offer her a gentle hug and tell her she is really a lovely person. "Thanks," she sniffles. "But do you think I'm cool? Because it means a lot that I'm cool."

I think you're cool. And let me tell you, Rebekka Armstrong, I know what cool is.

Lynn Harrell
Award-Winning Concert Cellist

Photo credit: Dan Porges

Described as one of the great cellists of this generation, Lynn Harrell's performances go beyond his superb intonation and rhythm. They are deeply personal, emerging from the painful circumstances of his childhood path to his instrument. As a young boy, Harrell wasn't interested in the cello at all. It was something his parents insisted he do every day, just as they insisted that his brother and sister play the clarinet and the violin. At age 12, Harrell moved from New York City to Dallas. Not only did he find himself severely uncomfortable adjusting to the junior high school lifestyle, his father also became seriously ill about this time. Uncomfortable with both his parents and with his adolescent world, Harrell reveals that he "turned to the cello as my friend, my companion, as something I could pour my feelings into."

Harrell was not able to share with his parents. They were cool and aloof, and Harrell was embarrassed that his parents were top professional musicians and he was not. But as a teenager, circumstances called him into action. At 15, his father died. Two years later, his mother died from injuries sustained in a car accident. The breakup of his family and his search for self compounded with the tragedies galvanized Harrell into becoming the son of famous musicians who would have a musical career of his own.

It was an awakening. "Music, the cello, and my connection with it became my salvation," Harrell reports. "I would talk to my cello, and sense its personality and it would feel different from day to day. Maybe, it was transference. But it was something that I could share my deepest and innermost thoughts with. And the question always was and is, why wasn't I able to do that with my parents? I've come to realize the real me is when I'm sitting at the cello and that the problems I've had in relationships and life have to do with trying to be something other than who I really am, which comes out when I'm performing with the cello."

At first, Harrell was challenged by the difficulty. "I just wanted to learn to do it well. Then, at 13, I suddenly realized that if I was going to be a musician, I had better really get good at this. I didn't know if I would be able to make a living at it. I would cry going to sleep at night because I wasn't better that day." One must have a natural, physical affinity for playing an instrument. But a teacher can only take a pupil so far by developing the physical manipulation, the mechanical elements of the instrument. Ultimately, the individual has to use the physical skills to release a more profound gift. Harrell intensified the pursuit of his newly formed objective by digging deeply.

The driving force behind his effort was the composers who wrote the music. From the beginning, that has been the guiding light. When challenged by friends to find a mentor, Harrell comfortably replied, "I have. But they would say, 'Yes, but they're all dead,'" Harrell laughs. "I feel uplifted, changed, awakened as I get to know the likes of Schubert through his music. It has always been my burning desire to understand more from the music and then show it through my performance."

Like all musicians, Harrell is entrusted with the responsibility of taking the composer's intentions off the printed page and presenting it. Like all remarkable musicians, he has developed his own viewpoint and personality in the process. "I haven't done that consciously at all. I've done it just by being honest and being receptive to the really great performers who were before me."

Instrumentalists have been given the opportunity to remind us about how extraordinary the composer is. Without them, Beethoven is lost. That is an incredible responsibility. But no matter what musicians do, it is not going to be like Beethoven, nor should it be, because Beethoven was playing for 19th Century individuals who had 19th Century concepts of how music ought to sound and what life was like. Our musical ears now include jazz and big band and our worldviews now include flight and computers, which indicates to Harrell, "We have to do something different with the music. We are the middlemen, so there is a great deal of responsibility, but there is also a great deal of freedom. And much more than I used to, I believe it's our ballgame too, not only the creator's."

When Harrell is playing, he transforms the game. He handles the instrument so that it is totally one with himself, far beyond the craft of handling something else well. There are no seams. But that's only the starting point. Through the physical skills he has developed so well, he displays the more profound gifts of intelligence and sensitivity to what the music is saying about life and human relationships and brings that message to life. "The doors open from the subconscious. You just react and you play in a way that is different than you've discussed or worked with yourself, but that you feel from the spirit, from somewhere very deep down, and you're in a place in your life where you have that sense of autonomy and security in yourself and you can say, 'I trust that,' and you go with it."

What the audience feels is Harrell giving them Harrell. It is also the music. The doors of the subconscious wouldn't open without the music. But, sitting there, Harrell knows when it is happening. "There are times when I'm playing and I look out and see in the dark light of the hall a man put his hand on his breast and realize this person is tremendously moved. I just want to put the cello down and put my arms around the person. And I feel this *Miracle Grow* feeling, this adrenaline of, 'This may be the last time you'll ever be able to play. It may be the only time that person is going to be in that concert hall. You have to do it great.' But you have to just let it happen. The moment you really try to do it, it's like trying to pitch a no hitter. It won't happen."

Harrell may be the Nolan Ryan of the cello. But despite his extraordinary performances, the classical music profession does not have a large enough audience to make him a superstar. There are musicians, however, who seem to leap out beyond that small audience and captivate even those people who are not aficionados of the art form. Cellist Yo-Yo Ma comes to mind for Harrell as for most. "I have faith that artists who display aesthetic integrity and honesty in their work will come through in the long run. But there are public relations distractions that are necessary. Occasionally I think I should work the room at the concert party and do things that some of my more famous colleagues are adept at. But, then I realize they're not doing it only for fame, it's their personality. Some people are just naturally political creatures, and some are just more retiring. So the thought doesn't last very long before I realize that's just not me."

> "None of us artists have normal lives ... Until I can let it all come out with the instrument, I am frustrated, sometimes lonely, and forsaken."

The constant reference to Ma and other musicians who excite the music public is not lost on Harrell. It has improved his playing. Impressed by Rostropovich and Ma and many young players, Harrell purchases their recordings and goes to hear them in concert. "There are times I think, 'That's a very interesting approach but it's not what I believe' and I feel what I'm doing is valid," Harrell affirms. "But, there are situations when I listen to someone and I think, 'Hmm. That's very good. I'd better go back and practice because that's better than I can do at this point.' I've done that a number of times in the past 25 years and it definitely helped. Look at the whole golf profession. Everyone is playing better because of Tiger. They just have to. The bar has been raised to a higher standard. Same in music."

The reference to Tiger Woods is not accidental. Harrell is an avid golfer and admires the results Woods has achieved. He also resonates with Wood's visible self-confidence. "I have an absolutely humongous ego. I show it every time I get up on stage," Harrell admits comfortably. "I just spent a whole week where I hardly thought about the Shostakovich Concerto I'm going to play tomorrow. I'm thinking a lot about my short irons and my putting. And, I come here and say, 'OK, now it's time to concentrate.' I get out a metronome and the score, get super focused, and get my fingers going. At the bottom of it is, one, the knowledge I can snap it together and, two, that I can snap it together at a level, that even if I played badly, would be better than just about anyone else in the world. This is incredible ego but it's used for the benefit of doing one's work."

Harrell has not displayed such self-confidence throughout his career. For years he felt insecure and unworthy, and it would rattle him. He spent much of his early career trying to perform well behind a psychological eight ball. It did not work. It was not what Harrell wanted. It was not what the people who hired him wanted. It was not what the audience wanted. His approach to himself and to his music changed while he was watching tennis on television. "John McEnroe, while commenting on a video of his match a few minutes before with Bjorn Borg said, 'I remember this point. I got really insecure about his backhand.' Backhand came and went. Ball was in. And I thought that's one of the really big names in tennis, and there's this moment where he's not so sure. That was a great lesson. I realized I could be better, then came to I'm OK, now to I'm damn good."

Building confidence provides security and allows for a healthy ego. By balancing the three, performers don't get cut off from the artistic vulnerability they need to open the doors of the subconscious. But the process is labor intensive. "It is very slow, sand grain by sand grain, and takes a long time to get. When you're young, you go out and play and you recognize you didn't play nearly as well as you played at rehearsal, it can become a problem. You've got to find a way to get over that." Acquiring a healthy ego is critical as well as developing confidence."

Beyond confidence, becoming a virtuoso requires a significant amount of assertiveness. Again, for many years, Harrell did not possess the personality force needed to look in the mirror and avow, "I want to be the best there's ever been, and all that stuff. I just didn't feel that," Harrell acknowledges reflectively. Harrell did have ambition and drive but he covered it up. He lied to himself about it and qualified his motivation as wanting "to be as good as my father was. I just wanted to make my dad proud…He died and he didn't know that I was even going to become a musician."

Often you hear that artists produce their greatest work out of the sorrow in their lives, that pathos enables them to find the deepest and truest roots of who and where they are. Harrell accepts the notion. "None of us artists have normal lives," Harrell says without embarrassment. "I bring out intensity and purity and distillation in my work, and if I had had good conversations with really close friends over most of the year, I could not be so intense, so distilled. My work would be diffused. Until I can let it all come out with the instrument, I am frustrated, sometimes lonely, and forsaken. But those are psychological patterns that were set in motion many years ago."

Studying the cello at both the Juilliard School in New York and the Curtis Institute in Philadelphia, the 18-year-old Harrell was invited by

George Szell to join the Cleveland Orchestra. Two years later Szell appointed him principal cellist, a position he held until 1971. During his tenure with the orchestra, Harrell read a book called *Up the Organization*, by Robert Townsend, the new head of Avis. In describing the path to corporate success, Townsend suggested that executives should stay in a particular position for five years and then change, having learned all they can learn in that role. Harrell took the suggestion to heart. "I had made the cello section a good cello section. I realized that I had accomplished that. But when Szell died, I also realized I had to move on. I couldn't just stay comfortable. I had to accept slight insecurity as a way of life. The envelope always has to be at its edge. Constantly pushed. You have to. That's what the requirement is. Even Beethoven would agree as he bemoaned at one point in his life that it didn't matter what pieces he had written, it was the next piece he was going to have to write that was always the problem."

The man who feared he might not make a living with the cello has made a pretty good one. The recipient of numerous awards including the Piatigorsky Award, the Ford Foundation Concert Artists' Award and the first Avery Fisher Award (jointly with pianist Murray Perahia), Harrell has obviously opened fully the doors to his subconscious. But he still wants more. "I am tremendously revitalized by playing great music of the Twentieth Century. I'm more fascinated than ever in Jazz. I would like to conduct more. It's going to take me to the grave. If I didn't have music as my outlet, I just would not be able to function as a normal person, or somewhat normal person. It's the protein, carbohydrate, and fat of my existence." Yes, definitely, it's an obsession. Absolutely. But Harrell is more than comfortable with that. "We all are obsessed with something. I feel terribly for people who cannot make a living with theirs."

In the spring of 1998, Harrell nearly lost his ability to make a living. His fingers were going numb. It's every string player's nightmare. "My voice, my very being, or so I thought, was in my hands. For two months, I told no one, barely myself," Harrell reveals. "What is more astonishing is that my fingers carried on of their own accord, as if they didn't know what was happening to them. I have played the cello for almost all of my life; music and memory are embedded in my body."

Even now Harrell shudders at the reason for his silence, his fears, and the months that passed when he did not play his prized Stradivarius. "It's the longest time I had locked it away in the years I've owned it. It was Jacqueline du Pre's Stradivarius. I bought it from her when she was still alive, her unique voice silenced by Multiple Sclerosis. I have always believed that the spirit of everyone who has played a cello lives on within it. It is the blessing of an old instrument. I asked myself whether it could also be its curse. Were my numbing fingers the beginning of a long descent into the hell she knew?" Harrell finally faced his problem and went to a neurologist. How does one of the world's great cellists trust a surgeon to cut open the hands that hold his being? "I trusted him because my heart told me to. It was nothing to do with reputation, tales of success. I looked into this man's eyes and put my hands, my being, into his."

Harrell has some advice for those who would follow a path to achievement. "Don't walk in my footsteps. Believe you can make your own. They will be better anyway, because you've got to have a belief in yourself." It has taken Harrell a long time to come to know that. During his journey, he has also come to know the footsteps must keep walking. "Don't stop, don't give up. There's this expectation that you go to school and graduate, get into a profession, become successful, and then you've arrived. That is death. You keep going. Every day you must strive to achieve something so your education never ceases. It requires vitality and commitment to the art, an intensity of purpose from within, a constant working, that never ends in your lifetime to deepen and broaden and improve, that strengthens and enlarges the personality, so that the personality comes out through what you are doing."

Photo credit: Dan Porges

Easier said from a distance. After all, as a child Harrell wanted to be a professional baseball player and later he wanted to be a tennis star like Jimmy Conners. Sports were very important to him, "but they were not supported in our family at all," Harrell laments. "My brother Fulton swam at SMU and he was in the Olympic trials for swimming when he was 16, and from the time he was twelve, when he got interested in swimming, all the way to the trials, my parents didn't go to one meet." There is still pain in the darkness. But there is also perspective. "Hey, I was lucky, too. I used the money that came from the settling of (my parents') estate to buy my Montagnana cello. When I bought it, I paid $25,000. Now it's worth close to $3 million."

Harrell's hands have mended. The fear and trembling about his beloved outlet is over. And without so much as a cello in the room, he opens the door of his subconscious. "How much have I learned? I've had to face the fact that I am not my hands. They are only part of me. I learned too that you have to face your own terror and pain. I have only allowed myself in the past to see mine in the reflection of other men's music. And I brought something else into the light that I already knew: that to trust another human being, to be vulnerable and open, is one of the greatest rewards of life."

Diana Nyad
*Ultra-Distance Athlete and First Person
to Swim from Bahamas to U.S.*

Photo credit: Carin Baer

At dawn on August 19, 1979, Diana Nyad entered the Atlantic Ocean from a beach in the Bahamas. Covered in latex and wearing several swim caps to keep warm, she methodically stroked her way toward Florida. Despite powerful ocean currents, aching muscles, mental and physical fatigue, and the poison sting of a jellyfish, she persisted, counting her strokes and singing songs to wile away the 27-hour journey. Nyad touched ground a few minutes after 8:00 a.m. on August 20, two days before her thirtieth birthday. She was greeted by several hundred friends and admirers as she became the first human to ever complete the 102.5-mile swim. For ten years, from 1969 to 1979, Nyad was the greatest long-distance swimmer in the world. In 1986, she was inducted into the National Women's Sports Hall of Fame.

During her long-distance swimming days, Nyad traveled around the world — from Argentina, swimming with sea lions, to Egypt, swimming in the Nile. The Caribbean swim was her last. "I was about to turn thirty and before I left marathon swimming (which had all been a wonderful adventure), I wanted to set an ego-maniacal, unmatchable record," Nyad admits with gusto. "I wanted to swim across some piece of ocean, like a hundred miles. I'll be the first to admit, I like recognition when I do something fantastic."

Nyad grew up in South Florida and had many Cuban friends. Through them, she had come to know Cuba as a beautiful island broken by Communism with thousands gazing at America for their freedom. "I imagined on the clearest day they could see Key West and see themselves getting to freedom and finding their self-respect." A lot of the interest in endurance sports is the magic of geography. Nyad could swim a hundred miles in a pool but no one would care. But if she crossed a sea that was once conquered by explorers a thousand years ago, then she would be doing something everybody could feel and they would join in. She was also a woman of her times. Billy Jean King had just beaten Bobby Riggs in tennis a few years before and Janet Guthrie had just become the first woman to drive the Indy 500.

"I wanted my last swim to be inspiring. I didn't make the Cuba swim because we couldn't get into the country, but I did make the Bahamas swim and that swim wound up being inspiring. The letters I got talked about what it meant to women and what they thought they could do in their lives because of it."

The public perceives athletes like Nyad as having a vision of their future achievements when they are very young and having parents who are former sports stars pushing them. But there was no one there for Nyad to urge her to do something with her life. "I was a kid in a very bad home situation with a father who was sexually inappropriate with me and a mother who was a very remote, uninvolved person," Nyad reports with little emotion and no hesitation. "We were on our own, ate our meals alone, and all of us were looking for a way to get out of the house." At ten, Nyad's sister found a boyfriend and became a part of his family. They made a bedroom for her and she slept and ate there and was gone.

Nyad found swimming. "I was good at it and beat everybody. That always motivates a person to keep going. But I found a way to get out of the house at 4:30 in the morning, because swimming starts early, and I didn't have to come home for dinner, and I had meets all the time, so I found a swimming family away from the house."

As a child, Nyad lived in Ft. Lauderdale, Florida. Many ex-Olympic swimmers had settled there to raise their families near the newly built Swimming Hall of Fame. Nearby, Chris Evert was at Holiday Park playing tennis. "I was in a milieu that was world-class and very mainstream but in my private life there were shadowy moments that didn't feel mainstream at all." Therapists say that a common response of children who went through sexual abuse is they become perfectionists. The underlying psychology is they believe they must have done something wrong so for the rest of their lives they have to be the best at everything. Their friends have to think of them as their best friend and employers have to think of them as the most nurturing people in the office.

Nyad looks back and sees the syndrome in her own life. "Besides the pats on the back for breaking records, I was very driven by a psychology of 'I'm not a bad person but I must have done something terribly wrong and I'm going to show everybody I'm the best human being alive.' I wanted to be canonized as the best human being. I'm talking about it in hyperbole because at fifty I hope I'm past that."

But there was a lot to get past. Nyad found swimming through a fifth grade geography teacher who was an ex-Olympic swimmer, an ex-all American football player, a very charismatic personality. "Within two months into his swim program, he said 'You're going to be the best swimmer in the world.' It wasn't the grandiosity of that statement, it was that an adult, someone I looked up to, an Olympian, was talking to me about my life, which my mother and father never did and that somebody cares about my spirit and my life and what's going to become of me. So I found this guy who was so accomplished and everybody loved him, and he was always there with hugs and talking to you. He was so intense and I have that in my personality as well, and so I just drew to him like a magnet." And, in part the hope was fulfilled. At fourteen, Nyad was the best in the state of Florida, a regular at the U.S. Nationals, among the top ten in the country. But at fourteen, she also suffered a violent and unforgettable molestation at the hands of her coach.

The circumstance is classic: a relationship with someone who has taken over the parental role. It happens most often in cases where the child is not close to the family and when the child is certain the person would never do anything to hurt or anything that was wrong and so the child does whatever is asked. The violent episode occurred the day of the state high school championship meet. Nyad was resting at the coach's house, a common practice for all the swimmers as their families knew his family well and baby-sat for his children.

> "We all have tremendous fear of failure and need to have the courage to try anyway."

"I was in a state of shock. I cleaned myself up and even had to sit in the car as he drove us back to the pool. I was stunned silent, barely breathing." Nyad swam the 100 backstroke that night and it was the first time she had lost since she started as a ten year old. Her teammates attributed the performance to the flu. As the team prepared to leave the meet to go out for pizza and cokes, Nyad went over to the diving well and dove to the bottom of the pool. "I yelled, 'No!' at the top of my lungs. If I'd been on the surface you could have heard me around the world." Nyad is and was a survivor. While submerged in the safety and silence of the water, she decided, "I was going to make a life for myself. I'm not going to let this ruin me. It did tonight. I lost. But I'm just going to sweep this under the rug like a tough little soldier."

Over her high school years, Nyad was coerced into a sexual liaison with her coach. "The first time was just rip, ram, fast, oh my god! The other times he said, 'You don't understand this because you're just a kid, but you will one day, and I love you so much and this is what I need, and we have the most special thing in the world; nobody else can know about it, they wouldn't understand, you'll never become a champion if anybody hears about this. This is our bond." While the relationship was secret, her feelings of embarrassment alienated her from her team. And she began to pound on herself for her failure. "It's so difficult to forgive yourself because I wasn't five years old, as I was with my father. I was tough and strong and a swimmer and with lots of will so why didn't I just say, 'No, you dirty jerk, get away from me, I'm going to the principal!' As I try to understand and try to forgive myself for not saying no, I believe I didn't because I had him on a pedestal of goodness."

Nyad is gay and has been public about it for thirty years. While there are no answers to the reasons of such a sexual orientation, Nyad does not shy away from the implications of her childhood experiences. "If none of this had happened, I would have naturally gravitated to having boys as friends. As it turned out, it's taken me till now to really realize that there are nice men. But during that period of time between him and my forties, I felt the whole male gender was out to hurt me, to get what they selfishly needed for themselves. It was just a big penis-fest." Nyad is candid about the impact of those experiences on her relationships in general. When she found the love of her life, she found herself acting like the two men. "That's all I knew; that's what I patterned myself after. I was sexually really messed up, in terms of being open and relaxed and feeling the female and feminine side of myself. I've come a long way in that too."

Nyad's drive toward perfectionism and her repeated self-flagellation were evident as far back as that horrifying fifth grade classroom. Nyad has tucked away in her drawer of mementos an essay she wrote that was recently sent to her by her fifth grade teacher. The essay talks about what she was going to do with the rest of her life. "There is this tremendous sense of urgency. I wrote I never knew my grandparents but they lived to be eighty-eight, and that most likely that was how old I would get and I said, 'I'm ten now, that only gives me seventy-eight more years' and I wanted to speak languages and I wanted to be a doctor and I wanted to be a great athlete. So there was this drive of time, a clock ticking by." The urgency was to fulfill potential. While Nyad enjoys a beer with friends, she is not ready to just sit all night and talk through a lengthy dinner. "That doesn't fulfill my potential. It's such a waste of this precious life if I don't use my brain, my body, my spirit, my will. That's the drive."

Since retiring from long distance swimming, Nyad has pushed as many adventures into her life as the clock will allow and the drive can fuel. In addition to being an author, Nyad has worked her way up the ladder of sports television. She is now the senior correspondent at Fox Sports News, respected for her insightful investigative journalism. For twelve years, Nyad has also been a columnist on National Public Radio's *Morning Edition*. Her skilled, intelligent, and passionate coverage of diverse topics has garnered numerous awards and wide recognition. But she has not done so at the expense of her adventurous spirit. On January 1, 1998, because of Nyad's vision and through her effort, 75 extraordinary individuals came together for the Vietnam Challenge, an athletic and goodwill event covering 1,200 miles through the heart of Vietnam.

The Vietnam Challenge bicycling team, composed of persons with and without disabilities, included many veterans of the war in Vietnam from both sides of the conflict. With world-renown cyclist Greg LeMond and Nyad leading the way, the Challenge became a three-week journey of discovery of past and present-day Vietnam. Through the Asia Society's AskAsia, a Web site dedicated to providing K-12 resources on Asia, students in classrooms around the world followed their progress and communicated with team members along the way. "The trip was a peaceful journey of joined hands, to bring about a sense of forgiveness and reconciliation."

In order to provide the capital resources for these adventures, Nyad had to "deal with suits who were in the world of women's sports looking for properties to support and win over the sums of money you need to engage in your dreams," Nyad states boldly. She acted boldly as well. When Nyad was training for the Cuba swim, she read that Rocky Aoki, owner of the

An exhausted Diana Nyad is tended to after one of her grueling ultra-distance swims

Benihana restaurant chain was a sports enthusiast, raced powerboats, trained every day, and loved American athletes. Nyad discovered he had an office in New York and made an appointment to see him. "I marched into his office and said, 'Mr. Aoki...' and he stopped me dead in my tracks and said, 'No, no, no, call me Rocky.' So I said, 'Rocky, I'm going to swim from Cuba to Florida. It's a dream of mine. I can't sleep at night I want to do it so badly. I'm swimming ten hours a day and I want you to come tomorrow to see me train.'" Nyad took him to Coney Island. He cruised in a boat while she swam up and down the channel. Then she tossed out the figure for her dream. "I said it's going to cost $300,000, but it's going to mean something to the whole country, it's going to be a woman doing something a man's never done, it's going to be like escaping from a Communist country and swimming to the freedom of Florida. It's going to be big."

Naoki wrote out a check for $150,000 dollars on the spot, after knowing Nyad for only two days. Nyad also struck the deal for the television coverage of her Vietnam Challenge. She went to *Sports Illustrated Television* and in a half hour walked away with the show. "I told them how moving it was going to be, their first time back in thirty years, they've lost the use of their legs, and they're going to ride through the villages with the Vietnamese that they injured, on hand cycles, with Greg Lemond. You can't ask for a better story."

Nyad has packaged her adventures and accomplishments into a motivational speaking tour. At first, she called the program The Courage to Succeed. She subsequently changed it to The Courage to Fail. "Not many people are afraid to succeed," Nyad explains. "But we all have tremendous fear of failure and need to have the courage to try anyway." Nyad uses her career in broadcast journalism as an example. Hired to appear on a live Washington insider show called *Equal Time*, Nyad was slated to debate conservative host Bay Buchanan, presidential candidate Pat Buchanan's sister. She agreed but warned the producers that she could debate anybody about anything except economics. They agreed to steer the week's shows toward other topics. The day of the first show, President Clinton presented his budget proposal to Congress and the producers decided they had to go with the budget and the budget only.

"Shit!" Nyad exclaims like it was all happening again. "I made some calls and started reading the Wall Street Journal. I don't even know the vocabulary to use in finance and economics. Got into my chair before Bay came in the studio, put my notes in front of me, and the guy putting on my microphone says, 'We're live in ninety seconds.'" Her heart was pounding. Bay, a Ph.D. in mathematics, was the Treasurer of the United States under Ronald Reagan. "I was so incompetent to debate this with her that I decided to just be confident, listen to what she said, and respond to her for average folks around the country. I had fears I wouldn't be up to it, but, hey, Robert MacNamara was hired as Secretary of Defense from the Ford Motor Company. He had only been in the Air Force for two years. All of us tend to elevate other people and say they are so brilliant. But if you made a list of people you admire, you could do what they do if you apply yourself. So whatever fears of incompetence or doubt I have usually go away quickly after I talk with myself and say I can do what they are doing. I wasn't brilliant that day against Bay, but I held my own."

All achievement requires some genetic gifts. Many people would love to run as fast as Carl Lewis, but as much as they train will never do so. He has the fast-twitch fibers you need for explosive power. But Nyad believes most people have gifts that can carry them to high levels of achievement; they just don't embrace them. "Most anyone can do anything," Nyad asserts. "I had a friend who saw a comedy act and said, that's what he should be doing because everybody tells him he's the funniest person they know. Sure, but there's one real difference between him and the people on stage: they're doing it. It's so sad, people get to the end of their lives and say they always wanted to write a novel and never did because of fear of failure and a lack of confidence."

Confidence is about examining self. Ego is about evaluating others. Ego looks at the competition and says there is not enough room on the sidewalk for two, so get off, I am going to walk by. Confidence says I deserve to be on the sidewalk because there is room for both of us. Ego is part of our Western notion of keeping other people down in order for us to go up. "When I started to taper off from ego competition," Nyad confesses, "I found compassion and respect for others, and my own vision of self started to soar."

Since Nyad has come to find value in others, the unforgiving pounding she had unleashed on her self for thirty years has begun to fade. Not completely, but it is diminishing. Seated in her cycling clothes in the living room of her art strewn Hollywood home, she is starting to feel free of the past. "Hey, I didn't get up that hill today while training as fast as I said I was going to. Screw it! Not that big a deal," she rationalizes. She takes another swig from her water bottle and philosophizes. "I'm better than I used to be. I would love to go back and develop myself as though I didn't know those two men, but I can't." Nyad is not formally a Buddhist, but of all the world's ideologies it is the one that makes the most sense to her. She likens her improvement to that of Buddha himself. "When Siddartha finished meditating for seven years and came out of the forest, his disciples said, 'Who are you? Are you the second Christ? Are you the Messiah?' Siddartha said, 'No, I'm just awake.' And I am transforming myself away from that oh-my-god-time's-running-out, I've got to be somebody, got to prove myself. Today, for me, success is just being awake, being very conscious, from the second I wake up till the second I go to bed."

> "It's so sad; people get to the end of their lives and say they always wanted to write a novel and never did because of fear of failure and a lack of confidence."

As she awakens, Nyad is changing her goals for achievement and, in doing so, coming face to face with the fears and enemies of her past. "I want to have a great love," Nyad whispers. "I had a great love and I blew it because I was afraid of the intimacy and did everything I could to sabotage it. I want to have a baby too. I don't feel lonely at the moment but there are only thirty years to go. That's not very many and it's fewer than I've already lived. And I want to feel all the sweetness and the tenderness of protecting each other and making a home together and raising a child together. At least a beagle!" she roars with laughter.

Through her athletic and broadcast endeavors, Nyad found a way to be heard without shouting. "You find your voice by being engaged," Nyad asserts. "It's the key to solving adolescent depression. Parents are working and the kids fix their own dinners. They have unlimited access to television and computer games. They don't feel needed, they don't feel valuable, they don't have any voice so nobody can be listening to them. They're not engaged, they're depressed. To find a voice and to start feeling passionate about what you think and what you have to say, you have to be engaged. Engaged in writing where thoughts are streaming out, or in theater and acting them out, or sports and physically expressing them."

Having been engaged in her athletic and journalistic quests for thirty-five years, Nyad is finally able to look back and understand where she has been and where she is going. "The biggest mistake I've made in my television career is trying to present myself as mainstream when I'm not. I have been trying to be Diane Sawyer, trying to be the people I admire and I see as successful. But the best job I've ever had in the media has been the column I do for National Public Radio. The reason that I've lasted for more than ten years and won awards is I haven't been mainstream at all. Been very brash. I just really need to be myself and not be afraid that it isn't mainstream enough. You don't have to be on the *Today Show* and perky to be a success."

Nyad's life outside the mainstream began in the still deep waters of a diving pool and tumbled along the turbulent currents of her troubled psyche. The bitterness of earlier times is fading, replaced by a more enlightened, comfortable soul that puts the journey into perspective.

"Through all of the adventures, the only things in life I missed were the beer drinking, and drugs, and partying, all things that come under that category of getting high. I'm high on what I do. But swimming was largely a metaphor for me for escaping, immersing myself away from the hellish stories I have mentioned. Because of emotional pain, some people use drugs and alcohol; I used sport. Training was the anesthesia to block it all out. But as a metaphor, I was only half awake. Now I'm fully awake. I regret not having been as awake as I am now my whole life."

You're not alone. Most of us have been asleep as well.

Pam Shriver

Winner of the 1988 Olympic and 20 USTA
Grand Slam Titles in Doubles Tennis

Photo credit: Jonathan

After becoming a professional tennis player in 1978, Pam Shriver reached a career-high No. 3 in the world singles rankings six separate times from 1984 to 1988. She ended No. 1 ranked Steffi Graf's 46-match win streak at the 1988 Virginia Slims Championships after stopping No. 2 ranked Chris Evert in the quarterfinals. In all, Shriver won 21 singles titles and became one of only eight women to win more than 500 career matches. Despite the marvelous record, Shriver is best remembered as a dominant doubles player. She and Martina Navratilova teamed to win 20 of her 22 Grand Slam doubles titles and 79 of her 93 doubles titles overall. The duo won 109 consecutive doubles matches from April 1983 to July 1985. All three records still stand today. Teamed with Zina Garrison, Shriver won the gold medal in doubles tennis at the 1988 Olympic Games in Seoul. But a shoulder injury in late 1989 required surgery in June 1990. Following the procedure, her singles ranking fell from No. 5 to No. 66. Despite the hard times, Shriver continued playing professional tennis for six more years.

Doubles tennis takes a back seat to the singles show that drives the sport. In 1968 when open tennis was created, organizers sliced up the sport and men's singles got the largest piece of the pie. Women's singles took a smaller pie, and doubles got only a morsel. "They divided the prize money with a big inequity to doubles, and it didn't take top players too long to figure out all the financial success and attention is on the singles," Shriver explains. Doubles was attractive for Shriver whose game has always been built around the classic doubles serve and volley. But the ultimate draw for her was companionship. "I found the partnership exciting. As a singles player I was lonely on the court. I longed for someone to talk to. I was more comfortable and didn't get as uptight or nervous because I was sharing the spotlight with somebody else."

That is how she is remembered, similar to another doubles specialist, Peter Fleming, who is best known as John McEnroe's partner in the late 70s and early 80s. A relative unknown in his own right, Fleming was ranked in the top 10 in singles only once in his career and won very few tournaments.

The comparison riles Shriver. "People often categorize me in his company. If I wanted to argue, I have tons of ammunition: 21 singles titles, ranked as high as 3 in the world, in the top 10 for most of the 80s, wins over virtually every top player who ever played during my era. Thank you. I rest my case."

But, when you win 22 Grand Slam doubles titles and not one Grand Slam singles title, it is inevitable that you will always be known as a doubles player. "I am proud of my doubles record. I can live with being considered a doubles specialist," Shriver concludes.

Shriver's love of the game started very early, when she was five. With a true passion for tennis, she spent the next 10 years developing her skills. But there are a lot of people that love tennis and spend time working on it who don't get over the hump and become successful. "It took good coaching and supportive parents," Shriver lists as primary contributors to her success. There always is a parent in the wings for No. 1 ranked players. Back then, Gloria Conners guided Jimmy, Jimmy Evert helped Chris, Peter Graff aided Steffi. Today, Martina Hingis has her mother, Melanie, and Serena and Venus Williams have their father, Richard.

The No. 3 ranked Shriver had no one. "Neither of my parents took a primary role. They took a supporting role. They drove me to tournaments." Shriver does remember her father showing her some agility drills but he was a "B" player on the tennis club ladder. "I discounted him a little bit instead of having respect for him as a coach. We both knew he was never going to be my primary coach, not that he wanted to. I'm actually so thankful that throughout my whole career, my dad had his job and it was important to him and he didn't for one minute think that I was going to become his job."

Tennis doesn't give you a lot of years in which to succeed; the body only possesses the firepower for so long. So most of today's players and their parents argue they need to start very young in order to fulfill their destiny in the few years they have. But Shriver's friend and doubles partner Martina Navratilova did not win a Grand Slam singles title until she was 21 when she won at Wimbledon in 1978. Her subsequent and extraordinary run of Grand Slam titles occurred between the ages of 24 and 28. "Too much has been placed on succeeding at an early age," says the still relatively young 38-year-old Shriver. "I played my best tennis after I'd been on the tour for 10 years. You need a foundation when you're young but you don't need to beat the world up."

The war raged by young aspirants on their competition and on themselves is part of the all-consuming requirements of success in athletics. Once you get towards the top, say No. 3 in the world and you're trying to get to No. 2, it is unavoidable. "There were times when I was obsessed with my tennis, trying to get just a little bit better. I crossed over the line, especially my last two years of juniors and the first 10 years professionally," Shriver acknowledges. "It's OK in doses to cross over the line as long as you can get back, and there were certain warning signs that would tell me it was time to take a break for a couple of months. I remember doing that a couple of times. But, over-all I actually had a pretty good balance of friends and other activities."

She also had a lot of doubts which created fear that motivated her to work harder and thirst for success. "I'd ask myself whether I enjoy winning or hate losing and which motivated me. The thrill of winning should be the overrid-ing emotion versus thinking negatively but, man, I definitely felt a lot of fear and the number one players today don't." Indeed, the top women players of the new millennium possess supreme confidence. They have a very strong goal to be and a stronger belief in their ability to become number one. "They are comfortable talking about it," Shriver says in amazement. "It's so brash that it makes other people uncomfortable because we're used to a little bit of diplomacy and not coming right out and saying it. Serena and Venus Williams and Anna Kournikova and Martina Hingis openly talk about and believe in their heart they can get to the top. I could never put myself there. I lacked that last bit of confidence. Or, maybe, it wasn't put into me."

Such ambition is a great motivator, but it can also distort the way an indi-vidual looks at oneself. Shriver's deficiency in ambition may have inhibited her climb to the top but it may have also enabled her to accept her fall. "It took me awhile before I did not lose self-esteem because my tennis results were poor. But, at the end of my career when I was not that successful on the tour, I kept my self-esteem up,"

"I was never ambitious. I wanted to be as good as I could be, but I didn't translate that into being the best. I wonder if my parents and my coach had reinforced that I could be the best and should reach for No. 1 instead of some blurry thing, if that would have made the difference."

Research shows conclusively that specific, highly difficult but attainable goals are substantially superior to vague ones but in the end, at least for Shriver, it may not have mattered at all. "I don't think so," Shriver adds, quickly answering her own question. "When I look at my talent compared to Martina Navratilova, Steffi Graf, Crissy Evert and Monica Seles — and those were the number ones during most of my career — I didn't stack up. Number one is so rare. Where I reached was pretty rare, but where they were was like wow!"

Unlike those in most other occupations, pro athletes cannot hide when they are not good. A resounding defeat can send you from the penthouse to the doghouse just like that. It can also take the psyche with it. "After one loss you suddenly get all these doubts and you need other people to help you get back on track." Shriver's big derailment was her shoulder injury in 1989 and she "never could find out how to get back on track. I let go after 11 years of chasing the top. I just said, 'I can't do it anymore, I'm exhausted,' and I let go of my singles dream and announced my retirement." She was 27.

Shriver regretted her decision, believing it was premature and tried to get back aboard. "I never, never got back," Shriver states with a twinge of pain. "There are degrees of falling off. And there is the absolute fall when you just let go. It's like opening floodgates. Once you open them, they are hard to shut because everything just rushes through. You send off all these signals to your opponents that you are not competent any more."

Shriver leans back in the sofa and stretches her arms over her head and twists to look out the window. She appears antsy. Whether it is from her reflections during the conversation, or her anxiety about the charity exhibition match with the teenage Russian sensation Anna Kournikova just 30 minutes away, is hard to tell. It appears it was the conversation as Shriver returns preoccupied with what might have been. "I don't have any anger about my tennis career," Shriver says, "because I went in with fairly modest expectations. I far exceeded my dreams. I do wonder if I'd gone into that final US Open match with an attitude of 'I could win this match' instead of 'Oh, my God, I hope at least I put up a respectable fight,' if that would have made a difference. But I think it would have put so much pressure on me and I put too much pressure on myself anyway. Literally, at times, I felt I was suffocating and if I had put additional pressure on me I could have just snapped."

> "I'd ask myself whether I enjoy winning or hate losing and which motivated me. The thrill of winning should be the overriding emotion versus thinking negatively..."

There have been some pretty high profile snaps in women's tennis. Shriver was not among them. Neither did she reach the top. "You have to continually narrow your focus to a tighter and tighter beam until you're just looking at that number one. My beam was too broad. I could see that number one, but the light was spread out so that I could see all this other stuff. I was the most distracted person in the top ten. There were a lot of other things going on. Tennis is a part of my whole but I had many different activities. That is the way I am."

Indeed, Shriver has been busy. In 1988, at the height of her career, she was the honorary chair of Athletes for Bush/Quayle and served as a member of the President's Council on Physical Fitness and Sports during the Bush Administration. Shriver was elected the sixth president of the Women's Tour Players Association in 1991 and served three years as a player representative on the board. In 1993, she was part of a group headed by Peter Angelos that purchased the Baltimore Orioles baseball team. She remains a board member for the United States Tennis Association and a vice president of the International Tennis Hall of Fame. Shriver also hosts an annual tennis exhibition, the Celebrity Charity Tennis Challenge, that has raised more than $2 million for Baltimore-area children's charities, one of several activities that have resulted in the USTA Service Award, a similar honor from the Women's Tennis Association and *Family Circle* magazine's Player Who Makes a

Difference Award. She is also an accomplished television commentator, having worked as a tennis analyst for ESPN, ABC, CBS, the BBC and 7 Sport in Australia.

The tab for Shriver's success and involvements was a tender one. "In my late teens and early 20s, I regretted I was not around more boys," Shriver admits. "Before three years in a public high school, I attended all-girl schools. If I had never switched and then went on to the women's tennis tour I would have been a total novice socially around men. As it is, I was a little insecure. I never dwelled on it because honestly I was very happy following this dream of trying to be as good as I can be."

> "You have to continually narrow your focus to a tighter and tighter beam until you're just looking at that number one."

While she recognizes she made some sacrifices in pursuit of her dream, the benefits from tennis outweighed them. "Tennis is a huge part of my identity. It gave me a lot of tangibles," Shriver says referring to more than $5 million in earnings, "and it also gave me a lot of intangibles, access to things that I never, ever would have had access to. Tennis opened a lot of doors and you can't open those doors as a used-to-be player like you can when you're number three in the world and reigning everything doubles champion."

Tennis was a vehicle for Shriver to see the world and meet some rather remarkable people, including presidents and royalty. It also took her from being with others, including a sister who passed away from cancer. "I spent time with her, but I could have spent more time. That is the only thing I regret in my career," Shriver notes softly and quickly and then looks to ameliorate the introspection. "On the other hand, you have to be true to yourself. I needed to invest in my tennis. I needed to come to a closure that I was content and since I stopped playing, I'm content that I put that last bit into it and I closed the door and I haven't wanted to go reopen it."

With center court and the roar of the crowd behind her and her marriage and family life ahead of her, Shriver is making changes. "I feel unbelievably lucky. I've found someone to spend the rest of my life with. Ten years ago, I thought maybe I'd never be married. It's amazing how once you get past a certain segment of your life, things open up. Once I got past tennis, more of life opened up for me and I expect that to continue. I've always been mature beyond my years in some areas and immature in others and I'm going to be a late bloomer when it comes to personal life and family." Among Shriver's after-tennis goals are personal fitness, her broadcasting career and "to have a successful marriage."

Shriver embarked on the latter by marrying Joe Shapiro, the former general counsel for the Walt Disney Company. They had a celebrity-filled wedding in December 1998 at Palm Springs, California, with plans to split their time between Los Angeles and Baltimore.

The media have arrived and spectators are beginning to mull about the grounds wondering if the light rain will hold long enough for the exhibition match to occur. A group of young tennis fans approach Shriver for autographs. The momentary celebrity actually surprises her. "In my every day life, I am not a celebrity," Shriver smiles. "But there are times when obviously you are. During Wimbledon very much so. I always had this neat relationship with British people because I had a lot of tragic losses on center court, so they felt badly for me and they fell in love with this six foot tall, duck-footed, outgoing, emotional wreck on the court. Other than that, you could drop me in any mall in this country and I could walk around and shop all day and maybe one person might say, 'Aren't you … ?' But then they wouldn't remember the name."

The rain starts to come down harder than before and the organizers scramble to pull everyone inside for a talk session with the two players. Shriver directs her remarks to the young players, many of whom are decked out in white tennis togs to serve as ball retrievers for a match that appears won't happen. "Keep your options open and don't burn any bridges," she advises the enthused juniors seated at her feet. "There are several different ways to reaching your goal. Education is so important. And you are listening to someone that didn't go to college and in this country college is such a big thing. People still ask me every day, 'What college did you go to?' Well, I was in the final at the US Open the day before my senior year of high school so that sort of ruled out college. Education is part of keeping your options open."

It is a typical day in the life of a used-to-be tennis star and the last day in a series of appearances before she wings her way to the west coast. As she picks up her gear and heads for her car she shares, "I had the day from hell today. Everything went wrong. I was running late for your interview, got lost finding the place, a rain-damaged match. But everything works out. I'm going off to LA and that will be enjoyable because there are no demands from the community. LA is a place where there's Maria Shriver. There's no Pam Shriver. And that's just fine because I can do what I want to do and be with Joe."

On September 23, 1999, Joe Shapiro died after a five-year battle with lymphoma, less than a year after they were married.

Chapter 11

It's Using Your Life
To Make a Difference

Margaret Allen

First Woman to Perform Heart Transplant Surgery

In 1967, Dr. Christiaan Barnard was the little-known senior cardiothoracic surgeon at Groote Schuur Hospital in Cape Town, South Africa, where he had introduced open-heart surgery and other pioneering procedures. Barnard's patient, 55-year-old Louis Washkansky, was a diabetic with incurable heart disease and not much time left. The surgeon gave Washkansky a choice: either wait for certain death or risk a heart transplant, something which at that point had never been attempted in a human before. Washkansky chose the latter.

On December 3, 1967, assisted by a team of 30 medical specialists, Barnard replaced Washkansky's diseased heart with that of a young woman who was killed in an automobile accident. Double pneumonia exacerbated by a suppressed immune system claimed Washkansky later that month, but the transplant gave him an extra 18 days of life. A month later Barnard performed a second transplant; the patient lived for over a year.

Barnard's accomplishment was a milestone in medical science and made him an international celebrity. He later wrote, "For a dying man, a transplant is not a difficult decision because he knows he is at the end. If a lion chases you to the bank of a river filled with crocodiles, you will leap into the water convinced you have a chance to swim to the other side. But you would never accept such odds if there were no lion."

More than 30 years later, and with little public attention, Dr. Margaret Allen continues to save people from the lions. "I was interested in science because of my father who was a great outdoorsman," Allen remembers. Seated in the large living room of her Victorian home she is engulfed by the enormous Seattle skyline that rises up behind her along the windows. "We had a farm in Iowa and he and I used to go canoeing and take hikes in the woods, and look at pond life under the microscope at home."

Allen took her interest in science to Swarthmore College in suburban Philadelphia, where she majored in zoology with minors in literature and art. Undecided about her long-term career, she applied to graduate schools in both physiology and medicine. She was accepted to both but enrolled in medical school at the University of California, San Diego. "I can remember my father advising me against it because he didn't want me to be disappointed later on if the obstacles in my way were insurmountable. But, I didn't listen to that. I knew I could overcome anything in my path," Allen states without the slightest hesitation or the slightest bit of arrogance. "The thing that worried me most was that I would be bored by age 40. Everybody I could see that had gone into medicine was boring and uninteresting."

In 1970, most of the "everybody" going into medicine was male. The number of females in general surgery was even smaller and you could count on one hand the number of women exploring cardiothoracic surgery. Allen clearly had no role models and, frankly, doesn't care. "I don't think it is necessary," Allen says, smiling with anticipation as only she knows the next remark. "There is a lot of emphasis on role models. But when I found out that I was supposed to have a role model, I picked Tina Turner." Allen bursts out laughing and then adds, "I wanted mine to be someone who was doing well and enjoying life even when they got older."

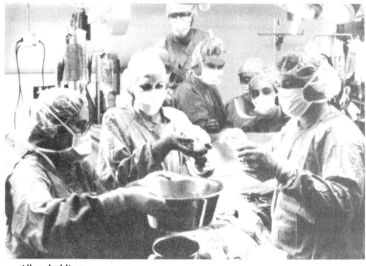

Allen, holding heart, conducting the first transplant in the Pacific Northwest in the mid-1980s

Whether she was motivated by Turner's 1971 hit "Proud Mary" or the 1991 smash "Simply the Best," she won't say, but Allen kept moving forward. "Perseverance makes the difference. It's much more important than intelligence or creativity. I never listen to people who tell me I cannot do something. The way I have always done things in my life is I look into the future and see where I want to be and then whatever it takes to get there, I just do it and get there. The times that are most troubling are when I can't see myself in the future."

On those occasions, Allen stops mid-journey and takes time to fix her current location and identify the next step. During one such period between 1981-1982, Allen chose to work as a general surgeon at Kerema District Hospital in Papua New Guinea's Gulf province. She selected a primitive country so that she might learn what a Stone Age culture thought about modern civilization. From her Third World medical outpost, she discovered lessons for the United States about health care delivery that enabled her to see her end point in cardiothoracic surgery.

She returned to the US to take a position at Stanford University Medical Center. She also returned with trunk loads of native artifacts to keep the lessons she learned alive in her mind and to transform her living room into a wonderful gallery of cultures. "Once you can see into the future, the route to get there is clear. That vision of one's self in a future is inside everyone and the key is to bring it out. Too often, people are afraid to think of themselves as being something other than what they are. Fear of dreaming, more than socioeconomics, is what holds back inner city youth, and it is an eminently solvable problem. You have to open up your mind and everyone can do that if they really want to."

During her cardiothoracic surgery training at Stanford, Allen worked and studied with Drs. Norman Shumway and Richard Lower who spent their careers developing transplantation procedures. Allen is quick to point out that while Barnard bolted to the forefront with his headline surgery, the silent work of Shumway and Lower made the procedure a routine part of modern medicine. Among her accomplishments at Stanford, Allen became chief resident in cardiac transplantation and unknowingly became the first woman to perform a heart transplant.

In 1985, Allen moved to the University of Washington Medical Center where she founded the Regional Cardiac Transplant Program. It is no small undertaking. The American Heart Association estimates 60 million Americans have some type of cardiovascular disease. One in three men will develop major cardiovascular disease before 60. One in 10 women will share the same fate. Each year, an estimated 20,000 to 40,000 Americans could benefit from a heart transplant.

But finding a treatment center, a donor, and a way to pay for it all can be overwhelming. As of January 2000, there were 141 heart transplant programs operating in the US with 4,135 people on the national waiting list, almost double the 2,345 who actually had a transplant the year before. The average waiting time for a transplant is more than seven months. In parts of the country, as many as 40 percent of the patients die while waiting. The trend is expected to get much worse.

> "You have to deal with fear and go ahead and if you can't then there are certain fields you shouldn't go into."

A cost-benefit analysis of the procedure suggests if the lion doesn't get you, the crocodiles will. Based on heart transplants performed between 1994 and 1997, 83 percent of the patients survived one year. That number drops to 78, 74 and 71 percent respectively after years two, three and four. In 1996, the estimated first-year cost for a heart transplant was $253,200 and the annual follow-up cost was $21,200. Not unreasonable sums to pay for the surgeon, cardiologist, nurse, dietician, pharmacist, social worker, and psychologist that form the typical transplant team.

For most of her medical career, Allen has been standing at the surgical table. Beneath her is her patient, replete with IV lines for drugs that lower the immune system and prevent the body from rejecting the new heart and a neck catheter to measure pressure in the heart's chambers. As Allen goes to work, the breastbone is split in half, the old heart removed and the main vessels carrying blood to and from the heart are connected to a heart-lung bypass machine to maintain circulation. Most heart transplant surgeries are done "orthotopically," that is, leaving the residual cuff of the inflow chambers of the patient's heart in place and sewing the donor heart inflow chambers to this cuff and then attaching the donor's main arteries.

As mechanical as the heart may be, serving as the body's pump, and as clinical and calculating as the procedure appears, Allen draws foremost on her love of art to complete her main *d'oeuvre*. "Operating is not a technical thing. For me, it's like making art. The heart is beautiful in its shape. It's such a masterpiece of tissue engineering how a graceful curve in a new coronary graft nestles right around the heart and ensures it won't kink; how a tuck in the valve commeasure makes the leaflets close perfectly." And beyond its structure, Allen marvels at its beat the way a conductor muses over a classical masterpiece. "What is so special about hearts is that they beat on their own. I don't make a heart beat; I just help it beat better. The contractions are inherent in every heart cell. You can put a heart cell in a dish and it will start beating on its own. It's like watching life start from a primordial soup. And we each have that little original sparkplug inside us. I operate like an artist, looking for ways to let nature work and, in nature, orchestrated function is beauty."

> "Now I have to think about what I want to do in my future, what is the most important thing that I can do, where I can make a real difference."

Beautiful as it may be, it is also delicate and precarious work. "I don't like fear. You have to conquer that," Allen declares. "You have to deal with fear and go ahead and if you can't then there are certain fields you shouldn't go into. They say surgeons are supposed to be fearless but I don't think that's good either because they're not the ones who suffer. They make decisions that are risky for the patient, not for themselves. Dr. Shumway always said, 'You have to trust the cardiac surgeon more than you do the airplane pilot, because at least the pilot is on the same plane as you are.'"

Confronted with the life or death struggle of her patients, Allen cannot be controlled by fear but she does believe the risk inherent in her work is an important element in her life. "Holding someone's life in your hands forces you to be completely honest with yourself. You can't get away with blaming problems on someone else. You have to take responsibility otherwise you can't live with yourself." Another deeply philosophical benefit of the occupation is that it gives Allen insight into people. "It is a privileged position to be with people at this all-important time in their lives. It is something that in your own lifetime only happens a few times, like the death of your parents or spouse. You have to appreciate that and really want to get to know your patients and empathize with them."

One might argue that surgeons must only be objective, unemotional, and distant, but masterful at the mechanics of what they are doing. Allen stridently disagrees. "Experiencing with your patients how they handle their illnesses and disabilities is a way of increasing your own wisdom," Allen argues. "You can read about others' experiences and hope there is something that will make you wiser. If you read a lot, you will gain some wisdom, but it's not as good as first hand experience. I've learned from my patients how to live and how to face very difficult situations."

In keeping with her philosophy, Allen contacts her patients before surgery to tell them that "after they're asleep, I'll be acting for them, making the decisions that will most likely get them through. I make a contract with that patient. I have my judgments on what to do, but I also know what the patient wants and I will carry this through no matter what it takes. Sometimes I've invented new operations." Allen is so committed to her role as surrogate, she actually dresses the part. At meetings, Allen wears a skirt, but as a doctor and surgeon, she wears pants. "I don't want patients to think of me as male or female. I want to be a generic human being because it is so important for patients to be comfortable enough to tell me everything. If patients look at me, and my gender is in front of them, suddenly and unconsciously they skew what they say because they're talking to a stereotype. I need to know everything because you never know when a small something might be the key to the diagnosis."

Ever mindful of the big picture at the end, Allen does not view transplantation as the end in itself. "It's a route towards future treatment that would be available to a larger number of people because it would not be limited to human donors or where devices would take the place of hearts. These ideas sound off the wall, but I have that big vision." Not all that off the wall. In the first half of Allen's career, pacemakers were large and implanted through the abdomen. Now they are the size of a quarter and have a battery that lasts 12 years.

"What seems impossible to us now, may soon be the routine heart replacement or device one gets when you're sixty-five to take you through the last thirty years of your life." But the biggest vision is accessibility, not technology. When Allen first arrived in Seattle, a newspaper article covering the new transplant program commented it was going to be a very expensive proposition. Allen decided otherwise.

When she opened the transplant program, she did not charge for transplant operations. She also convinced the other physicians who were part of the transplant team to eliminate their charges. There are lab and hospital charges but Allen worked to ensure they would be covered through state Medicaid. "Everyone should have this option. It shouldn't be something just for the elite few."

Since 1990, Allen has been one of the leading voices in making transplantation an option to a broader range of patients. She is a member of UNOS (United Network for Organ Sharing), the non-profit organization that contracts with the federal government to match donated organs with recipients and sets policy for organ allocation. Allen became aware that minority patients waited much longer for kidney transplants than white patients. She quickly set her sights on changing that. Her vision and ideas resulted in a series of UNOS leadership roles that culminated in 1994 when she was elected president. Under her watch, UNOS began a re-examination of its organ allocation policies and, using computer modeling experts, addressed ethical questions on a rational level, producing a paradigm shift in the field. Among the changes, UNOS increased the number of points on the kidney allocation schedule for people who had waited a long time and reduced the number of points for certain matches that didn't improve survival rates.

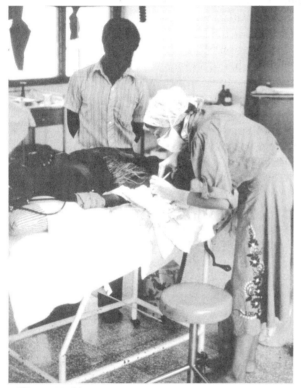

Allen reattaching a thumb in Papua, New Guinea, in 1981.

Allen also put patients on the Board so that they had a voice in implementing policy. "That's an example of seeing the end and getting from one place to that end," Allen comments proudly. "One of the strongest forces in making change in medicine is an informed public. AIDS patients successfully put pressure on the FDA to get drugs for HIV released when physicians were ineffective in doing that. It is extremely important that patients are their own informed advocates. That will make as much of a difference as anything else. Being successful in medicine includes keeping the cost down and making the procedures accessible to everyone."

After 11 years as director of the heart transplant program, Allen again is looking out into the future. For the first time in a long time, she is uncomfortable. The destination is not as clear as before, and the path has not been charted. "Having worked with UNOS, I found myself helping make policies effecting 60,000 people instead of one. That was an eye opener," Allen admits. "As a physician, you look back at what you've done in your life and you have this row of patients that you have taken care of. Policy making is a way to affect a lot more people, but you don't get to know them."

There is also a dark cloud on the horizon that obscures her view to the future. Unexpectedly, Allen was replaced as head of the transplant program she had founded and that was working effectively with its highest caseload and lowest mortality rate ever. "That was pretty devastating," Allen concedes quietly. "It wasn't that they had a reason and had brought me in and said, 'You should have done this or that.' It really bothers me that a couple of people could change my life without any reason. I like to be the one in control of my own life. But the decision caused substantial introspection, and I realized I had begun to define myself as my job. This was my job, not my life, and it was important not to get the two mixed up. It was time for reassessment."

Since the decision was made, Allen has tried regular cardiac surgery without transplants but that did not produce the same satisfaction. She is now working in gene therapy research. It is very difficult for her to be in the division and not to be operating. In a culture where litigation is one of the main methods of obtaining satisfaction, Allen could contest her termination with a lawsuit and probably win. "I don't want to spend my time fighting. It is a waste of my time," she responds. "But then I feel like I'm giving up and I never give up. I could get a private practice job in the city, but I am stubborn. I don't want to do something just to be doing something or just to be making money. I don't want to do something that I am not happy with. I like taking care of patients. I want to do what I want to do and I don't like to be stopped by small-mindedness. Life's not that long and I want to spend all of it doing what I want to do. Now I have to think about what I want to do in my future, what is the most important thing that I can do, where I can make a real difference."

Jaime Escalante

Award-Winning Math Teacher and the Subject of the Movie Stand and Deliver

In 1988, Edward James Olmos, Lou Diamond Phillips, and Andy Garcia starred in the Warner Brothers movie *Stand and Deliver*. While only a modest financial success, the film won widespread critical acclaim for the electrifying performance of Olmos as Jaime Alfonso Escalante Gutierrez, the high school teacher whose underprivileged Hispanic students at Los Angeles' Garfield High set standards in mathematics unequaled in American education. The fascinating, unforgettable, and inspiring story gave the world a vivid picture of genius in the classroom and a teacher as a hero.

"I am just a teacher," Escalante protests in his thick, Latino accent, "helping my students achieve. I don't think I am a hero." Describing Escalante is a matter of semantics but there is no debate that his persistent, challenging, and controversial methods helped a school plagued by low funding, violence, and poor working conditions become one of the most highly ranked secondary institutions for calculus in the United States.

Escalante was hired to teach basic mathematics in 1974. Four years later, he began his first advanced placement calculus course and steadily increased the size of the calculus program. In 1982, suspicious of the eighteen Hispanic students from Escalante's class that successfully passed the national AP exam, the Educational Testing Service ordered them to retake the test. They all passed the second time. In 1987, Escalante's program grew to 129, setting a Los Angeles school record. Within two years, the program had grown to more than 200 students, the largest in the country. "Every time I explain something I want the kids to get a crystal clear picture," Escalante says, "so I use many examples. I use basketball, for instance. A player in the NBA goes to the free-throw line and concentrates many seconds on the rim; the rim, not on the ball. He concentrates on the success he is going to make happen."

At the moment, nothing successful is happening for a small Latino boy who throws his pencil in disgust and pushes his calculus book off his desk. Escalante quietly steps forward and kneels down on one knee to confront him face to face. The boy tells Escalante he can't do it. "You see that guy?" Escalante asks while pointing to one of the several dozen athletic posters that crown the walls of his room at ceiling level. The poster, like everything in Escalante's room is dated: a 1965 glossy of Wilt Chamberlain. In a voice that sounds like a priest whispering from behind a confessional screen, Escalante continues. "He is a superstar and he used to intimidate the other team. Used to block lots of shots, pull lots of rebounds. The relationship between him and this class is simple. Don't let the word calculus intimidate you. Don't let any homework assignment block your mind. You have to pull lots of rebounds, because only A's and B's are accepted here and you're going to be able to do it."

If they don't do it, Escalante will probe and dig and find out what's lacking, what part of the equation they do not have. "I concentrate on the weakness of the student," Escalante touts. "And they work while sitting at tables. We're the only class that has tables. I put four kids together and they have to help each other to get it. They all have to succeed, not just one." If that doesn't sound like anything you ever heard from your mathematics instructor, it is because you probably didn't.

Escalante was born in La Paz, Bolivia in 1930. Both of his parents were teachers who worked in the small Aymara Indian village of Achacachi. He attributes his pedagogy to his mother who was his teacher in elementary school. "I was seven years old and my mom asked me to take some oranges in a basket to the classroom. I didn't want to do it but I had no choice." In class, Escalante's mother asked him to pass one to each child. He didn't know she had already cut the oranges so they were easy to peel. "I passed out the oranges and went back to my seat and she said, 'Look, if you do this' — and she peeled off the skin — 'you have a circumference.' Then she took the knife and cut right in the middle so there were two equal halves and she said, 'This is what we call symmetry. What you see on this side you see exactly on the other side.' I always remembered that picture."

Although his parents were not wealthy, they found enough money to send Escalante to a top Jesuit high school. After graduation and mandatory military duty, he enrolled in a teachers college because his family could not afford the tuition required to attend an engineering school. "When I was twenty-one, my high school physics teacher was a big shot in the government and he called me up and said he wanted me to teach at a new school. I didn't have credentials but he said he would give me emergency credentials. He told me 'You have to teach just one thing, but teach well and make sure the kids understand what you said.'"

Escalante started teaching but forgot his mentor's advice. As the first year ended, he was completely frustrated. "I thought I did a good job," Escalante remembers sadly, "but when I gave the questions in the final test, the kids were ignorant. I just wasted time. I was covering what I had to do without emphasizing what my teacher told me. I blew it and I decided to do better." Escalante started cutting pieces of cardboard and creating ways for students to see real models of the theoretical concepts. "I discovered the easy way, the fast way.

Visualize and you become a better teacher. Every time you teach something you have to adjust yourself to the things kids like to do or to what is familiar. For instance, variables. I take a piece of wood and ask, 'Can you estimate this in inches?' One kid's going to say four inches and another says five and so I say, 'That's what we call variable. We don't know exactly so that's why we use x or y.' I ask, 'Do you know what illegal defense means in basketball?' And they can explain it much better than me. I tell them that terminology has come to math. It's illegal to divide by zero; that's an illegal defense. If you find an equation with a zero in a denominator, it's illegal, you cannot do that."

During his twelve years as a teacher in La Paz, Escalante developed a reputation for excellence as his students consistently won contests against other local schools. In 1962, Escalante traveled to Puerto Rico to attend a special U.S. State Department program for Latin American teachers. During a U.S. tour following the program, he agreed to his wife's life-long desire to join her relatives in California. Escalante's first decade in America was horrendous. Without an American college degree, he could not teach. He worked as a cook and electronics technician while accumulating night school credits for a degree in mathematics and a teaching credential from California State University in Los Angeles.

> "Visualize and you become a better teacher. Every time you teach something you have to adjust yourself to the things kids like to do or to what is familiar."

"The main thing is commitment," Escalante preaches. "I tell the kids, set your goals otherwise you're never going to make it. You have to have some vision. What you have in your mind is what you're going to be in life."

Escalante's educational platform uses love to combat socio-economics. Thousands of children have ideas of what they'd like to be but they never get there. What separates the ones with the ideas from the ones that make it is the family. "Parents should be interested in their kids, but in minority schools, students come not motivated. They don't see that education is the ticket to success." That is when the teacher plays the lead role. In such cases, Escalante becomes, and demands that his colleagues become, an "intensive care teacher, helping kids after school, before school, during lunch. Teachers have to emphasize that no one person has the authority over your destiny, you're the one to decide. You have to build that at an early age. That's when you create the picture in their mind — 'This is what I'm going to be.' I don't just teach mathematics, I teach first, self-esteem, believe in yourself; you're going to be able to do it. With that and the help of the parents, I could accomplish something, because the school alone cannot educate."

Children come to school and talk about three things: drugs, sex, or music. To eliminate that, to redirect the energy, Escalante believes teachers have to help students believe school is the place that is going to set the stage for their tomorrow. That does not happen in a day. Doesn't even happen in a year. Escalante requires his students to stay in his classroom for all four years. "During that period of time the kids know where I'm driving. I wouldn't achieve anything if next year the student goes to another teacher." There are no placement tests to get in. The only requirement is students must be "willing to follow my instructions, for four years, plus four summers."

The instructions are laid out from day one. They are neither new nor mysterious. They are time-tested and basic, like Escalante. "One, you have to believe you can do it. Two, determination — which means you don't give up, you go all the way — and hard work makes the future. You do not enter the future, you make the future, you make things happen. And then discipline, that is the most important. That means you listen to your mom, your dad, your coach. If we work together we're going to accomplish something. That gives you the way to success and success is victory. Anybody can do it if they have the desire. That's why I have that sign that says *ganas*." The word is in twenty-four inch letters spread across the front of the classroom just above the chalkboard. Ganas is Spanish for desire, although it means much more than that. It translates to a thirst or quest for victory.

The room is noisy. Each table of students is working on something different from the other. Escalante moves about like a foreman surveying and cajoling his crew. But he is no longer in Los Angeles. That was then. This is now. Escalante is in Sacramento. "I have a problem with the LA teachers union," Escalante shrugs with little remorse or guilt or worry. The union and the mathematics teaching staff complained that he directed all of his attention to his calculus program and neglected other duties. "My idea is to help the students, not the teachers." The teachers wanted Escalante's help in controlling the mushrooming class size of public school classrooms. "I used to have more than thirty students. I used to have sixty. I couldn't stop the kids, saying no more. The principal provided me a beautiful room — it used to be a music room. And that was against the contract the union had. They told me that I make it difficult for others."

Escalante was department head and made matters even more uncomfortable by creating a policy that limited failing grades to six percent of the students enrolled. "You have to find out why these kids are not doing well," Escalante ordered his staff. "There's three sources for that. A conference, sure. But, if you don't get positive response you have to go to the barrio, to the home. Maybe it's mom and dad who are fighting. This could be one of the reasons why the kid's not doing well. If that doesn't work, you have to prove the kid can do it. They didn't like that." In the war zone of inner city schools, the teachers regularly failed more than half of the class. Consequently, many dropped out. "They have to make it attractive to every student. But they didn't like that philosophy. They said it's wasting time. Some kids are motivated and they are willing to help them out. But they're not going to work with the others. Teaching to me is helping the kids that need help, not the ones already ready to go. The ones that are lazy are the ones that need more help from us and I have to focus on that."

Escalante's criticism is not limited to teachers. The whole system needs a major change. Escalante points to a teacher who couldn't control the class and opted out of the classroom to become a counselor. "What kind of counselor is this when he couldn't even control the class?" Escalante winces. The story gets worse. The counselor became a principal and today is a superintendent. "They take some classes to get the credentials, but they don't have a good education experience. The first and most important teacher you have is experience. And look at teacher preparation. You have to be with one teacher, student teaching they call it, and they're assigned a lousy teacher and that student teacher does not get anything from him."

Ask Escalante's students for a critique and the response is overwhelming. Anita is a wiry sophomore from Romania. "He knows how to explain stuff so he explains it well. And he doesn't give busy work. He actually wants you to learn the stuff we're doing." Sam is a soft-spoken Eurasian. "He comes here every Saturday to help us. He's not paid to come. He comes on his own time. He makes you feel special. I admire him for it." Walja is in her first year from Afghanistan. "He makes it fun. He keeps it interesting. He's not up there just writing numbers. He makes you laugh so you stay interested for the full two hours. He doesn't just teach math, he teaches life. He talks about what he's gone through and how he became things because he knew stuff." Jason is an African-American who seems withdrawn. "If you do poorly on an exam, he makes you do it again. He makes you work hard." What is the one thing that best describes their professor? In near unison, "He cares."

He truly does. Walja once told Escalante that he expects too much from her. He replied, "No, I expect the same from you I expect from everybody. What's wrong is that the other teachers don't expect anything." Jason is in his fourth year with Escalante. In his second year, he told Escalante that he didn't think he could make it and he was going to drop the class. Escalante said, "That's fine. Have you talked to your mom?" Jason answered, "No. I don't want my mom to know because she will tell me I can't drop the class." Escalante quickly suggested, "Oh, then I would like to talk to your mom." Jason begged Escalante not to do so and agreed to try another year. "I am doing fine," Jason smiles.

By his own admission, Escalante is a rogue. "I am a trouble-maker because I want my kids to be the best and I want to do better than other teachers teaching the same textbook. I want to be that kind of teacher in whose class the kid can do it." His instructions to himself are as crystal clear and simple as those to his students. "I look for three things in my teaching. First, I look for excellence. That means to me to do the right things. Second,

I look for innovation. Innovation is the light that makes you win the competition. The last one is I must be in the right place at the right moment. Sometimes kids come with no sense of education and they use foreign language. I have to be prepared for the next question they ask and the kind of answers they give."

To do as much as Escalante does for his students, there has been little time left for himself. And it has always been that way. "I have a beautiful wife," Escalante says proudly, tenderly. "She understands perfectly. I've been doing this for our whole life together. When I was in Bolivia I stayed at the school, and even after my soccer team was done playing I used to take them to the classroom to learn. If you concentrate only on your subject, like mathematics, you build an image as a math teacher. Image is important. It is the big killer of the teacher. I tell jokes or let them tell stories. I teach the freedom to ask questions. Then I take advantage of that situation instead of concentrating on the topic so I capture the attention of the kids. You must be a bit of an entertainer."

A fitting remark for a man immortalized in film. But the immortality has not changed one bit of the short, gnarled man from Bolivia. "I am not famous. And I am not great," Escalante laughs. "Famous are the people who did something, like Newton. Maybe people call me famous because they don't find another word to say I'm doing better than the usual teacher. Some people, when they get this kind of recognition, they believe it and they create themselves in their own image. Cassius Clay used to say, 'I'm the greatest.' That was his ego, but to me no, no, no, no, no. To me it's much better to be humble. If I'm at the level of the students, I feel like I'm doing the job."

There is an old Spanish saying that to be famous is to wear a tie and suit and walk like a million dollar man with one penny left. It will never happen to Escalante, attired in khaki pants and a plaid shirt and an array of odd caps he changes nearly every day. "It's much better to be like we are. The students say to me 'Why don't you dress like other teachers?' No, I'm a common man. I don't have to show I have a new jacket, no, no. Don't concentrate on the miles you're walking. It's much better to look in the direction you're going. Some of these kids feel that they won't make it. I tell them 'Don't put limits to your knowledge, you can go beyond that.' That is when really I feel famous. I'm changing the direction of the kid. I call this the click. Sometimes I have to wait a year to get the click. Sometimes I wait for two years and then I get the click. But I insist and I don't give up. It's just to see the kid could do it."

> "The main thing is commitment. I tell the kids, set your goals otherwise you're never going to make it. You have to have some vision. What you have in your mind is what you're going to be in life."

Escalante's charm is his power. He genuinely believes everyone can do it. As he always says, "I don't believe in the gifteds," Escalante's endearing term for students tracked into honors curricula. "I was not familiar with this because in South America we don't use that terminology because everybody's gifted. I learned that word at Garfield High, because one kid came to me and he told me, 'I don't want to sit next to him.' I said, 'Why? His color or what?' The kid said, 'No, he's gifted. He knows more than me. I don't want to be with him.' I eliminated that word. That's why my kids don't have that complex of inferiority."

Time is running short. There is a writer from *Reader's Digest* waiting his turn. A dozen years after the movie, many of the kids are somewhat befuddled by all the attention lavished on their teacher. But Escalante diverts it with his profound simplicity. "Kids, the movie *Stand and Deliver* was made because I was the only one who got the right equation to calculate IQ. These men want to know the equation. I can't explain it because the equation I have is so complex that it takes at least four weeks to calculate the IQ for each student and it seems I am the only one who got it right. So I don't make mistakes. And when I calculated your IQ's, you're all gifted."

He starts toward the door to greet his next guest. As he does, he passes one of his female students. "Who picked the color of the blouse? It's a beautiful color. I bet your mom did," he says all the while moving toward the door. "No, I did," the coed shouts back, flattered and delighted with the attention. "You have good taste." She says with pride, "I have another one I'll wear tomorrow."

Dreams accomplish wonderful things. We are made full by dreams. Escalante dares his kids to dream and ignites a confidence in themselves in their ability to make those dreams come true. Most of the kids who enter the impoverished, inner city, ethnically troubled domain of Escalante's classroom have no dreams or have let them die.

A boy wearing black leather and chains arrives to enroll. The neatly attired class stares with anticipation and Escalante goes to work immediately. "There is one thing missing," Escalante comments about the boy's fashion. "You need to have a symbol to go with your clothes. I have some symbols. Pick one of these." Escalante shows the new student a board with various medallions. Somewhat confused but not concerned, he picks one. "OK, sit over there," Escalante orders as he escorts the boy to the far corner of the room. "Why? Because it shows these kids how different you are; you're the only one with that symbol." "Then I'll take another one," he argues. "No, you already picked; just stay here." Escalante turns to his two classroom guests and whispers, "Tomorrow he will come in different fashion, and I will let him sit any place he wants."

You *are* a trouble-maker, Mr. Escalante. Thank goodness. Unfortunately, in June of 1998, Jaime Escalante retired from teaching. He and his wife returned to Bolivia.

Rev. Theodore M. Hesburgh
President Emeritus of Notre Dame,
and Medal of Freedom Winner

The offices of the Rev. Theodore M. Hesburgh, president emeritus of the University of Notre Dame, are located on the 13ᵗʰ floor of the library that bears his name. As a testimony to Hesburgh's career, he and his staff occupy a thousand square foot complex tucked inauspiciously behind library archives but, as he had wished, overlooking Notre Dame's legendary golden dome and tree-lined campus in South Bend, Indiana. Although ostensibly retired, as the nation's senior and arguably most illustrious university administrator, he spends much of his time traveling, writing articles and delivering speeches.

Fame and greatness are different. They're certainly cousins, maybe first cousins, but there's a difference. You can be famous as a successful actor in highly popular films. That is being great within that genre of activity. True greatness carries with it a certain moral dimension. "The greatness of Franklin Roosevelt or Winston Churchill is a much broader thing," explains Hesburgh. "It's not the notoriety or admiration. It's the fact that something truly important, truly essential for society happened. Through those two, we got world peace out of a world war, which is really something."

Hesburgh stepped down as president of Notre Dame in June 1987, ending the longest tenure among living American university presidents. One of his first post-retirement projects was the completion of his autobiography, *God, Country, Notre Dame*. Published in 1990, the book became a national bestseller, reaching number 11 on the *New York Times* nonfiction list. The book made clear that his agenda was — and is — service, not stardom. "Seeking greatness is not important," Hesburgh summarizes. "Getting the job done is. If six million people, because they're black, can't vote, you have to figure out a way to get them the vote. If there isn't a single black in school, and there wasn't when I came here in 1934 as a freshman, you have to figure out a way to change that. We did those things. That was an important social breakthrough. That's what I mean by getting the job done."

The public service career of Hesburgh includes 15 presidential appointments, most recently to the U.S. Institute for Peace, involving him in virtually every major social issue from nuclear disarmament to civil rights. His presidential conference room is lined with numerous awards he has received, highlighted by the nation's highest civilian honor, the Presidential Medal of Freedom, bestowed on him by President Lyndon Johnson in 1964 for his leadership in passing the Civil Rights Amendment. We often forget that there were only a few jobs blacks could apply for before 1964 and there were dozens of things they could not do that today we just take for granted. Going into a restaurant of their choice to get a meal, going to a movie theater, to the toilet, going swimming at a state park, getting a drink of water out of a fountain, or being buried in a white cemetery.

"Activism is not something you put on like a new suit and throw it away after a year or two. It's something that's in your very being, something you feel a compulsion to do."

Hesburgh is genuinely passionate yet remarkably humble about the achievement. "Now how silly can it get?" Hesburgh remarks. "That is all gone. It was an almost impossible task, a 250-year-old problem, solved not because I was involved in it but because we were all involved in it right up to Lyndon Johnson. You can be shocked by the nature of the job that has to be done, but you figure out a way of doing it and you do it. History may call that greatness, but the important thing is we were happy to get it done."

But greatness was not Hesburgh's objective. There are people that set out to be great. Biographies portray John and Robert Kennedy that way. Their father did everything he could to help get them there. There probably is an inherent reach for greatness in the British monarchy. With all the aspiration that might have been there in both cases, it has not come out as intended. "Maybe," Hesburgh poses, "aspiration is the enemy of greatness."

Hesburgh was born of humble origins in 1917, the son of a modestly successful executive of the Pittsburgh Plate Glass Company. Like his brother, Hesburgh initially studied at Notre Dame but ultimately obtained a bachelor degree of philosophy from the Gregorian University in Rome. He was ordained a priest on the Notre Dame campus in 1943 and believes his achievements occurred because he said yes too often. "Everything I did I didn't really want to do," Hesburgh admits. "The only thing I really wanted to do was be a good priest."

Following his ordination, Hesburgh wanted to be a chaplain in the Navy. But he was told by his order to get a degree in philosophy or theology. He had taken a vow of obedience and followed the mandate begrudgingly choosing theology, which he liked better, but was determined to continue on to military service. "The degree was a four-year course and I did it in two because

I wanted to get to the Pacific and be a chaplain. But when I finished, they asked me whether I would rather be in teaching or in pastoral work. I said pastoral work, so they gave me teaching and told me to start teaching at Notre Dame. That meant I had to get a doctorate, which I didn't particularly want to get. But I got a good one and came out here and started to teach."

Hesburgh's personal ambitions were put on hold. His life of service to voices other than his own had officially begun. So had the contradictions, the connections, and the contributions. As Hesburgh sees it, "Through the vow of obedience, you get assigned to things rather than doing things you want to do personally, selfishly. But here is the heart of it. Here's the best part. It works out the right way." No sooner had Hesburgh started teaching in July 1945, than the war began and he wound up being the chaplain of veterans. And as it turned out, the doctor's degree was essential for an unseen future, since it is unlikely he would ever have been a university president without it.

Despite his earlier objections, Hesburgh enjoyed teaching, was really quite good at it, and he began to imagine his future as a college professor. "I was prepared for a lifetime of teaching which I loved when the President one day asked if I would like to go in administration. I said, 'Oh, golly, that's the last thing I want to do. I want to be out there with the kids, where the problems are.' Well the next year, he made me executive vice president. Three years later his term was up and the board made me president." Hesburgh was only 35.

He would remain president for 35 years. During the Hesburgh era, enrollment at Notre Dame increased from 4,979 to 9,600, faculty from 389 to 950 and degrees awarded from 1,212 to 2,500 annually. To accommodate the new university Hesburgh was overseeing, the annual budget increased from $9.7 million to $176.6 million, endowments grew from $9 million to $350 million, women were admitted as undergraduates for the first time and governance was transferred from the religious community to a lay board of trustees.

As the university's 15th president, Hesburgh set a course of educational innovation and humanitarian service that dramatically altered the character of the institution and cast him into the forefront of higher education and social activism. In 1954, President Dwight Eisenhower put him on the National Science Board. The Board's purpose was to engage in research in astronomy, atomic energy, and weather. Hesburgh told the President, "I think you've got the wrong guy; my background is in philosophy and theology," to which Eisenhower replied, "I want a philosophical and theological point of view on the Science Board." While serving on the Board, two years later, Eisenhower appointed him to the U.S. Commission on Civil Rights.

In the field of education, he served on commissions that examined everything from public funding of independent colleges to the role of foreign languages in the university curriculum. His stature as elder statesman in American higher education is reflected in his 144 honorary degrees, the most ever awarded to one person. His leadership in international education and his efforts to resolve the problems of science and technology in the Third World included an ambassadorship that Hesburgh was hesitant to accept. Again he begged to differ, telling President Jimmy Carter, "There has never been a Catholic priest ambassador in the United States, and I think I should bring that to your attention before you make this appointment. Carter replied, 'It doesn't bother me if it doesn't bother you. And I'm Baptist so if I'm willing to do it, why not? Anyway, I'm the President.'"

Hesburgh has never looked for a job in his life. "I just have never developed the capacity to say no to the President of the United States," he says with a smile. As a result of his obedience, Hesburgh has had two or three jobs simultaneously most of his life. And the philosopher-theologian-educator-administrator continually found himself in situations far outside the realm of his training. He approached each with the conviction that if you are willing to commit yourself you can manage any task. In each case, he finds that what you have to do is read up on the problem and recruit people who know more about the problem than you do. Hesburgh adds, "You've got to be able to manage the organization in a way that they get credit for what they do and you're not around grabbing all the credit."

"The world is not going to be the same when you die as it was when you were born. And what field you're in doesn't matter. What matters is that it's important to human life that you've tried to make a difference."

Hesburgh sees Americans as great volunteers with the potential to solve any problem. The history of catastrophe illustrates that Americans don't wait for the state, or the government, or the President. They take care of the trouble then and there. When a neighboring farmer's house burns down, the farmers from the area gather around and begin building it the next day, maybe even add another barn if he needs it. For Hesburgh "activism is not something you put on like a new suit and throw it away after a year or two. It's something that's in your very being, something you feel a compulsion to do. You can't see something that needs to be changed without getting in there and helping change it."

That sense of social activism has been the driving force of his life's work, and he encourages his staff and students and all who listen to follow it. "Education, public service, and peace making are really the same thing," says Hesburgh. "It's using your life to make a difference." And don't let Hesburgh ever hear you say that you can't make a difference. We can all make a difference. Whether as an educator, or a politician, or a musician, or an author,

Hesburgh believes everyone can make a difference. "The world is not going to be the same when you die as it was when you were born. And what field you're in doesn't matter. What matters is that it's important to human life that you've tried to make a difference."

For Hesburgh the solution to problems is found in building a network of capable, well-read, socially concerned individuals, a band of committed people who know what the problem is. There is a world of these people and you constantly run into them. And it tends to be cumulative. If you do a reasonably good job in one place, you are going to be asked to do one in another and the network gets bigger and stronger. But Hesburgh cautions his troops that the starting point should be calculated and manageable. "Everybody potentially can make a difference. You don't have to be a Rockefeller or Einstein to do that," Hesburgh states. "Do something that's needed where you are with what you've got. Begin locally because locally you've got every problem in the world."

Hesburgh explains his illustrious career in terms of faith in action. For Hesburgh, people are children of God and deserve to be treated with dignity. The dignity that God gives them requires our respect despite their ethnicity, religion, or circumstances. "It may sound silly," Hesburgh preaches, "but whether it's an old lady in a shawl in Santiago, Chile, a young black guy in a fireman's uniform in Mobile, Alabama, or a little white kid who's been abandoned in a parking lot, when they reach for your help, I don't care if they're Christian, or Jewish, or Muslim, they own you."

Building and energizing solution teams are Hesburgh's strategic forte. But it all begins from the heart. "Service is at the heart. Networks and mobilization are at the mind. If we hadn't cared, hadn't pulled together all the right leaders, blacks wouldn't be able to vote, U.S. and Soviet missiles would still be aimed at each other, millions of refugees would be dead. What other choice do you have but to help?"

There is a remarkable tradition of educational excellence at Notre Dame and a better world today than there might have been. A lot of people would attribute the tradition and the changes to the work of Theodore M. Hesburgh. "One can say that, but I wouldn't. America has always been a great country and Notre Dame has always been a great place. They're just really beginning to hit their stride."

It appears that the same is true about Hesburgh. On July 13, 2000, at 83 years of age, he was awarded the Congressional Medal of Honor paying tribute to his career-long interest and work in civil rights.

Frederica von Stade
Six-Time Grammy-Nominated
Mezzo-Soprano and Opera Star

Photo credit: Marcia Lieberman

Described by the *New York Times* as "one of America's finest singers," Frederica von Stade enters the fourth decade of her remarkable career and continues to reign as one of the music world's most beloved figures and one of the great opera stars of our time. Since her 1970 debut with the New York Metropolitan Opera, von Stade has appeared with every leading American opera company and such European institutions as La Scala, Covent Garden, the Vienna State Opera, and the Paris Opera. Every year, von Stade is invited by the world's top conductors to appear in concert with the world's leading orchestras.

Not bad for a woman who did not even plan to be a performer. "I had a very Catholic home, and the Catholicism I grew up in was very much a part of my love of theater," von Stade reminisces. "There was a lot of magical imagery in the church: incense, the Holy Ghost, the Virgin Mary. And I went to a convent school in Washington D.C. and we always had beautiful celebrations outdoors in the spring and laid fresh lilies at the foot of Mary's statue. It was special and very beautiful and part of the theater I grew up in. I was always looking for visions and apparitions. My imagination was stirred by that."

The pageantry of von Stade's childhood was not limited to religious festivals and the mass. Nor was singing only a matter of hymns. She seemed to find herself on stage repeatedly. "My mom was a wonderful, crazy mother, and she was very encouraging of anything we did that was the least bit special, and even in my early plays, she made a big fuss over me," von Stade recalls. During her teens, von Stade's mother took the children to listen to jazz and to see Broadway shows. Already displaying a gifted voice, von Stade was always performing at school and at parties. "It was a happy experience. It was all something I loved so much and was so much a part of my imagination but I didn't have an ambition to do it. I thought it was too good to be true; that it would never be possible for myself."

Since her professional career began as a twenty-five year old, she has made nearly forty recordings with every major label. Her discography has garnered six Grammy nominations, two *Grand Prix du Disc* awards in France, the *Deutsche Schallplattenpreis* in Germany, Italy's *Premio della Critica*

Discografica, and "Best of the Year" citations by *Stereo Review*, *Opera News*, and other music publications. Remarkably, von Stade had the distinction of holding simultaneously first and second place on the national sales charts for recordings she made of tunes from *Showboat* and *The Sound of Music*. Despite the extraordinary success of her music, the woman who goes by the nickname "Flicka" still does not see herself as a star. "Not at all. Not at all," she repeats giggling at the description. "In my particular corner of the music industry, you can be very well respected and not be known. The only true celebrities who are opera singers are Luciano Pavarotti and Andrea Bocelli."

At the moment, von Stade appears much more like "Flicka" than a celebrity. Dressed in workout apparel that is not name brand let alone color-coordinated, she is on her way to the hotel exercise room, a regular part of her performance lifestyle. She appears lean, fit, but physically tired although emotionally energized. The image is a sharp contrast to the elegant woman who appears frequently on television. In addition to regular *Live from the Met* performances, von Stade celebrated the art of American song with Thomas Hampson, Marilyn Horne, Dawn Upshaw and Jerry Hadley in a program at New York's Town Hall titled, *I Hear America Singing*, which was televised by PBS. She has also presented PBS holiday specials, *Christmas with Flicka*, shot on location in Salzburg, Austria, and, with Kathleen Battle and Wynton Marsalis, a *Carnegie Hall Christmas Concert*, broadcast internationally.

But neither the television and stage productions nor the recordings and the awards have convinced von Stade that she is "there" yet. "The trouble with the performing business is there is no 'there.' There are stages of 'there,' but no sooner are you in a position of importance or significance or acclaim, than you risk falling off it," von Stade philosophizes. Performers tend to pursue one of two different ambitions. One is to seek more celebrity. Wary of that path, von Stade notes, "It's very easy to get spoiled in this business. You're as great as your gift. But there must be a sense of responsibility about it. I've been given this gift and I must take care of it, not exploit it and not exploit others because of it." The other is to continually develop the talent and that is von Stade's road to "there." "I realized I had a wonderful gift from God that could be developed yet I have been consistently dissatisfied with its development because I just couldn't understand the exact mechanics of the voice. Understanding — that is my ambition."

A frequent hazard for singers is that they can only go so far with the gift, the voice. Then, at some age or for some reason, it breaks down. A few years ago, von Stade experienced the crash. "I was doing a lot wrong and I really had to go back to square one," von Stade says out loud what most singers do not dare to whisper. And then she turned to Jan Randall, a music teacher in Oakland, California, nearby von Stade's home. "She was a spiritual person as well," von Stade adds. "And singing is very spiritual. It requires a lot of trust, because you can't see the instrument, you can't tune it. You can't even protect it. No matter how good you are, a cold can set in. You don't take your voice out of a nice velvet case and know that it's going to be the same instrument you put to sleep the night before. It's out there in the elements all the time, subject to simple things like air-conditioning and complicated things like thought." If something is the matter with a singer's voice there is great shame that accompanies it. Football players get an injury and it's just an injury. It goes with the game. In high school they're even proud of it. But when singers get an injury, "they wear hair shirts and beat their chests," von Stade reports, offering a stylized gesture of mea culpa.

With Randall's assistance, von Stade has begun to understand how her voice functions. "I feel so blessed," von Stade remarks, deeply grateful for the revelation. "Now it doesn't mean I can always do it. But I know what it is. And my dream was to leave the business with that knowledge." It has taken von Stade thirty years to find it. But singing is not a skill that starts early and remains on autopilot like riding that bicycle you learned at age eight. Singers usually do not even discover their voices until they are in their twenties, a time when learning things is usually set aside for doing things. "Most singers don't have a child's relationship to singing. As adults, you've lost that childish abandon with which children learn. We have so much noise in our brains that points out we can't do it, that we don't do what we're told, and learning becomes vastly more complicated. So my ambition has been to approach a true understanding of the mechanism of the human voice. And, I'm definitely on the right path."

Most successful people are incredibly driven, and von Stade is no exception. There is that predictably neurotic part that all of us raised in the magical Catholic theater understand. "Trying to please people is one of the drives, and is somewhat negative," von Stade acknowledges. "The positive drive is that singing is fun. Doing opera is fun. Opera is like sport. It's fun and you get addicted to performing. It's a high." Like baseball, opera is a production. The music, costumes, set, and performers all contribute to the outcome and to an exhilarating team spirit. "You know the whole thing isn't resting on you," von Stade explains. "And the camaraderie of being joined by others is such a nice feeling." But recital is a bit like baseball too, only the count is 0-2 and the game is on the line. "In recital, I concentrate on the words with all my energy and the tension has to go someplace. Last time I sang, it was in my feet like I was gripping the earth. In either case, you're standing in the best place to hear the orchestra playing and it's wonderful to spend your life with absolutely beautiful music."

But the wonderful world of beautiful music, like sport, is ultimately about contracts. Contracts for recitals, contracts for operas, contracts for recordings. The wonderful world of beautiful music is very competitive. "There's a certain natural competitiveness between us all. But what can you do about it? You can't force people to hire you. And you can't force the public to like you. So there is an awful lot of our business which is in the mouth of wolves and you can't tell whether they're going to eat you or bite you or what's going to happen." It is a part of the industry that von Stade avoids. She seldom reads reviews. Like most performers in any medium, there is very little that she can be told that she doesn't already know. She knows when she has not sung the right note or run out of breath. She has made friends with her foibles. "My task is to keep working on my voice and my music, and get up there and do it as best I can."

It appears she does. In addition to the accolades from the entertainment community, von Stade holds honorary doctorates from Yale University, Boston University, the Georgetown University of Medicine, and her alma mater, the Mannes School of Music in New York City. In 1983 she was honored with an award given at the White House by President Ronald Reagan in recognition of her significant contribution to the arts.

But seated in the lobby of the Four Seasons Hotel 30 years away from the beginning and a thousand miles away from home, the accomplishments and tributes did not come freely. "The travel costs you a lot," von Stade says with a furrowed brow. "The separation from family is the biggest cost. It costs me and it costs them. It's not easy to be married to or be the child of a performer. It costs everybody in the household — the performer because you have to be away and the family members because you're not there. And no matter how much you are there, there are going to be ten times when you're not there." Having spoken so painfully, the logical question follows whether she would do it all again. "I don't know," von Stade divulges and furrows her brow tightly. "The overriding regret for me is not being home. I would want to be there more. But that would mean giving a lot of it up."

"It's very easy to get spoiled in this business. You're as great as your gift. But there must be a sense of responsibility about it. I've been given this gift and I must take care of it, not exploit it..."

Through all the sadness von Stade embraces for having missed special moments with her children, she has certainly offered them other things. They were frequent companions on her tours. Their worlds must surely have been expanded in ways and to an extent that might never have been achieved had she stayed home. She takes solace in that possibility and embraces even more fully what she views as providence in her life. "I may have been frustrated if I had stayed home. I don't know. I do believe I am fulfilling my destiny," von Stade says. "It happened this way, so it must have been part of a plan. My favorite saying is, 'If you want to make God laugh, tell him your plans.' I feel I'm part of a plan that is mine to a certain extent, but has to have been somebody else's plan too.

I'll take responsibility for what I can take responsibility for. But I think there's a bigger plan in there."

Call her spiritual or call her religious, in any case, von Stade is very attached to Irish Catholic roots. "I'm not a very intellectual Catholic, but I love it," von Stade shares openly and easily. "I've found so much comfort in Catholicism, just going into churches, being able to have the option as a human being to say, 'Help me out of this. I can't manage this. I don't see a solution.'" She offers numerous examples of such circumstances from events ranging from the death of local fire fighters to the unrelenting bombing of Yugoslavia. Absent any plausible solution to the pain of the planet, von Stade turns over the world and her own world "to a higher power that is in charge of all that is going on in the earth. It's way too complicated. No matter how intellectually astute we've become, how we've developed every part of the earth, people still die and there are things we still can't control. And that lack of control gives us a marvelous opportunity to turn over to spirituality, to God, to a relationship with God just for the basic joy of being able to say HEEEEELP!!"

The conversation turns back to family and to children, the place where von Stade always goes when she reaches for things that matter. "There are those who made huge marks in history: Martin Luther King, presidents, scientists," von Stade outlines. "And there are those like me who have had some achievements. Then there are those who just share their faith in God and go about their life just taking care of their family. That's truly greatness." The woman who has been on nearly every major stage in the world offers her next-door neighbor as the real profile of success. She has spent her whole life dedicated to her family and to her community. "They call her 'footsteps in the sand' because you don't even know that she's been there but she does so many things all the time that you can't even assess them. She is a great woman. There are many people like that offering small gestures of extraordinary kindness. The biggest frustration of many people is the world's failure to recognize them. The greatest human tragedy may be looking for recognition and not getting it. Achievement and recognition don't dictate greatness at all."

It is perplexing that we spend money for fertility drugs to bring children into the world and then don't really spend much time to bring them up to live it sensibly. The push for achievement limits our ability to give children attention. Parents are pulled in every direction, including von Stade. "The great achievements of the future should be about creating a good world for kids. Anybody who doesn't see it is nuts."

Maybe we knew that. If so, we seem to be forgetting it as a nation.

Chapter 12

The Heart of Success

The Heart of Success

My fascination with extraordinary achievement has never diminished ever since attending my first college football game in 1953. On the contrary, it has become more acute because of my professional pursuits. But it has also become more prudent because of the perspective gained by those years and the close proximity to achievers. As a result of a lifetime of watching and working with passionate, committed people, it is clear to me that there are extraordinary achievers: individuals who have done what we only dream to do and individuals who have done what we dare not even dream. It is also clear to me that today such people have been swallowed up by a culture whose appetite for the extraordinary denigrates the term itself.

In the media madness of our age, we are assailed by lists: Person of the Year, National Best Seller, Rock Top Forty, NCAA Final Four. Everywhere we turn, one institution or another is heavily marketing its definition of success. In an earlier era, a .280 hitter was a minor leaguer, today he is a millionaire. Great theater had a story, not a star. We live in a time when the rich and famous are the objects of an entire generation and the very word star is made hollow by superstar. But overusing such superlatives, like overusing any words, squanders their meaning. Soon, we may need to create super-super-stars to distinguish their success from superstars. That, of course, may explain why USC running back Aramis Dandoy, whom I mentioned in my introduction, has been forgotten. He was only a star.

Equally important, Americans appear obsessed with revelation and have chosen the distasteful elements of celebrities' lives as their leading interest. In the past, the public preferred to keep the distasteful aspects of their icons hidden from view, and the media shielded the people about whom they reported. There are few photographs of President Roosevelt in a wheelchair because the respect for the man, the office, and the right to privacy protected him. Today, the media pay little heed to privacy. While interviews with extraordinary people are not recent phenomena, in an earlier time reporters did not peek into their bedrooms or dredge up tales from their pasts. Biographers have changed too. In the past, they tried to flatter their subjects. Today, they reveal all of the unpleasant aspects they can find.

More than any other factors, tabloid journalism and the American passion for it are responsible for the revolving door through which pass our icons and the change in the meaning of success. After all, the closer we examine a painting, the more we are likely to discover its flaws. Similarly, the closer we get to extraordinary individuals the more they seem to be human, with marvelous abilities in one area, but nonetheless with failings. Today, it seems the media concentrate on the failings rather than the successes. But, such journalism would not exist if there were not a market for it. Perhaps, we want to see extraordinary people stripped of their extraordinariness. Perhaps we entertain the fantasy that, given their failings, we are not really that far from being like them after all.

That is not the way it was. Earlier in our history, acclaim was awarded to people whose deeds imparted great social benefit upon us and, on rare occasions, to those whose lives reflected the finest qualities of humankind. Americans once focused on adventurers that opened new views of the planet, entrepreneurs that improved the way we lived, politicians who corrected social ills, soldiers that kept us free, scientists that sustained our health, and moralists who expressed something marvelously profound. It was a pretty good standard. But as we entered the new millennium, success as measured by achieving or living with impact was replaced by a whole new set of criteria. Notoriety is prerequisite for success in America today.

No better place to find successful people, then, but in sports and entertainment. Sports and entertainment produce stars, the contemporary currency for success. The production is cybernetic; publicity surrounding stars fuels the celebrity, which in turn increases their economic value. This again feeds the celebrity because contemporary Americans are also fixated on money. This publicity cycle can be traced to the growth of mass communication. Television has made the extreme accessible. Cable and direct television have made it ordinary.

The excess of personal entertainment has also increased the number of celebrities and thus the number of nominees for success. On rare occasions, the nominations are unanimous. Marilyn Monroe and Michael Jordan are examples. Along with their extraordinary talents, they possessed the ability to touch people emotionally. Coupled with their good looks, notoriety, and wealth, they formed the quintessential American icons of success during the last half of the 20th Century. Perhaps it is time to remember Andy Warhol's remark that everybody is famous for fifteen minutes. But being famous is not necessarily the sign of success. Perhaps it is time to remind ourselves of what is.

What we know is that deep in the recesses of achievers there are personal qualities that enable their gifts to reach the light of day, that propel their dreams into reality, that transform their lives from ordinary to extraordinary. Like the achievers in this book, it begins with discovering your talent, possessing a deep desire to make your gift your life, and to developing that talent throughout your life.

But talent alone is insufficient. To be successful, you must truly enjoy what you do and possess a passion for using your gift. Without that intense emotional focus, nothing significant ever happens. As children we were all fascinated by the magnifying glass. Holding it steady on a cool fall day, we could harness the sun's rays 93 million miles away and center them on one spot until a pile of leaves burst into flames. It was a dynamic example of intense focus. Everybody who achieves has the capacity to do so, totally. Watch **Mike Eruzione** on the ice. **Chaim Potok** in his study. **Karen Thorndike** at the helm. **Bill Walsh** on the sidelines. Look at their eyes.

Such focus demands an incomprehensible amount of self-discipline. You must be honest in your effort. You cannot succeed if you fall to the temptation for shortcuts. Grammy-nominated violinist **Hilary Hahn** practices her instrument and attends to her schooling amid an overwhelming schedule of travel and concerts. **Mills Lane** hasn't stopped training despite a life seated on the bench. After his gold medal performances, swimmer **John Naber** transformed the lessons of the pool into lessons about life. Justice **Sandra Day O'Connor** is still driving a truck, now for America instead of for cowboys.

Success is as much a direction as it is a destination. To accomplish extraordinary things, you must see life differently but accurately and take others to that point of view. Call it curiosity or intuition, instinct or insight, physicist **Leon Lederman** used it and changed the way society views matter. Marketing and entertainment leader **Mark McCormack** used it and changed what mattered in society. It is an internal probing that seeks answers to complex problems and the results are as different as the marvelous unpredictability in a **Mark Morris** dance to the miraculous precision in **Belding Scribner's** shunt.

But the marvelous and the miraculous do not come easy. Successful people possess enormous energy. As defined by physicists, energy is the capacity to do work. In order to be successful, you must have enormous energy to do enormous amounts of work. If it were possible any other way, everybody would be successful. Baseball manager **Sparky Anderson** and General **Harry Brooks** demanded it from their troops and expected it of themselves. Despite nearly forty years in science, biologist **Paul Ehrlich** is still in the lab and still flying to the jungle. Despite two batting crowns, plenty of money, and an aging body, baseball player **Edgar Martinez** is still in the weight room and flying (albeit less quickly) around the bases.

While everyone who succeeds benefits from a bit of luck along the way, high achievers triumph when it is absent. No adversity is too severe to resolve. Tragedy is accepted, enemies are circumvented, loss is transformed, and obstacles are overcome. Conductor **James DePreist** brought dignity to his life in a wheelchair and grace to the stage. Pianist **Vladimir Feltsman** proved to a totalitarian regime and to critics that passion is mightier than the sword. Gymnast **Kathy Johnson Clarke** broke the bonds of age and injury. Sailor **Dawn Riley** navigated a new channel for women on the high seas. To be successful, you must pass all the barriers. Despite your calamity, you keep going forward.

You must also be very patient and persistent. Successful individuals embrace their journey with a determination so deep that when their bodies are so tired they can't take another step or their minds are so weary they can't try another time, somehow, they rise above it all and they do. Triathlete **Mark**

Allen had to ignore his place among thousands of competitors and the fatigue of eight hours of exercise to know when it was time to take the lead. World land-speed king **Craig Breedlove** continues to endure weather, mechanical and financial trouble to wait his turn for yet another chance at destiny. For filmmaker **Ken Burns**, it takes five years to make one documentary. For former Senator **Bob Dole**, it has taken a lifetime to become the subject of one.

But shear doggedness must be accompanied by periodic and strategic moments of risk. To be successful, you need to stretch your personal and professional envelope. Entrepreneur **Paul Brainerd** risked his life savings and became a multi-millionaire. Mountaineer **Tom Hornbein** risked his life and became a legend. Saxaphonist **Don Lanphere** transformed his life and singer-guitarist **Roger McGwinn** transformed his style. They are both at peace with themselves and performing long after their counterparts have stopped.

But like everything else in life, nothing personally or professionally extraordinary happens in isolation. You succeed with and/or for others. Legendary basketball coach **Red Auerbach** sits in an office surrounded by photographs of his players, not the trophies they helped him win. Public Relations guru **Daniel Edelman** is more proud of his ability to influence the lives of his employees and colleagues than the client list that gave him such stature. Promise Keeper's **Bill McCartney** preaches humility and interdependence, love and affiliation. Maestro **Hugh Wolff** talks about antennae and input. All of them know success is as much about process as it is about product.

Successful people find within themselves the courage to overcome their fears and doubts whether those apprehensions arise from the past, from the moment, or from the future. To be truly successful, you need to learn who you are, like model **Rebekkah Armstrong**; put aside the baggage of the past like cellist **Lynn Harrell** and athlete-commentator **Diana Nyad**; and face the setbacks and tragedies of the moment like tennis player **Pam Shriver**.

Finally, despite the fact that the achievement is a personal quest, truly successful people are unselfish. They have the ability to convey a sense of community or family, to express genuine care and concern for the larger world like physician **Margaret Allen** as she pressed to bring medicine to the impoverished or for the smaller world like teacher **Jaime Escalante** as he fought to bring the impoverished into medicine. They have a willingness to serve and the capacity to make things happen with absolutely no concern about who gets the credit like **Theodore Hesburgh** as he mobilized a nation for civil rights and global peace. They have, at their core, like singer **Frederica von Stade**, a genuine love for people and a fervent hope for tomorrow that are even more extraordinary than their accomplishments.

For me, the journey was incredible. I talked at length with men and women who represent everything I wanted to be. From their admonitions, their introspective musings, and their rebuttals to my questions, I have found answers to the plaguing universal questions about achievement. From their smiles, their tears, their silence, I have also found answers to personal ones about me that finally end my quest for success.

I have come to learn that success grows from the inside out and celebrity goes from the outside in and that there is very little interest in celebrity among truly successful people. Most successful people aren't celebrities. I have met such people in my work all around the world. People who have helped others because in their hearts that is who they are and they have a vision of what is important in life. Few will ever hear of them, they will never be in this book, and yet most of the good that is done in the world is done through these people.

I have come to learn that success is achieved one step at a time. We must remove the things that stop us from becoming successful. Society does not encourage that. Instead we are told talent and opportunity make it happen and the media report the results. But that is really all about celebrity. Whether or not you win a Nobel Prize, are inducted into an athletic Hall of Fame, or receive an Emmy, you can still be successful. But most people drop by the wayside as they sedate themselves with hopes for celebrity.

I have come to learn that the potential for success is within everyone. Achieving it requires peeling away all of the impediments that stand between that plane and our daily lives. You can find it through a powerful moment when you are on the Road to Damascus and you are knocked to the ground. You can find it through the conscious search of your very existence. Success can sneak up on you while you are achieving your goals. Whichever way, it is not a transformation that takes you from being one thing to being another; it is becoming what and who you really are. And once you have discovered who that is, you have to work at being that every day.

Finally, I have come to learn that success is becoming and being content with what and who you really are. Everyone has some gift through which he or she can discover that sense of higher life and living fully. Everyone has had that experience at one time or another. The time you got the "A" on that history test, hit the homerun in Little League, or sang beautifully in the chorus. Immediately you knew. For one moment you traveled beyond the limits of your daily life and you realized you must pursue your own lifelong journey without worrying about the results, not dying if you fail or glorying if you win, but rejoicing in the process.

Because we live in a media culture, everything reduces to phenomenology. The essence of phenomenology is if a tree falls in a forest and no one is there to hear it, it did not make a noise. Of course it made a noise. Similarly, one does not need to be recorded in the annals of human progress, which today unfortunately means newspapers and magazines and TV, to be a success. Just because the media have not pointed their lights on you does not mean that you are not successful. Success does not need to be recognized.

Cinematographer Ken Burns, one of the recorders of human progress, says it best. "It's OK that we look at geniuses and athletes and entertainers and celebrate them. That's wonderful," Burns says. "But what makes them a success has nothing to do with the fact that there is a system that recognizes it. The fact that they move people is the proof that they are. Daycare center workers right in your neighborhood may be producing future healthy adults because of the kindness they bestow on the children under their care. And that makes them a success."

What's at the heart of yours?

Afterword
By John Wooden

When I think of who are the truly extraordinary people, I think of the ones whose actions have had a decided effect on others. There are stars like Babe Ruth who have done great things. He may be the greatest baseball player of all time. But I wouldn't want youngsters to emulate him. There needs to be a spiritual dimension whereby you can give and you can forgive — lose self in the group. My definition of team spirit is an eagerness to lose one's self in the group for the good of the group. Extraordinary people are very thoughtful of others. I tried to bring out the importance of unselfishness, to make my players more considerate of others because it was going to make them better players. But more important, it was going to make them a better person.

I tried to show my players what they needed to do to be truly successful in the Pyramid of Success. I worked on it for 14 years. In doing so, I felt the two most important things for anyone trying to accomplish anything were industriousness and enthusiasm, and those two became the cornerstones of a five-block foundation. The three blocks in between include other people: friendship, loyalty, and cooperation. With those as your framework, you build the next level: self-control, alertness, initiative, and intentness. Then you get to the heart of success, three things that some feel pertain more to sports but I think pertain to everything.

It begins with conditioning. You have to be conditioned for what you're doing. And there's more than physical condition. There is mental and moral conditioning. All three are used in everything. Next is skill. You have to know what you're doing, you have to do it well, whether you're a surgeon or an athlete. And since achieving involves others, there must be team spirit. You must be considerate of others. Those three blocks are the heart. And if you have these, they will take you to the next level. They will give you poise, which is doing what you're capable of doing. And they will give you confidence— knowledge that you can function at your level of competence. The result is that you will be competitive; you will be the best you can be.

Now, I'm really more concerned with being ready for what happens today, but you do have to have goals. Never make the goals impossible to attain but they should be difficult. As a general rule, things easily achieved aren't really worthwhile. The goal should be to do the best possible job you are capable of doing at a particular task. If you do that, you are successful. In my years at UCLA we had to win the conference to enter the NCAA tournament, so my goal was not to win the NCAA; it was to win the conference. Then we had a chance for the encore.

You have to make the most of your moment. You can't do a thing about yesterday. But you can have an effect on tomorrow by what you do today. Today is the day that counts. It will have an effect on the future, adversely or positively, depending on how you prepare yourself today. Preparing to fail begins by failing to prepare. Once I put on the bulletin board a poem titled, *Today*. It reads:

> I've shut the door on yesterday, its sorrows and mistakes.
> I've locked within its gloomy walls past failures and heartaches.
> And now I throw the key away to seek another room
> And furnish it with hopes and smiles and every springtime bloom.
> No thoughts shall enter this abode that have a hint of pain
> And envy, malice and distrust shall never come again.
> I've shut the door on yesterday and thrown the key away.
> Tomorrow holds no fears for me for I have found today.

I believe today is the only time you have to do what you need to do. If you let things over which you have no control affect you, they are going to affect you adversely. Notoriety or fame affects you adversely. You've got to keep things under control. If you would look back at the players after each of the ten national championships we won, you'll find very little exultation. Fortunately in all of the championship games there was a time out right near the end of the game and we've got the game won, so I would say, "You've done a wonderful job, I'm very proud of you, but now when it's over let's not make fools of ourselves." I never wanted my team to get too high over winning, nor did I want excessive dejection if we were defeated. I wanted them to get that peace of mind from knowing we did what we could. That was often why we won but if we lost, well, we just weren't good enough on that day but now we're going to try to get better.

Now, I wanted winning, as it is generally considered, that is outscoring people. But I wanted that to be the by-product of other things, a by-product of success. I wanted to outscore opponents, but I wanted my players and I wanted myself to know that this isn't always going to happen. We've got to accept it when it doesn't happen. We're not all going to be equal as far as ability's concerned and most of the times when someone outscores us it's because they're better than we are and let's just accept that and try to get better. Maybe we can't …but maybe we can.

There's nothing wrong with ambition. I want people to be ambitious. But it must be kept under control. You have no control over somebody else, but you have control over yourself and that's what you must concentrate on. Don't make your ambitions the idea of getting ahead of somebody else, make your ambitions the idea of doing the best you can possibly do. That's the heart of success.

Known as the "Wizard of Westwood," John Wooden is one of only two men to be honored in the Basketball Hall of Fame as both a player and a coach. A standout player at Purdue in the 1930s, Wooden was head coach of the UCLA men's basketball team from 1949 to 1975 and won 10 national championships – including seven straight from 1967 through 1973. The John Wooden Award, given to the best all-around college basketball player of the year by the Los Angeles Athletic Club, is named in his honor.